# THE
# 50 GREATEST PLAYERS
## IN
# CHICAGO BEARS
## HISTORY

# THE
# 50 GREATEST PLAYERS
## IN
# CHICAGO BEARS
## HISTORY

### ROBERT W. COHEN

**LYONS PRESS**

Guilford, Connecticut

An imprint of The Rowman & Littlefield Publishing Group, Inc.
4501 Forbes Blvd., Ste. 200
Lanham, MD 20706
www.rowman.com

Distributed by NATIONAL BOOK NETWORK

British Library Cataloguing in Publication Information available

**Library of Congress Cataloging-in-Publication Data**

Names: Cohen, Robert W., author.
Title: The 50 greatest players in Chicago Bears history / Robert W. Cohen.
Other titles: Fifty greatest players in Chicago Bears history
Description: Guilford, Connecticut : Lyons Press, 2020. | Includes
   bibliographical references. | Summary: "Sports historian Robert W. Cohen
   ranks the top 50 players ever to perform for one of the NFL's most
   historic franchises"— Provided by publisher.
Identifiers: LCCN 2020003619 (print) | LCCN 2020003620 (ebook) | ISBN
   9781493046980 (hardback) | ISBN 9781493046997 (epub)
Subjects: LCSH: Chicago Bears (Football team)—Biography. | Chicago Bears
   (Football team)—History. | Football
   players—Illinois—Chicago—Biography.
Classification: LCC GV956.C5 C655 2020 (print) | LCC GV956.C5 (ebook) |
   DDC 796.332/640977311—dc23
LC record available at https://lccn.loc.gov/2020003619
LC ebook record available at https://lccn.loc.gov/2020003620

♾️™ The paper used in this publication meets the minimum requirements of American National Standard for Information Sciences—Permanence of Paper for Printed Library Materials, ANSI/NISO Z39.48-1992.

# CONTENTS

# ACKNOWLEDGMENTS

I wish to thank Troy Kinunen of MEARSonlineauctions.com, Kate of RMYAuctions.com, Richard Albersheim of AlbersheimsStore.com, Pristine Auction.com, SportsMemorabilia.com, George A. Kitrinos, Mike Morbeck, Jeffrey Beall, Chris Usalis, Kevin Moore, Joe Glorioso, John Martinez Pavliga, and the grandchildren of Leslie Jones, each of whom generously contributed to the photographic content of this work.

# INTRODUCTION

## THE BEAR LEGACY

One of only two charter members of the National Football League still in existence, the Chicago Bears have their roots in Decatur, Illinois, where they spent the 1920 season competing in the newly formed American Professional Football Association (APFA) as the Decatur Staleys after the league office granted team representatives a franchise in exchange for the standard entry fee of $100 on September 17, 1920. Named after their sponsor, the Staley Starch Company, the Staleys excelled under the leadership of player-coaches George Halas and Edward "Dutch" Sternaman in the league's inaugural season, compiling a record of 10-1-2 that earned them a second-place finish in the 14-team circuit. After acquiring full control of the team in 1921, Halas moved the Staleys to Chicago, where he guided them to a mark of 9-1-1 and their first league championship. With the APFA renaming itself the National Football League prior to the start of the 1922 campaign, Halas similarly chose to change the name of his team to the Bears, in deference to the more established Chicago Cubs, whose home ballpark, Wrigley Field, served as the venue for Bears home games for the next half-century.

Remaining competitive from 1922 to 1924, the Bears posted the NFL's second-best record in each of those three seasons, compiling an overall mark of 24-6-5. Yet, despite the success they experienced on the playing field, the Bears found themselves plagued by the same financial difficulties that afflicted the rest of the teams in the infant league, prompting Halas to sign star University of Illinois running back Red Grange to a unique contract in which the latter agreed to participate in a 19-game barnstorming tour in exchange for the then-exorbitant fee of $3,000 per game, plus a share of the gate receipts. Halas's brilliant idea proved to be a boon to the league, with

Grange's presence altering the mindset of many Americans, who previously took an extremely dim view of professional football. Boosting the prospects of many debt-ridden teams, Chicago's 1925 tour likely saved several NFL franchises, including the New York Giants, who benefited greatly from Grange's appearance at the Polo Grounds.

Halas retained his duties as player-coach until 1929, when he retired as an active player and replaced himself at the helm with former Lake Forest Academy head coach Ralph Jones, who guided the Bears to their second NFL championship in 1932, when, after finishing tied for the league's best record during the regular season, they defeated the Portsmouth Spartans by a score of 9–0 in an "unofficial" championship playoff game. However, with every NFL team struggling to make ends meet during the Great Depression, Halas returned to the sidelines for a second tour of duty in 1933, after which he led the Bears to five Western Division titles and three league championships over the course of the next nine seasons.

With the NFL having adopted a new two-division setup in 1933, the Bears posted a regular-season record of 10-2-1 that earned them their first Western Division title. They then laid claim to their third league championship by defeating the Giants by a score of 23–21 in the NFL championship game. The Bears followed that up by going a perfect 13-0-0 during the 1934 regular season, outscoring their opponents by a combined margin of 286–86 along the way. But the Giants exacted a measure of revenge against them in the NFL title game, recording a 30–13 victory in what became known as the "Sneakers Game." After a two-year hiatus, the Bears made another championship game appearance in 1937, only to lose to the Washington Redskins by a score of 28–21. However, they avenged that loss in 1940, defeating the Redskins by a score of 73–0, in what remains the most lopsided playoff game in NFL history. The Bears repeated as NFL champions in 1941, claiming the Western Division title with a 33–14 victory over the Green Bay Packers in a one-game playoff, before defeating the Giants by a score of 37–9 in the league championship game.

Remaining one of the NFL's elite teams after Halas entered the military to serve his country during World War II, the Bears captured the Western Division title in both 1942 and 1943, with Hunk Anderson and Luke Johnsos sharing coaching duties. After losing to Washington by a score of 14–6 in the 1942 NFL title tilt, the Bears claimed their sixth league championship with a 41–21 victory over the Redskins the following year.

Clearly establishing themselves as the NFL's dominant team from 1932 to 1943, the Bears became known for their powerful running game that featured the league's most physically intimidating player, fullback Bronko

Nagurski, whose aggressive style of play came to epitomize the Bears of that era. Also known for their ferocious defense and exceptional line play on both sides of the ball, the Bears acquired the nickname "Monsters of the Midway" for the havoc they wreaked on opposing teams during the 1930s and 1940s. On offense, the Bears featured Nagurski, quarterback Sid Luckman, end Bill Hewitt, and standout linemen Dan Fortmann, Joe Stydahar, and George Musso. All six men also starred on defense, with Nagurski excelling at linebacker, Hewitt at end, Luckman in the secondary, and Fortmann, Stydahar, and Musso on the line.

Making a successful return to the coaching ranks in 1946, George Halas guided the Bears to a regular season record of 8-2-1 and their seventh league championship, which they captured with a 24–14 victory over the Giants in the NFL title game. Halas remained at the helm for another nine years, leading the Bears to an overall record of 67-40-1 during that time, although they failed to make another playoff appearance. Standout performers for the team during Halas's third term as head coach included center/linebacker Clyde "Bulldog" Turner, offensive tackle/linebacker George Connor, defensive end Ed Sprinkle, and wide receivers Ken Kavanaugh and Harlon Hill.

The Bears posted a regular season record of 9-2-1 under new head coach Paddy Driscoll in 1956, earning in the process their first division title in 10 years. However, they subsequently suffered an embarrassing 47–7 defeat at the hands of the Giants in the NFL championship game, before going just 5-7 the following year. Dissatisfied with his team's performance, Halas returned to the sidelines in 1958, remaining there for the next 10 seasons before retiring from coaching for good at the end of 1967. Although the Bears advanced to the playoffs just once during Halas's final tour of duty as head coach, they made that postseason appearance a memorable one, winning their eighth NFL title by recording a 14–10 victory over the Giants in the 1963 league championship game, with their exceptional defense, which featured lineman Doug Atkins, safeties Richie Petitbon and Rosey Taylor, and linebackers Bill George, Joe Fortunato, and Larry Morris, rekindling memories of the "Monsters of the Midway."

The Bears subsequently entered into an extended period of mediocrity, posting a winning record just four times between 1964 and 1983. Particularly inept from 1966 to 1976, the Bears compiled an overall mark of just 54-96-4 over the course of those 11 seasons, as Halas (1966–1967), Jim Dooley (1968–1971), Abe Gibron (1972–1974), and Jack Pardee (1975–1977) all took turns coaching the team. Yet, despite their lack of success, the Bears fielded some of the league's most talented players during those lean years, with tight end Mike Ditka, halfback Gale Sayers, line-backer Dick Butkus, and defensive back Gary Fencik all earning numerous individual accolades. Meanwhile, Walter Payton established himself as the NFL's premier running back, ending his career as the league's all-time lead-ing rusher.

With the Bears in the middle of the darkest period in franchise history, they elected to change home venues in 1971, leaving Wrigley Field for the friendly confines of Soldier Field, a historic stadium built in the 1920s as a memorial for World War I veterans that has hosted many memorable sporting events through the years, including the 1927 heavyweight boxing championship rematch between Jack Dempsey and Gene Tunney. Located on Lake Shore Drive, on the Near South Side of Chicago, next to Lake Michigan, Soldier Field has now served as home to the Bears for nearly half a century.

After Jack Pardee left the Bears to coach the Washington Redskins following the conclusion of the 1977 campaign, former Minnesota Vikings defensive coordinator Neill Armstrong replaced him at the helm for the next four seasons, leading the team to an overall record of just 30-34. Things finally began to turn around, though, shortly after George Halas replaced Armstrong with Mike Ditka at the end of 1981. Ditka, whose gritty personality had earned him the nickname "Iron Mike" during his earlier six-year stay in Chicago, proved to be just what the Bears needed, with his toughness, determination, and single-mindedness helping to alter the team's losing mindset. Before long, the Bears emerged as an NFL pow-erhouse, capturing five straight NFC Central Division titles from 1984 to 1988, appearing in three conference championship games, and winning their ninth NFL championship with a resounding 46–10 victory over the New England Patriots in Super Bowl XX.

Although those Bear squads featured Walter Payton and arguably the NFL's best group of linemen on offense, the key to their success proved to be their overwhelming "46" defense, which they used to batter their opponents into submission. Devised by legendary defensive coordinator Buddy Ryan, Chicago's scheme on that side of the ball emphasized putting an inordinate amount of pressure on opposing quarterbacks, which expert defenders such as Richard Dent, Dan Hampton, Steve McMichael, Mike Singletary, Otis Wilson, and Wilber Marshall did an exceptional job of. Particularly dominant in 1985 and 1986, Chicago's defense surrendered only 198 points to the opposition in the first of those campaigns, before allowing just 187 points the following year. And, en route to winning the NFL championship in 1985, the Bears allowed a total of only 10 points during the postseason, shutting out both the New York Giants and the Los Angeles Rams in the NFC playoffs.

Sadly, George Halas did not live to witness his beloved team's return to glory. After spending the previous 15 seasons serving the Bears exclusively as owner and front office executive, the man affectionately known as "Papa Bear" died of pancreatic cancer at the age of 88, on October 1, 1983. Almost all the success the Bears experienced between 1920 and 1983 can be attributed to Halas, who, in addition to owning, coaching, and playing for the team, fulfilled several other roles at various times, including serving as traveling secretary and head of public relations. Generally considered to be the "father of professional football," Halas retired in 1967 with a total of 324 coaching victories that stood as the NFL record until Don Shula finally surpassed it in 1994.

Following Halas's passing, his oldest daughter, Virginia McCaskey, became principal owner of the Bears, with her husband, Ed McCaskey, succeeding Halas as the chairman of the board. Mrs. McCaskey later replaced her husband with her son, Michael, who remained chairman of the board until 2010, when his brother, George, assumed that position. Meanwhile, Mrs. McCaskey, who is 97 years old as of this writing, continues to hold the honorary title of "secretary of the board of directors."

Mike Ditka led the Bears to two more playoff appearances between 1989 and 1992, before being relieved of his duties after the team finished just 5-11 in the last of those campaigns. Former Dallas Cowboys defensive coordinator Dave Wannstedt succeeded Ditka as head coach, achieving very little success over the course of the next six seasons, with the Bears compiling an overall record of 40-56 and making the playoffs just once. Team ownership then turned to onetime NFL defensive back and former Jacksonville Jaguars defensive coordinator Dick Jauron, who guided the Bears to just one winning season between 1999 and 2003, although they managed to capture the division title in 2001 by going 13-3 during the regular season, before losing to the Philadelphia Eagles by a score of 33–19 in the divisional round of the postseason tournament.

The Bears finally began to perform at a consistently higher level after longtime college and NFL assistant coach Lovie Smith assumed head coaching duties in 2004, winning three division titles and one NFC championship under his leadership from 2004 to 2012. Particularly impressive in 2006, the Bears outscored their opponents by a combined margin of 427–255, en route to compiling a regular-season record of 13-3 that represented the best mark in the NFC. They then earned a hard-fought 27–24 overtime victory over the Seattle Seahawks in the divisional round of the postseason tournament, before winning the NFC title by defeating the New Orleans Saints by a score of 39–14 in the conference championship game. However, they came up short against Peyton Manning and the Indianapolis Colts in Super Bowl XLI, suffering a 29–17 defeat at the hands of their AFC counterparts. Although the Bears remained extremely competitive under Smith the next six years, posting a winning record three times and capturing another division title in 2010, team ownership ultimately decided to go in a different direction, replacing their longtime head coach with Marc Trestman, who had spent nearly three decades coaching quarterbacks, running backs, and offense at both the collegiate and professional levels. Smith left behind him a legacy that included overseeing the development of outstanding players such as linebackers Brian Urlacher and Lance Briggs, running back Matt Forte, cornerback Charles Tillman, and wide receiver/return man Devin Hester.

Trestman ended up lasting just two seasons in Chicago, leading the Bears to an overall record of 13-19 from 2013 to 2014, before being replaced by former Carolina Panthers and Denver Broncos head coach John Fox. The Bears performed no better under Fox the next three seasons, compiling a composite mark of 14-34. A 5-11 finish in 2017 sealed Fox's fate, prompting management to replace him with Matt Nagy, who had spent the previous two seasons serving as offensive coordinator of the Kansas City Chiefs. Experiencing a resurgence under Nagy in 2018, the Bears claimed their first division title in eight years by finishing the regular season with a mark of 12-4. However, they exited the playoffs quickly, losing to the Philadelphia Eagles in the wild card round of the postseason tournament by a score of 16–15 on a last-minute touchdown pass from Nick Foles to Golden Tate. Perhaps still suffering from the after-effects of their unexpected playoff loss, the Bears performed erratically in 2019, concluding the campaign with a record of just 8-8.

Nevertheless, with a strong defense anchored by All-Pro linebacker Khalil Mack, the Bears figure to be perennial contenders in the NFC North Division for the foreseeable future. Their next division title will be their 23rd. They have also won two NFC titles, nine NFL championships, and one Super Bowl, with their nine league championships placing them second only to the Green Bay Packers (13). The Bears have also recorded more victories than any other NFL franchise. Featuring a plethora of exceptional performers through the years, the Bears have retired the numbers of 14 former players. Meanwhile, 33 members of the Pro Football Hall of Fame spent at least one full season with Chicago, with 27 of those men wearing a Bears uniform during many of their peak seasons.

## FACTORS USED TO DETERMINE RANKINGS

It should come as no surprise that selecting the 50 greatest players ever to perform for a team with the rich history of the Chicago Bears presented quite a challenge. Even after narrowing the field down to a mere 50 men, I still needed to devise a method of ranking the elite players that remained. Certainly, the names of Walter Payton, Dick Butkus, Gale Sayers, Mike Singletary, Bronko Nagurski, and Brian Urlacher would appear at, or near, the top of virtually everyone's list, although the order might vary somewhat from one person to the next. Several other outstanding performers have gained general recognition through the years as being among the greatest players ever to wear a Bears uniform, with Sid Luckman, Bill George, Mike Ditka, and Dan Hampton heading the list of other Bears icons. But, how does one compare players who lined up on opposite sides of the ball with any degree of certainty? Furthermore, how does one differentiate between the pass-rushing and run-stopping skills of linemen such as Doug Atkins and Richard Dent and the ball-hawking skills of defensive backs such as Gary Fencik and Charles Tillman? And, on the offensive end, how can a direct correlation be made between the contributions made by standout lineman Stan Jones and skill position players such as Rick Casares and Gale Sayers? And then there are early greats Bronko Nagurski and Dan Fortmann, both of whom starred on both sides of the ball for the Bears throughout their respective careers. After initially deciding whom to include on my list, I then needed to determine what criteria I should use to formulate my final rankings.

The first thing I decided to examine was the level of dominance a player attained during his time with the Bears. How often did he lead the NFL in a major statistical category? Did he ever capture league MVP honors? How many times did he earn a trip to the Pro Bowl or a spot on the All-Pro Team?

I also chose to assess the level of statistical compilation a player achieved while wearing a Bears uniform. I reviewed where he ranks among the team's all-time leaders in those statistical categories most pertinent to his position. Of course, even the method of using statistics as a measuring stick has its inherent flaws. Although the level of success a team experiences rushing and passing the ball is impacted greatly by the performance of its offensive line, there really is no way to quantifiably measure the level of play reached by each individual offensive lineman. Conversely, the play of the offensive line affects tremendously the statistics compiled by a team's quarterback and running backs. Furthermore, the NFL did not keep an official record of defensive numbers such as tackles and quarterback sacks until the 1980s (although the Bears kept their own records prior to that). In addition, when examining the statistics compiled by offensive players, the era during which a quarterback, running back, or wide receiver competed must be factored into the equation.

To illustrate my last point, rule changes instituted by the league office have opened up the game considerably the last two decades. Quarterbacks are accorded far more protection than ever before, and officials have also been instructed to limit the amount of contact defensive backs are allowed to make with wide receivers. As a result, the game has experienced an offensive explosion, with quarterbacks and receivers posting numbers players from prior generations rarely even approached. That being the case, one must place the numbers Jay Cutler compiled during his time in the Windy City in their proper context when comparing him to Hall of Fame signal-caller Sid Luckman. Similarly, the statistics posted by Brandon Marshall and Alshon Jeffery must be viewed in moderation when comparing them to previous Bears wideouts Ken Kavanaugh and Harlon Hill.

Other important factors I needed to consider were the overall contributions a player made to the success of the team, the degree to which he improved the fortunes of the club during his time in Chicago, and the manner in which he impacted the team, both on and off the field. While the number of championships and division titles the Bears won during a player's years with the team certainly factored into the equation, I chose not to deny a top performer his rightful place on the list if his years in the Windy City happened to coincide with a lack of overall success by the club. As a result, the names of players such as Doug Buffone and Matt Forte will appear in these rankings.

One other thing I should mention is that I only considered a player's performance while playing for the Bears when formulating my rankings. That being the case, the names of Wilber Marshall and Khalil Mack, both of whom had many of their finest seasons with other teams, may appear lower on this list than one might expect. Meanwhile, the names of Hall of Fame players Bobby Layne and Alan Page are nowhere to be found.

Having established the guidelines to be used throughout this book, the time has come to reveal the 50 greatest players in Bears history, starting with number 1 and working our way down to number 50.

# 1

# ― WALTER PAYTON ―

Dick Butkus provided stiff competition to Walter Payton for the top spot on this list, with Butkus's eight Pro Bowl selections, six All-Pro nominations, two NFL Defensive Player of the Year awards, and ability to dominate a game from his middle linebacker position making him an extremely worthy contender. However, Payton compiled a similarly impressive list of accomplishments during his time in the Windy City, earning nine trips to the Pro Bowl, eight All-Pro selections, and one league MVP trophy, while establishing himself as the most complete running back in NFL history. The choice was a difficult one, and Butkus would have made an excellent selection as well. But, in the end, the all-around brilliance of Walter Payton enabled him to edge out the legendary linebacker for the foremost position in these rankings.

Called "the very best football player I've ever seen, period, at any position" by former Bears head coach Mike Ditka, Walter Payton did everything one could possibly expect from a great running back, ending his career with NFL records for most yards rushing, touchdowns scored, yards from scrimmage, all-purpose yards, and receptions by a non-receiver. Truly excelling in every aspect of the game, Payton even threw eight touchdown passes and did an outstanding job of blocking for his teammates, with his magnificent all-around play helping the Bears win four division titles, one NFC championship, and one Super Bowl. In addition to rushing for more than 1,000 yards 10 times and gaining more than 1,500 yards on the ground on four separate occasions, Payton amassed more than 1,500 yards from scrimmage 10 times, reaching the 2,000-yard plateau in that category four different times. The holder of numerous Bears records, Payton continues to rank among the NFL's all-time leaders in six different offensive categories more than three decades after he played his last game, with his long list of accomplishments earning him spots on the NFL's 75th Anniversary Team and the NFL 100 All-Time Team, a top-10 ranking from both the *Sporting News* and the NFL Network on their respective lists of the 100 Greatest Players in NFL History, and a place in the Pro Football Hall of Fame.

Born in Columbia, Mississippi, on July 25, 1954, Walter Jerry Payton displayed a strong affinity for music while growing up in the segregated South, playing and singing in jazz-rock combos after school as a teenager.

Although Payton continued to express his love for music while attending Columbia High School, playing drums in the school band, he began to exhibit his tremendous athleticism as well by participating in track as a long jumper, while also starring in baseball, basketball, and football, garnering All-State honors for his performance on the gridiron at running back. After running 65 yards for a touchdown the very first time he carried the ball as a junior, Payton ended up scoring at least once in every game he played over the course of the next two seasons, establishing himself in the process as one of Mississippi's top running back prospects. However, with Southeastern Conference colleges accepting few black players at the time, Payton ultimately elected to follow in the footsteps of his older brother, Eddie, and enroll at historically black Jackson State University.

Walter Payton retired as the NFL's all-time leading rusher. Courtesy of MearsonlineAuctions.com

Continuing to make a name for himself in college, Payton rushed for more than 3,500 yards, averaged 6.1 yards per carry, and scored 65 touchdowns and 464 points for the Tigers, with his outstanding play earning him Black College Player of the Year honors twice and All-America recognition once. Turning in his finest individual performance during his sophomore year, Payton scored seven touchdowns and tallied a total of 46 points during a 72–0 win over Lane College. While at Jackson State, Payton also acquired the nickname "Sweetness" for his affable personality and graceful athleticism.

Selected by the Bears with the fourth overall pick of the 1975 NFL Draft, Payton posted relatively modest numbers his first year in the league, rushing for 679 yards, amassing 892 yards from scrimmage, accumulating 1,336 all-purpose yards, and scoring seven touchdowns for a Chicago team that finished just 4-10. Emerging as the NFL's premier running back the following season, Payton began an extraordinary 11-year run during which he posted the following numbers, with only the strike-shortened 1982 campaign being excluded from this graphic:

| YEAR | RUSH YD | REC YD | YD FROM SCRIMMAGE | TD |
|---|---|---|---|---|
| 1976 | 1,390 | 149 | 1,539 | 13 |
| 1977 | **1,852*** | 269 | **2,121** | **16** |
| 1978 | 1,395 | 480 | **1,875** | 11 |
| 1979 | 1,610 | 313 | 1,923 | 16 |
| 1980 | 1,460 | 367 | 1,827 | 7 |
| 1981 | 1,222 | 379 | 1,601 | 8 |
| 1983 | 1,421 | 607 | 2,028 | 8 |
| 1984 | 1,684 | 368 | 2,052 | 11 |
| 1985 | 1,551 | 483 | 2,034 | 11 |
| 1986 | 1,333 | 382 | 1,715 | 11 |

* Please note that any numbers printed in bold throughout this book indicate that the player led the NFL in that statistical category that year.

Despite playing behind an inferior offensive line the first few seasons, Payton managed to finish either first or second in the NFL in rushing six times, placing in the league's top five in three of the other four years. He also ranked among the league leaders in yards from scrimmage nine times, topping the circuit in that category twice. Payton's amazing performance in 1977, which saw him set single-season franchise records for most yards rushing, yards from scrimmage, and rushing touchdowns (14), earned him NFL Offensive Player of the Year and league MVP honors. He also earned nine trips to the Pro Bowl, eight All-Pro selections, and nine All-NFC nominations during that time. More importantly, the Bears gradually established themselves as perennial contenders, making five playoff appearances, capturing three division titles, and winning one Super Bowl over the course of those 11 seasons.

Employing an extremely aggressive style of running even though he lacked great size, the 5'10½", 204-pound Payton had a way of exploding into defenders, typically doling out as much punishment as he received. Rarely choosing to run out of bounds, Payton preferred to run over potential tacklers, reinventing the use of the stiff-arm, which had gone out of favor among running backs during the 1970s. Recalling one of his encounters with Payton, former Dallas Cowboys cornerback Everson Walls said, "I caught his stiff-arm once, under my chin. It bent my head back, and, where your head goes, your body goes."

Refusing to apologize for the way he punished defenders, Payton stated, "What about the pain they've dealt out to me? Pain is expected in this game."

Commenting on Payton's aggressive running style, former NFL head coach Jerry Glanville suggested, "He was a linebacker carrying the football."

Meanwhile, Jim Brown expressed his admiration for Payton's confrontational mindset by saying, "We were warriors, and he was a great warrior. If a guy runs out of bounds because a cornerback is coming up to hit him, that's not my kind of guy. Walter was definitely one of them because he was a powerful man. . . . Give me the heart of Walter Payton. There's never been a greater heart."

Blessed with tremendous physical strength, Payton had the ability to bench-press 390 pounds and do leg-press series with more than 700 pounds. In discussing Payton's granite-like physique, former Bears backfield coach Fred O'Connor once said, "The first time I saw Walter Payton in the locker room, I thought God must have taken a chisel and said, 'I'm going to make me a halfback.'" An extraordinary all-around athlete, Payton also could throw a football 60 yards, punt it 70 yards, kick a field goal of 45 yards, and walk across a football field on his hands.

Known for his grueling offseason training regimen, Payton worked himself into top shape by running up a steep hill near his Illinois home about 20 times a day for several months before the start of each NFL season. Convincing teammates or local college players to join him on his treks from time to time, the mischievous Payton admitted, "I enjoy seeing them try it once or twice and then vomit."

Payton's strength, conditioning, and tenacity also helped make him one of the league's finest blocking backs, with Los Angeles Rams Hall of Fame defensive end Jack Youngblood stating, "I remember a block he threw on me once, and I thought he opened a hole in my sternum, he hit me so hard. I said, 'Walter, what are you doing?' He said, 'You were in the way.'"

Although Payton lacked great breakaway speed, defenders rarely caught him from behind, due, in part, to his signature "stutter step," which he often employed to distract his pursuers during long runs. Feeling that this high-stepping maneuver caused his opponents to commit to an angle of pursuit based on what they believed he would do next, Payton made any necessary adjustments, allowing him to gain an advantage over players who possessed more straight-ahead speed.

A selfless team leader who preferred not to draw attention to himself, Payton chose not to take part in elaborate touchdown celebrations, instead handing the ball to an official or one of his offensive linemen because, he said, "They're the ones who do all the work."

The totality of Payton's game, coupled with his unselfish mindset, earned him the respect and admiration of everyone he competed with and against, with former Raiders linebacker Matt Millen saying, "You felt honored to tackle him."

Dick Butkus, who retired two seasons before Payton arrived in Chicago, called him "a perfect example of what a true back was supposed to be."

Longtime Dallas Cowboys head coach Tom Landry said, "Walter has two qualities that you don't have in one running back. He has great speed, but, not only that, he has great strength. You gotta' plug the hole up twice."

Former St. Louis Cardinals halfback Johnny Roland suggested, "When God created a running back, he created Walter Payton."

Meanwhile, Jim Finks, the late general manager of the Bears, once described Payton as "a complete football player, better than Jim Brown, better than O. J. Simpson."

After surpassing Brown as the NFL's all-time leading rusher in 1984, Payton helped lead the Bears to the league championship the following year by gaining 1,551 yards on the ground, amassing 2,034 yards from scrimmage, and scoring 11 touchdowns, with his contributions to the success of the team gaining him recognition as the NFL Player of the Year. Payton subsequently rushed for another 1,333 yards in 1986, before assuming a somewhat diminished role in 1987, when he rushed for only 533 yards and scored just five touchdowns in Chicago's 12 non-strike games. Choosing to announce his retirement following the conclusion of the campaign, Payton ended his career with 16,726 yards rushing, 492 receptions, 4,538 receiving yards, 21,264 yards from scrimmage, 21,803 all-purpose yards, and 125 touchdowns, with his 16,726 yards gained on the ground currently representing the second-highest total in NFL history. Extremely durable, Payton missed just one non-strike game his entire career, appearing in 190 out of a possible 191 contests, 184 of which he started.

When asked years later how he felt about having his long-standing rushing record broken by Payton, Jim Brown said, "Well, there are some individuals who, if they broke a record, and they did it the wrong way, they wouldn't hear from me. But the way that he was, his attitude, his ability, I have all the admiration in the world for him."

After retiring as an active player, Payton became involved in an unsuccessful attempt to bring an NFL team to the city of St. Louis that would have made him the first minority owner in league history. Having failed in that venture, Payton dabbled in the race car industry, acquiring part ownership of Dale Coyne Racing. He also opened a restaurant in Aurora, Illinois, that he called Walter Payton's Roadhouse.

Sadly, Payton found himself unable to enjoy his retirement for very long, disclosing to the public during an emotional news conference held in Chicago on February 2, 1999, that he had been diagnosed with primary sclerosing cholangitis, a rare condition in which the bile ducts become blocked. Although Payton subsequently received chemotherapy and radiation treatment to help prevent the disease from spreading, it soon became apparent that the cancer had progressed to a point that it had become terminal. Payton spent the next few months trying to raise awareness as to the importance of organ donation, before making his last public appearance at Wrigley Field in April 1999, when he threw out the first pitch at a Cubs game. Payton finally succumbed to his illness on November 1, 1999, passing away at only 45 years of age, after spending the final weeks of his life working with author Don Yaeger to create his posthumously published autobiography entitled *Never Die Easy*. One of the passages from that work reads: "If you ask me how I want to be remembered, it is as a winner. You know what a winner is? A winner is somebody who has given his best effort, who has tried the hardest they possibly can, who has utilized every ounce of energy and strength within them to accomplish something. It doesn't mean that they accomplished it or failed, it means that they've given it their best. That's a winner."

Expressing his love and admiration for his former teammate during the eulogy he delivered at a memorial service the Bears subsequently held for Payton at Soldier Field, an emotional Dan Hampton said, "I've got a little girl, she's four years old. Ten years from now, when she asks about the Chicago Bears, I'll tell her about a championship, and I'll tell her about great teams and great teammates and great coaches, and how great it was to be a part of it. But the first thing I'll tell her about is Walter Payton."

## CAREER HIGHLIGHTS

### Best Season

Payton had so many great seasons from which to choose, with the 1978, 1979, 1983, 1984, and 1985 campaigns all ranking among the finest of his career. Nevertheless, Payton turned in his most dominant performance in 1977, when he earned NFL Offensive Player of the Year and league MVP honors by topping the circuit in seven different offensive categories, establishing career-high marks with 1,852 yards rushing, 2,121 yards from scrimmage, 2,216 all-purpose yards, 14 rushing touchdowns, 16 touchdowns, and an average of 5.5 yards per carry.

### Memorable Moments/Greatest Performances

Payton scored the first touchdown of his career when he ran the ball in from 4 yards out during a 46–13 loss to Miami on November 2, 1975.

Payton went over 100 yards rushing for the first time as a pro during a 31–3 loss to the 49ers on November 16, 1975, finishing the game with 23 carries for 105 yards.

Payton amassed 300 yards of total offense in the 1975 regular-season finale, rushing for 134 yards and one touchdown, making five receptions for 62 yards, and returning two kickoffs for 104 yards during a 42–17 rout of the New Orleans Saints.

Payton led the Bears to a 19–12 win over the 49ers on September 19, 1976, by rushing for 148 yards and two touchdowns, the longest of which covered 20 yards.

Payton carried the ball 27 times for a season-high 183 yards during a 34–7 win over the Seattle Seahawks on December 5, 1976.

Payton led the Bears to a 30–20 win over Detroit in the 1977 regular-season opener by rushing for 160 yards and two touchdowns, with his longest run of the day being a 73-yard scamper.

Payton rushed for 205 yards and two touchdowns during a convincing 26–0 victory over the Packers on October 30, 1977.

Payton proved to be the difference in a 28–27 win over the Kansas City Chiefs on November 13, 1977, rushing for 192 yards and three touchdowns, with his most memorable run of the day coming on a 32-yard gain in which he bowled over several would-be tacklers before finally being brought down from behind by the ankles.

Payton turned in arguably the greatest performance of his career on November 20, 1977, when, despite displaying severe flu symptoms entering the contest, he ran for a franchise-record 275 yards and one touchdown during a 10–7 win over the Minnesota Vikings.

Payton helped the Bears celebrate Thanksgiving in 1977 by rushing for 137 yards and scoring two touchdowns during a 31–14 win over the Detroit Lions, with one of his TDs coming on a 75-yard pass from Bob Avellini.

Payton led the Bears to a 21–10 win over the Packers on December 11, 1977, by rushing for 163 yards and two touchdowns.

Although the Bears lost to the Broncos by a score of 16–7 on October 16, 1978, Payton rushed for a season-high 157 yards during the contest, gaining nearly half of those on a 76-yard run.

Payton starred during a 26–7 victory over the Vikings on September 9, 1979, rushing for 182 yards and two touchdowns, which came on runs of 43 and 26 yards.

Payton gave the Bears a 7–0 win over Buffalo on October 7, 1979, by scoring the game's only touchdown on a short run in the fourth quarter, concluding the contest with 155 yards rushing.

Payton accounted for all three touchdowns the Bears scored during a 30–27 loss to Minnesota on October 21, 1979, scoring twice himself and throwing a 54-yard TD pass to Brian Baschnagel.

Payton led the Bears to a 28–27 win over the 49ers on October 28, 1979, by rushing for 162 yards and three touchdowns.

Payton amassed 200 yards of total offense during a 42–6 mauling of the Cardinals in the final game of the 1979 regular season, rushing for 157 yards and three touchdowns, and making three receptions for 43 yards.

Payton contributed to a 22–3 victory over the New Orleans Saints on September 14, 1980, by rushing for 183 yards and one touchdown, which came on a 69-yard run.

Payton helped lead the Bears to a 61–7 thrashing of the Packers on December 7, 1980, by rushing for 130 yards and three touchdowns.

Although the Bears lost to Dallas by a score of 10–9 on Thanksgiving Day 1981, Payton rushed for a season-high 179 yards during the contest.

Payton once again starred in defeat on September 18, 1983, rushing for 161 yards and one touchdown, and completing a pair of TD passes to Willie Gault during a 34–31 overtime loss to New Orleans, with the longest of his TD tosses covering 56 yards.

Payton earned NFC Offensive Player of the Week honors by rushing for 179 yards and one TD during a 27–0 win over Denver on September 9, 1984, with his TD run covering 72 yards.

Payton led the Bears to a 20–7 win over New Orleans on October 7, 1984, by rushing for 154 yards and one TD, supplanting Jim Brown in the process as the NFL's all-time leading rusher.

Although the Bears suffered a 20–14 defeat at the hands of the Green Bay Packers on December 9, 1984, Payton rushed for a season-high 175 yards and one touchdown during the contest.

Payton led the Bears to their ninth straight victory without a loss the following season by rushing for a season-high 192 yards and one TD during a 16–10 win over the Packers on November 3, 1985, with his outstanding performance earning him NFC Offensive Player of the Week honors.

Payton earned that distinction for the third and final time in his career by rushing for 177 yards and one touchdown during a 13–10 overtime victory over Philadelphia on September 14, 1986.

## Notable Achievements

- Rushed for more than 1,000 yards 10 times, topping 1,500 yards four times.
- Surpassed 50 receptions twice and 500 receiving yards once.
- Surpassed 1,500 yards from scrimmage 10 times, topping 2,000 yards on four occasions.
- Scored more than 10 touchdowns seven times.
- Averaged more than 5 yards per carry once (5.5 in 1977).
- Led NFL in rushing attempts four times, rushing yards once, rushing touchdowns once, touchdowns once, rushing average once, yards from scrimmage twice, and all-purpose yards once.
- Finished second in NFL in rushing attempts twice, rushing yards five times, rushing touchdowns twice, touchdowns once, points scored once, yards from scrimmage once, and all-purpose yards once.
- Finished third in NFL in rushing yards once, rushing touchdowns once, touchdowns once, yards from scrimmage four times, and all-purpose yards three times.
- Led Bears in rushing 12 times.
- Holds Bears single-season records for most yards rushing (1,852 in 1977), rushing touchdowns (14 in 1977 and 1979), and yards from scrimmage (2,121 in 1977).
- Holds Bears career records for most rushing attempts (3,838), yards rushing (16,726), rushing touchdowns (110), touchdowns (125), receptions (492), yards from scrimmage (21,264), and all-purpose yards (21,803).
- Ranks among Bears career leaders with 4,538 receiving yards (4th), 750 points scored (3rd), and 190 games played (4th).
- Ranks among NFL's all-time leaders in rushing attempts (2nd), yards rushing (2nd), rushing touchdowns (4th), touchdowns (11th), yards from scrimmage (3rd), and all-purpose yards (3rd).
- Four-time division champion (1984, 1985, 1986, 1987).

- 1985 NFC champion.
- Super Bowl XX champion.
- Three-time NFC Offensive Player of the Week.
- Nine-time Pro Bowl selection (1976, 1977, 1978, 1979, 1980, 1983, 1984, 1985, and 1986).
- Five-time First-Team All-Pro selection (1976, 1977, 1980, 1984, and 1985).
- Three-time Second-Team All-Pro selection (1978, 1979, and 1986).
- Seven-time First-Team All-NFC selection (1976, 1977, 1978, 1979, 1980, 1984, and 1985).
- Two-time Second-Team All-NFC selection (1983 and 1986).
- 1977 NFL Offensive Player of the Year.
- 1977 NFL MVP.
- 1985 Bert Bell Award Winner as NFL Player of the Year.
- NFL 1970s All-Decade Team.
- NFL 1980s All-Decade Team.
- Pro Football Reference All-1980s First Team.
- #34 retired by Bears.
- Named to NFL's 75th Anniversary Team in 1994.
- Named to *Sporting News* All-Century Team in 1999.
- Named to NFL 100 All-Time Team in 2019.
- Number eight on the *Sporting News'* 1999 list of the 100 Greatest Players in NFL History.
- Number five on the NFL Network's 2010 list of the NFL's 100 Greatest Players.
- Elected to Pro Football Hall of Fame in 1993.

# 2

## DICK BUTKUS

Having fallen just short of earning the top spot on this list, Dick Butkus lays claim to the number two position, edging out longtime teammate Gale Sayers for that distinction. In discussing Butkus, former NFL center Bill Curry, who competed against him as a member of the Green Bay Packers and Baltimore Colts, said, "Dick Butkus is the greatest football player I ever saw. I'm convinced that he's the greatest football player who ever lived."

One of the most dominant and intimidating defensive players in the history of the game, Dick Butkus instilled fear into his opponents with his aggressive style of play, destroying anyone who stood in his path. Generally considered to be the finest middle linebacker in NFL history, Butkus earned eight Pro Bowl selections, six All-Pro nominations, and two NFL Defensive Player of the Year awards during his nine seasons in Chicago, before being further honored following the conclusion of his playing career by being named to the NFL's 75th Anniversary Team, the *Sporting News* All-Century Team, and the NFL 100 All-Time Team, receiving a top-10 ranking by both the *Sporting News* and the NFL Network on their respective lists of the 100 Greatest Players in NFL History, being inducted into the Pro Football Hall of Fame, and having his #51 retired by the Bears.

Born in Chicago, Illinois, on December 9, 1942, Richard Marvin Butkus entered the world weighing a robust 13 pounds 6 ounces. The son of

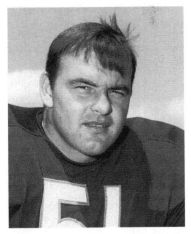

Most football historians consider Dick Butkus to be the greatest middle linebacker ever to play the game.
Courtesy of RMYAuctions.com

a Lithuanian immigrant father who spoke broken English and worked for the Pullman-Standard railroad company as an electrician and an American-born mother who worked 50 hours a week at a laundromat, Butkus grew up on the city's South Side hoping to one day play for his favorite NFL team, the Chicago Cardinals. In pursuit of his dream, Butkus elected to enroll at perennial football winner Chicago Vocational High School, rather than attend the school closest to where he lived.

Emerging as one of the area's most highly touted prospects under the tutelage of head coach Bernie O'Brien while at Vocational High, Butkus starred at fullback and linebacker, gaining recognition from the *Chicago Sun-Times* as Chicago's high school player of the year as a junior in 1959 by averaging 5 yards per carry on offense, while also making 70 percent of his team's tackles on defense. Choosing to remain close to home following his graduation, Butkus accepted an athletic scholarship from the University of Illinois, where he continued to star on the gridiron. Excelling at center and linebacker for the Fighting Illini from 1962 to 1964, Butkus earned All–Big Ten Conference honors as a sophomore, before being named First-Team All-America in each of the next two seasons. Butkus, who built up his strength by carrying cases of tile for hours on end in his summer job and pushing cars with the motor off on a dead-end street in his neighborhood, recorded 145 tackles and forced 10 fumbles as a junior, prompting Dan Jenkins to write in *Sports Illustrated*, "If every college football team had a linebacker like Dick Butkus, all fullbacks would soon be three feet tall and sing soprano. Dick Butkus is a special kind of brute whose particular talent is mashing runners into curious shapes. . . . Butkus not only hits, he crushes and squeezes opponents with thick arms that also are extremely long. At any starting point on his build, he is big, well-proportioned, and getting bigger." Performing brilliantly once again as a senior in 1964, Butkus recorded 132 tackles, en route to earning a third-place finish in the Heisman Trophy balloting and being named college football's Lineman of the Year and Player of the Year by both the *Sporting News* and the American Football Coaches Association.

Subsequently selected by the Denver Broncos with the ninth overall pick of the 1965 AFL Draft and the Chicago Bears with the third overall pick of that year's NFL Draft, Butkus chose to sign with George Halas and the hometown Bears even though the Broncos offered him more money. Making an extremely favorable impression on veteran middle linebacker Bill George once he arrived at his first pro training camp, Butkus drew praise from the future Hall of Famer, who later said, "The second I saw him on the field, I knew my playing days were over. Nobody ever looked that good before or since."

After beating out George for the starting middle linebacker job during the preseason, Butkus went on to perform magnificently as a rookie, earning Pro Bowl honors for the first of eight straight times and the first of his five First-Team All-Pro selections by leading the Bears with five interceptions, seven fumble recoveries, and well over 100 tackles, with his superb play helping them improve their record from 5-9 to 9-5. Although the Bears won only five games in 1966, Butkus had another huge year, gaining Second-Team All-Pro recognition by once again leading the team in tackles.

Already considered one of the league's top defenders after just two seasons, the 6'3", 245-pound Butkus possessed good size and strength, superb instincts, and excellent quickness, even though he lacked elite running speed, as former Bears roommate Ed O'Bradovich acknowledged when he said, "For Dick to run a 100-yard dash, it would take him three days. But I want to tell you something. From that middle linebacker position, 20 yards this way, 20 yards that way, and 20 yards that way, nobody, I mean nobody, was quicker than he was. . . . He made a lot of interceptions. If he was told, in pass defenses, to be in a certain area, he was there. He had great hands. The man was unbelievable."

Excelling in every aspect of the game, Butkus did an outstanding job of pursuing opposing ball-carriers all over the field, making tackles from sideline to sideline, and covering backs coming out of the backfield. However, Butkus impacted the outcomes of games with more than just his agility, ball-hawking skills, and tackling ability, with his nasty temperament, unmatched intensity, and barely controlled rage instilling fear in the hearts and minds of opposing players throughout the league. In explaining some of the psychological techniques he employed to work himself into a lather prior to the start of a contest, Butkus said, "When I went out on the field to warm up, I would manufacture things to make me mad. If someone on the other team was laughing, I'd pretend he was laughing at me or the Bears. It always worked for me."

Frightening his opponents with verbal threats and grunting sounds that often made them think he had animalistic tendencies, Butkus made a lasting impression on former Houston Oilers quarterback Dan Pastorini, who, years after his first encounter with the Bears middle linebacker, still seemed astonished by his behavior, recalling, "He [Butkus] is calling me everything in the book. He's threatening to kill me. He's threatening to kill my children. He's threatening to kill my mother and father. He's threatening to kill everybody!"

In explaining the method to his madness, Butkus stated, "If you can get someone who you're competing against either fearful or intimidated, it's going to make my job easier. For some reason, I was able to do that. Fear is lacking confidence, and I don't want people who I'm playing against to have confidence that they can beat me. So, let me try to make them fearful of me, not confident with me."

Revealing that Butkus did an outstanding job of accomplishing his goal, former Baltimore Colts running back Alex Hawkins admitted, "It was horrifying playing against him because he could intimidate literally an entire offensive team, and I mean good teams."

Suggesting that Butkus intimidated more than just the opposition, Bill Curry claimed, "Butkus dominated the game the way no other player ever has. He dominated officials. He'd take the ball away from the guy after the play and shake it in the official's face, and the official would point it their way. It was awesome."

Packers Hall of Fame halfback Paul Hornung said of his frequent foe, "He was the meanest S.O.B. I've ever seen in my life who played professional football. He didn't like anybody with a different jersey. I mean, he really disliked you. He went after you like he hated you from his old neighborhood."

Rams All-Pro defensive end Deacon Jones added, "He [Butkus] was an animal, and every time he hit you, he tried to put you in the cemetery."

Meanwhile, longtime Bears teammate Doug Buffone stated, "I always say to play professional football you have to have a Neanderthal gene. Dick had two."

Butkus, who led the Bears in tackles eight straight times, employed an unconventional tackling style that proved to be extremely successful. Instead of targeting his opponents' legs, he typically engulfed them in his viselike grip, picked them up, and slammed them to the ground, resulting in an inordinate number of fumbles. In discussing his technique, Butkus said, "When you are in a bearhug, it's hard to get your arms out to break your fall. And sometimes, you're going to be trying to break your fall with an arm that happens to be carrying the ball, and the ball pops out."

Commenting on the unusual manner with which Butkus brought down opposing ball-carriers, Colts Hall of Fame wide receiver Raymond Berry stated, "He was the most unique defensive player I ever saw come into professional football. The first year that he began to play, he began to do things to runners that no one had ever done before, in that he was tackling these guys with one hand and stripping them of the ball with the other. I'd never seen any linebacker in professional football, before or since, who did this."

Claiming that Butkus inflicted a considerable amount of punishment anytime he contacted someone in possession of the football, former Baltimore Colts general manager Ernie Accorsi said, "When he hit you, you stayed hit. He hit with violence. . . . There were more people in the training room after we played the Bears than any other opponent—everybody was bleeding, bruised, marked up. I remember looking at one of our assistant trainers and saying, 'Was it that tough out there?' And he looked at me and he said, 'Butkus.'"

Former Cardinals and Packers running back MacArthur Lane described what it was like being tackled by Butkus, stating, "If I had a choice, I'd sooner go one on one with a grizzly bear. I pray that I can get up every time Butkus hits me."

Paul Hornung noted, "Dick didn't just tackle you. He made just textbook tackles, but he didn't just tackle you. He engulfed you."

Saints wide receiver Dan Abramowicz added, "Dick was not satisfied with just an ordinary tackle. He had to hit you, pick you up, drive you, and grind you into the ground."

Yet, Minnesota Vikings Hall of Fame head coach Bud Grant suggested that Butkus depended on more than just brute force to establish himself as the premier defender of his time, saying, "Even though he had an intimidating way about him, he also had a way of being in the right place at the right time. He was there many times before the blockers were ready and did a lot of what he did not only because of the physical attributes, but I think he had great instincts. He was one of the most instinctive football players I think I've seen on the other side."

Although Butkus failed to gain All-Pro recognition for the first time in his career in 1967, he had another great year, recording 146 tackles (111 solo) and an unofficial total of 18 quarterback sacks. He followed that up by making First-Team All-Pro in each of the next two seasons, also earning NFL Defensive Player of the Year honors in 1969. Butkus continued to wreak havoc on opposing offenses in 1970, recording 132 solo tackles, 84 assists, and three interceptions, with his fabulous performance earning him NFL Defensive Player of the Year honors for the second straight time. Meanwhile, a poll taken of NFL coaches that year identified Butkus as the player with whom they would most like to start if they were building a new team from scratch.

Nevertheless, Butkus's aggressive style of play finally began to take its toll on him in 1970, with Detroit Lions tight end Charlie Sanders suggesting that the linebacker's reputation led to his eventual downfall when he said, "It was known around the league that no one wanted to take on Dick directly, so there was a lot of chop-blocking and hits below the knees on him, which contributed to his demise."

Butkus suffered his first serious knee injury during a 24–16 win over the Giants in the opening game of the 1970 regular season, with New York quarterback Fran Tarkenton marveling afterwards, "Butkus has the most concentration of any man in the game. He's fantastic. After he was hurt, he dragged that leg around the whole field. He was better after the injury than before—better on that one damn leg than with two."

After undergoing reconstructive surgery on his right knee during the subsequent offseason, Butkus played in pain in each of the next two seasons when the ligaments failed to heal properly. Still, he led the Bears in tackles both years, performing particularly well in 1971, when, in addition to making 117 stops and assisting on 68 others, he intercepted four passes and recovered three fumbles.

However, the pain became too severe for even Butkus to tolerate in 1973. After taking himself out of a game against the Atlanta Falcons in Week 5, Butkus limped off the field for the last time a few weeks later, failing to make an appearance in any of the Bears' final five contests. Announcing his retirement following the conclusion of the campaign, Butkus finished with unofficial totals of 1,020 solo tackles and 489 assists, giving him more total stops (1,509) than anyone else in franchise history. He also recorded 22 interceptions, amassed 166 interception-return yards, scored one touchdown, and recovered 25 fumbles on defense.

Following his playing days, Butkus began a career in acting and broadcasting, appearing in several commercials, movies, and television shows, while also serving as a color analyst on Bears games from 1985 to 1987, before replacing Jimmy "The Greek" Snyder on CBS's pregame show *The NFL Today* in 1988. He later retired to Malibu, California, where he remains an avid fan and frequent media image for the Bears.

Unfortunately, the injuries that Butkus sustained during his playing career have compounded with time, forcing him to undergo knee replacement surgery and an osteotomy that left him with one leg one-and-a-half inches shorter than the other, which has affected his hips, back, and neck. He has also lost much of the strength in his hands and undergone quintuple bypass surgery to remove blockages in his arteries. Still, Butkus maintains that football had a largely positive impact on his life, with longtime friend Ed O'Bradovich saying, "His whole damn life was football. Forget about it. It wasn't driving a pretty car. It wasn't going to the local bar and pounding your chest 'I'm the greatest.' It was the opposite."

Butkus once drew the following words of praise from former Rams head coach Tommy Prothro: "He is a legendary football player. I never thought any player could play as well as writers write that he can, but Butkus comes as close as any I've ever seen."

And, long after he retired from the game, Butkus continued to draw praise from those who saw him perform on the football field, with Ted Marchibroda, who spent 35 years coaching in the NFL, saying, "I think Dick, without question, in my mind, was probably the greatest linebacker that I ever saw."

Gale Sayers perhaps put it best when he said, "There was no one better than Dick Butkus."

## CAREER HIGHLIGHTS

### Best Season

Butkus performed brilliantly for the Bears as a rookie in 1965, leading the team in tackles, interceptions, and fumble recoveries, with his magnificent play helping them limit their opponents to 104 fewer points than they scored the previous season. Butkus also had a huge year in 1967, recording unofficial totals of 111 solo tackles, 35 assists, and 18 quarterback sacks, with Chicago statisticians later tabulating that he was involved in 867 of 880 defensive plays for the Bears. And, of course, Butkus earned NFL Defensive Player of the Year honors in both 1969 and 1970, concluding the second of those campaigns with 132 solo tackles, 84 assists, three interceptions, and two fumble recoveries. But Butkus recorded 182 tackles and three interceptions in 1968, with football researcher John Turney of *Pro Football Journal* writing in 2016, "after talking to people who studied Butkus, they feel 1968 was his best season overall." We will not dispute that opinion here.

### Memorable Moments/Greatest Performances

Although the Bears lost to the San Francisco 49ers by a score of 52–24 in the opening game of the 1965 regular season, Butkus excelled in his pro debut, recording 11 solo stops.

Butkus once again starred in defeat two weeks later, making 27 unassisted tackles during a 23–14 loss to the eventual NFL champion Green Bay Packers on October 3, 1965.

Butkus recorded the first interception of his career during a 31–6 win over the Los Angeles Rams on October 10, 1965, subsequently returning the ball 11 yards.

Butkus earned NFL Defensive Player of the Week honors for the first of four times by intercepting a pass and recovering a fumble during a 35–14 win over the Giants on November 28, 1965.

Butkus anchored a Chicago defense that allowed just 42 yards rushing and 168 yards of total offense during a 14–3 win over the Detroit Lions on October 15, 1967.

Butkus helped lead the Bears to a 38–7 thrashing of the Pittsburgh Steelers on November 9, 1969, that represented their only win of the year by making 25 tackles and recording a safety when he sacked quarterback Dick Shiner in the end zone, with his brilliant play gaining him recognition as NFL Defensive Player of the Week.

Butkus had another big game against the Steelers in the 1971 regular-season opener, picking off two passes during a 17–15 Bears win.

Butkus gave the Bears a 16–15 victory over the Washington Redskins on November 14, 1971, when, following a 40-yard touchdown run by Chicago's Cyril Pinder late in the fourth quarter, the linebacker broke a 15–15 tie by making a leaping catch in the end zone of a pass thrown by holder Bobby Douglass following a botched extra-point attempt. Butkus later called the play the favorite of his career.

Butkus carried the ball for the only time in his career during a 38–24 loss to the Lions on October 1, 1972, gaining 28 yards on a fake punt attempt.

Butkus contributed to a 35–14 win over the Houston Oilers on October 28, 1973, by intercepting a pass and scoring his lone career touchdown when he recovered a fumble in the end zone.

## Notable Achievements

- Recorded more than 100 tackles eight times.
- Intercepted five passes in 1965.
- Recorded unofficial total of 18 sacks in 1967.
- Finished second in NFL with seven fumble recoveries in 1965.
- Led Bears in tackles eight times.
- Holds Bears career records for most tackles (1,509) and most fumble recoveries on defense (25).
- Ranks among Bears career leaders with 22 interceptions (tied-11th).
- Four-time NFL Defensive Player of the Week.

- Eight-time Pro Bowl selection (1965, 1966, 1967, 1968, 1969, 1970, 1971, and 1972).
- Five-time First-Team All-Pro selection (1965, 1968, 1969, 1970, and 1972).
- 1966 Second-Team All-Pro selection.
- Two-time First-Team All–Western Conference selection (1966 and 1969).
- Three-time First-Team All-NFC selection (1970, 1971, and 1972).
- Two-time Newspaper Enterprise Association NFL Defensive Player of the Year (1969 and 1970).
- NFL 1960s All-Decade Team.
- NFL 1970s All-Decade Team.
- #51 retired by Bears.
- Named to NFL's 75th Anniversary Team in 1994.
- Named to *Sporting News* All-Century Team in 1999.
- Named to NFL 100 All-Time Team in 2019.
- Number 9 on the *Sporting News'* 1999 list of the 100 Greatest Players in NFL History.
- Number 10 on the NFL Network's 2010 list of the NFL's 100 Greatest Players.
- Number 70 on ESPN's 1999 list of the 100 Greatest Athletes of the 20th Century.
- Elected to Pro Football Hall of Fame in 1979.

# 3

# GALE SAYERS

His career shortened by a series of devastating injuries to his knees, Gale Sayers failed to compile the lofty career totals one would expect from one of the greatest running backs in NFL history. Nevertheless, Sayers proved to be just that during his relatively brief stay in the Windy City, establishing himself as the most exciting runner of his time in his seven years with the Bears. Blessed with great speed, tremendous acceleration, extraordinary peripheral vision, and exceptional cutback ability, Sayers remains, to this day, arguably the finest open-field runner ever to play the game. Despite playing only four full seasons and appearing in a total of just 68 games over the course of his career, Sayers managed to lead the league in rushing twice and all-purpose yards three times, amass more than 1,000 yards from scrimmage four times, and accumulate more than 2,000 all-purpose yards twice. The Bears' single-season record holder for most all-purpose yards, rushing touchdowns, and total touchdowns scored, Sayers earned four trips to the Pro Bowl and five consecutive First-Team All-Pro nominations while serving as a member of the team. And following the conclusion of his playing career, Sayers received the additional distinctions of being named to the NFL's 75th Anniversary Team, the *Sporting News* All-Century Team, and the NFL 100 All-Time Team, being included on both the *Sporting News* and the NFL Network lists of the 100 Greatest Players in NFL History, gaining induction into the Pro Football Hall of Fame, and having his #40 retired by the Bears.

Born in Wichita, Kansas, on May 30, 1943, Gale Eugene Sayers grew up in Omaha, Nebraska, where he attended Omaha Central High School. An exceptional all-around athlete, Sayers ran track and played football at Omaha Central, starring on the gridiron at running back on offense and middle linebacker on defense. Heavily recruited as a senior, Sayers initially signed letters of intent with 17 different colleges, including Iowa State, Northwestern, and Notre Dame, before ultimately choosing to enroll at the University of Kansas. He subsequently spent three years starring at halfback

Gale Sayers earned a place in the Pro Football Hall of Fame even though he appeared in a total of just 68 NFL games.
Courtesy of RMYAuctions.com

for the Jayhawks, concluding his college career with 2,675 yards rushing and 4,020 all-purpose yards, with his brilliant play gaining him consensus All-America recognition in each of his last two seasons. Sayers, whose tremendous speed earned him the nickname the "Kansas Comet," also excelled in track, competing in the high hurdles, the 100-yard dash, and the long jump, where he set a school record by leaping 24 feet, 10½ inches.

Impressed with Sayers's exceptional play at the collegiate level, the Bears selected him with the fourth overall pick of the 1965 NFL Draft, just moments after they claimed Dick Butkus with the third selection. Electing to sign with the Bears after also receiving a contract offer from the Kansas City Chiefs, who made him the fifth overall pick of that year's AFL Draft, Sayers immediately displaced Jon Arnett as the team's starting halfback upon his arrival in Chicago, after which he went on to have a fabulous rookie season. In addition to ranking among the league leaders with 867 yards rushing, 1,374 yards from scrimmage, and 898 kickoff- and punt-return yards, Sayers topped the circuit with 2,272 all-purpose yards, 22 touchdowns, 132 points scored, and a 31.4 yards per kickoff return average, earning in the process Pro Bowl, First-Team All-Pro, and NFL Rookie of the Year honors. Sayers followed that up with an equally impressive sophomore campaign, once again gaining Pro Bowl and First-Team All-Pro recognition by leading the NFL with 1,231 yards rushing, 1,678 yards from scrimmage, and 2,440 all-purpose yards, while also placing near the top of the league rankings with eight rushing touchdowns, 12 TDs, and a rushing average of 5.4 yards per carry.

Feeling that he needed very little room to free himself for a lengthy gain, the 6-foot, 198-pound Sayers once proclaimed, "Just give me 18 inches of daylight. That's all I need." Supporting his star running back's contention, Bears head coach George Halas said, "Gale detects daylight. The average back, when he sees a hole, will try to bull his way through. But Gale, if the hole is even partly clogged, instinctively takes off in the right direction. And he does it so swiftly and surely that the defense is usually frozen."

And, once Sayers broke into the open field, he proved to be the game's most exciting runner, thrilling fans around the league with his great speed, elusiveness, and cutback ability that made him extremely difficult for defenders to bring down. Blessed with an uncanny ability to stop on a dime and accelerate back to full speed in only one or two steps, Sayers drew the following words of praise from Dick Butkus, who said of his teammate, "He had this ability to go full speed, cut, and then go full speed again right away. I saw it every day in practice. We played live, and you could never get a clean shot on Gale. Never."

In describing his running style, Sayers said, "I had a style all my own. The way I ran, lurchy, herky-jerky, I kept people off-guard, so, if I didn't have that much power when I hit a man, hell, he was off-balance, and I could knock him down."

Sayers added, "I had great peripheral vision, there's no doubt about that. I could see everybody on the field, and so I knew where to run, where to cut. In the same way, I had a feel for where people were because I know many times, many runs I watched on film, there'd be a fellow coming from my blind side, and there was no way I could see him, but I could feel him."

Commenting on Sayers's unique ability to detect the presence of anyone in his general area, O. J. Simpson stated, "I've watched him [on film] put moves on guys coming up behind him, I mean four yards away. No back has ever been able to do that."

Sayers had another outstanding year in 1967, earning Pro Bowl and First-Team All-Pro honors for the third straight time by leading the NFL with 1,689 all-purpose yards, while also placing near the top of the league rankings with 880 yards rushing, 603 kickoff-return yards, seven rushing touchdowns, and 12 TDs, four of which came on special teams. Sayers got off to an even better start in 1968, rushing for 856 yards, amassing 1,463 all-purpose yards, and averaging a league-best 6.2 yards per carry through the first nine games, before suffering a season-ending injury to his right knee during a 27–19 home win over the San Francisco 49ers on November 10. With San Francisco cornerback Kermit Alexander delivering a blow directly to his knee as he looked to turn upfield after taking a pitch from Bears quarterback Virgil Carter, Sayers tore his anterior cruciate ligament, medial collateral ligament, and meniscus cartilage, forcing him to sit out the rest of the year after undergoing surgery immediately. Looking back years later at the damage done to his knee, Sayers said, "The injury was only serious because they had to saw through muscles and nerves. If they'd had arthroscopic techniques in those days, I'd have been back in a couple of weeks."

Upon his return to the Bears in 1969, Sayers seemed a bit slower, failing to display the same great speed and acceleration he possessed during the early stages of his career. Nevertheless, relying more on tough running and engaging tacklers for extra yards, he ended up leading the NFL with 1,032 yards rushing, while also finishing second with 1,487 all-purpose yards and placing third with eight rushing touchdowns, with his strong performance earning him Pro Bowl and First-Team All-Pro honors and recognition as the league's Comeback Player of the Year. When accepting the award in the spring of 1970, Sayers famously dedicated the honor to his close friend and teammate, Brian Piccolo, who died of cancer shortly thereafter.

Unfortunately, Sayers subsequently sustained an injury to his other (left) knee during the 1970 preseason that limited him to just two games, 23 carries, and 52 yards rushing, before forcing him to go under the knife once again. Sayers attempted a comeback the following year, but he suffered another knee injury during the early stages of the campaign, prompting him to announce his retirement at season's end. Over parts of seven NFL seasons, Sayers rushed for 4,956 yards and 39 touchdowns, caught 112 passes for 1,307 yards and nine TDs, amassed 6,263 yards from scrimmage, 3,172 yards returning kickoffs and punts, and 9,435 all-purpose yards, returned two punts and six kickoffs for touchdowns, and threw one TD pass. Sayers retired as the NFL's all-time leader in kickoff-return yardage (2,781), with his average of 30.6 yards per return still representing the highest mark in league history. His rushing average of 5 yards per carry also places him in the league's all-time top 10.

Yet, years later, Sayers continued to be haunted by the notion that he could have accomplished so much more had he been able to remain healthy, stating on one occasion, "Sometimes I cry about it because I didn't get a chance to play the game. I wish they had better doctors back then."

In explaining his decision to retire when he did, Sayers said, "I had no choice but to retire. My knees made the decision for me. I no longer had the explosiveness you need to get away from people. As a running back, the decision is probably easier than say quarterback, because we rely so much on our speed and maneuverability. Once you lose that, you should retire as a running back."

Following his playing days, Sayers, whose friendship with Brian Piccolo inspired him to write his autobiography, *I Am Third*, which in turn proved to be the basis for the 1971 made-for-TV movie *Brian's Song*, returned to the University of Kansas to receive his BA in physical education. Named the university's assistant athletic director in 1973, Sayers later became director of the Williams Educational Fund, the fundraising arm of the KU athletic department. After leaving Kansas in 1976 to become the athletic director at Southern Illinois University, Sayers remained in that post until 1981, when he moved back to Chicago and launched a sports marketing and public relations firm, Sayers and Sayers Enterprises. He also later started a computer supplies business that eventually became a huge success. Diagnosed with dementia in 2013, Sayers, according to his wife, Ardythe, remains physically healthy. However, he suffers from memory loss, making simple tasks such as signing his own name difficult.

Named the greatest halfback in NFL history as part of the league's 50th Anniversary celebration in 1969, Sayers received the additional distinction of being named to the NFL's 75th Anniversary Team as both a halfback and kickoff returner 25 years later, making him the only player to occupy two positions on the team. Called "the greatest player I've ever seen" by former teammate Mike Ditka, Sayers also drew praise from Pulitzer Prize–winning sportswriter Red Smith, who wrote, "His days at the top of his game were numbered, but there was a magic about him that still sets him apart from the other great running backs in pro football. He wasn't a bruiser like Jimmy Brown, but he could slice through the middle like a warm knife through butter, and, when he took a pitchout and peeled around the corner, he was the most exciting thing in pro football."

Despite the brevity of his career, Sayers gained induction into the Pro Football Hall of Fame the first time his name appeared on the ballot in 1977, entering the Hall at only 34 years of age. In explaining its decision, the selection committee stated, "There never was another to compare with him. What else is there to say!"

## CAREER HIGHLIGHTS

### Best Season

Sayers had a sensational year for the Bears in 1966, scoring 12 touchdowns and leading the league with 1,231 yards rushing, 1,678 yards from scrimmage, 2,440 all-purpose yards, and a 31.2-yard kickoff-return average. But Sayers put together arguably the greatest all-around season of any rookie running back in NFL history the previous year, helping the Bears improve their record to 9-5 in 1965 by finishing second in the league with 867 yards rushing, gaining another 507 yards on 29 pass receptions, placing near the top of the league rankings with 1,374 yards from scrimmage, 898 kick-off- and punt-return yards, and a 5.2 yards per carry rushing average, and leading the NFL with 2,272 all-purpose yards, 22 touchdowns, 132 points scored, and a 31.4-yard kickoff-return average.

### Memorable Moments/Greatest Performances

Sayers scored the first touchdown of his career on an 18-yard run during a 30–28 loss to the Los Angeles Rams on September 25, 1965.

Sayers starred during a 23–14 loss to the Packers on October 3, 1965, scoring both Bears touchdowns on a 6-yard run and a 65-yard pass from quarterback Rudy Bukich. He finished the game with 80 yards rushing and five receptions for 104 yards.

Sayers contributed to a 31–6 victory over the Rams on October 10, 1965, by collaborating with Bukich on an 80-yard scoring play.

Sayers led the Bears to a 45–37 win over the Minnesota Vikings the following week by amassing 297 all-purpose yards and scoring four touchdowns, all of which came in the second half. Displaying his tremendous versatility, Sayers scored his TDs on a 10-yard run, pass plays that covered 18 and 25 yards, and a 96-yard kickoff return.

Sayers topped 100 yards rushing for the first time as a pro during a 35–14 victory over the Giants on November 28, 1965, finishing the game with 13 carries for 113 yards and two touchdowns, which came on runs that covered 45 and 15 yards.

Sayers helped lead the Bears to a 13–0 win over a powerful Baltimore Colts squad on December 5, 1965, by rushing for 118 yards and one touchdown, which came on a 61-yard first-quarter run.

Sayers followed that up with a memorable performance against San Francisco on December 12, when, despite playing on a muddy field with poor traction, he led the Bears to a 61–20 rout of the 49ers by rushing for 113 yards, gaining another 89 yards on two pass receptions, amassing 336 yards of total offense, and scoring six touchdowns, which included a short swing pass that he converted into an 80-yard TD, a run of 50 yards, and an 85-yard punt return. Following the conclusion of the contest, Chicago head coach George Halas, who had been in the NFL since its inception in 1920, stated, "It was the greatest performance I have ever seen on the football field."

Sayers proved to be the difference in a 17–10 win over the Rams on October 23, 1966, rushing for 87 yards and returning a kickoff 93 yards for a touchdown.

Sayers helped the Bears forge a 10–10 tie with the Detroit Lions on November 6, 1966, by carrying the ball 21 times for 123 yards and one touchdown.

Sayers contributed to a 23–6 victory over the Atlanta Falcons on November 27, 1966, by gaining 172 yards on 19 carries and making five receptions for 65 yards.

Sayers led the Bears to a 41–28 win over the Vikings in the final game of the 1966 regular season by returning the opening kickoff 90 yards for a touchdown and rushing for 197 yards and another TD.

Although the Bears lost to the Steelers by a score of 41–13 in the 1967 regular-season opener, Sayers scored again on special teams when he returned a kickoff 103 yards for a touchdown.

Sayers rushed for 142 yards and one touchdown during a 14–3 win over the Detroit Lions on October 15, 1967.

Sayers helped the Bears complete a season-sweep of the Lions by returning a kickoff 97 yards for a touchdown during a 27–13 win over Detroit on November 5, 1967.

After scoring six touchdowns against the 49ers two years earlier, Sayers proved to be a one-man wrecking crew again when the Bears traveled to San Francisco on December 3, 1967. Playing on a rain-soaked field at Kezar Stadium, Sayers led the Bears to a 28–14 win by returning the opening kickoff 97 yards for a touchdown, scoring on a 15-yard run, and scoring a third time on a 58-yard punt return. Following the contest, 49ers head coach Jack Christiansen, who revealed that he ordered all his team's punts to be directed out of bounds after Sayers returned the opening kickoff for a TD, said, "It was a bad field, but it didn't stop some people."

Sayers supplied what little offense the Bears mounted during a 10–10 tie with the Vikings on December 10, 1967, carrying the ball 20 times for 131 yards and his team's lone touchdown.

Sayers again served as the focal point of the Bears offense when they defeated the Falcons by a score of 23–14 in the 1967 regular-season finale, rushing for 120 yards and scoring a pair of touchdowns on a 51-yard run and a 32-yard pass from Jack Concannon.

Sayers contributed to a 26–24 victory over the Vikings on October 27, 1968, by rushing for 143 yards and gaining another 33 yards on four pass receptions.

Sayers led the Bears to a 13–10 win over the Packers on November 3, 1968, by carrying the ball 24 times for a career-high 205 yards.

## Notable Achievements

- Rushed for more than 1,000 yards twice, topping 800 yards three other times.
- Surpassed 500 receiving yards once (507 in 1965).
- Surpassed 1,000 yards from scrimmage four times, topping 1,500 yards once (1,678 in 1966).
- Amassed more than 1,000 all-purpose yards five times, topping 2,000 yards twice.
- Scored more than 10 touchdowns three times, surpassing 20 TDs once (22 in 1965).
- Returned six kickoffs and two punts for touchdowns.
- Averaged more than 5 yards per carry three times.
- Led NFL in rushing yards twice, yards from scrimmage once, all-purpose yards three times, touchdowns once, points scored once, rushing average once, and kickoff-return average twice.
- Finished second in NFL in rushing yards once, all-purpose yards once, rushing touchdowns twice, and rushing average once.

- Finished third in NFL in rushing yards once, yards from scrimmage once, all-purpose yards once, touchdowns once, rushing touchdowns once, and rushing average once.
- Led Bears in rushing five times.
- Holds NFL record for highest kickoff-return average (30.6 yards per return).
- Holds share of NFL record with six touchdowns in one game (December 12, 1965, vs. 49ers).
- Holds Bears single-season records for most rushing touchdowns (14 in 1965), touchdowns (22 in 1965), and all-purpose yards (2,440 in 1966).
- Ranks among Bears career leaders with 991 rushing attempts (5th), 4,956 yards rushing (5th), 6,263 yards from scrimmage (5th), 2,781 kickoff-return yards (5th), 9,435 all-purpose yards (4th), 39 rushing touchdowns (5th), and 56 touchdowns (5th).
- Four-time Pro Bowl selection (1965, 1966, 1967, and 1969).
- Three-time Pro Bowl MVP (1966, 1967, and 1969).
- Five-time First-Team All-Pro selection (1965, 1966, 1967, 1968, and 1969).
- Five-time First-Team All–Western Conference selection (1965, 1966, 1967, 1968, and 1969).
- 1965 NFL Offensive Rookie of the Year.
- 1969 NFL Comeback Player of the Year.
- NFL 1960s All-Decade Team.
- #40 retired by Bears.
- Named to NFL's 75th Anniversary Team in 1994.
- Named to *Sporting News* All-Century Team in 1999.
- Named to NFL 100 All-Time Team in 2019.
- Number 21 on the *Sporting News'* 1999 list of the 100 Greatest Players in NFL History.
- Number 22 on the NFL Network's 2010 list of the NFL's 100 Greatest Players.
- Elected to Pro Football Hall of Fame in 1977.

# 4

## — BRONKO NAGURSKI —

A legendary figure from the early days of the NFL, Bronko Nagurski combined brute strength with tremendous acceleration to establish himself as the greatest running back of the 1930s. Virtually impossible for one man to bring down, Nagurski terrorized his opponents with his aggressive running style, with author Jim Dent writing in his book, *Monster of the Midway: Bronko Nagurski, the 1943 Chicago Bears, and the Greatest Comeback Ever*, "Bronko ran the football like he was boiling over with rage. He was one of the greatest big running backs in history." An outstanding defensive player as well, Nagurski proved to be equally intimidating on that side of the ball, delivering vicious hits to opposing ball-carriers from his tackle position. Leading the Bears to five division titles and three NFL championships, Nagurski earned All-Pro honors seven times between 1930 and 1937, with his brilliant all-around play prompting teammate Red Grange to call him the "best football player of all time." A member of the 1930s All-Decade Team, Nagurski later received the additional distinctions of having his number retired by the Bears, being named to the NFL's 75th Anniversary Team, receiving a top-40 ranking from both the *Sporting News* and the NFL Network on their respective lists of the 100 Greatest Players in NFL History, and being elected to the Pro Football Hall of Fame.

Born to Polish-Ukrainian immigrant parents in Rainy River, Ontario, Canada, on November 3, 1908, Bronislau Nagurski moved with his family to International Falls, Minnesota, at the age of nine. Spending his early years working on the family farm and delivering groceries for his father's grocery store, Nagurski developed his powerful legs as a youth by running to-and-from school four miles each day. After further developing his physique by laboring at nearby timbering operations as a teenager, Nagurski began competing in sports in high school, starring in football and basketball, while also excelling in track and field as a sprinter, discus-thrower, shotputter, and high-jumper.

Following his graduation from Bemidji High School, Nagurski accepted an athletic scholarship from the University of Minnesota after the school's head football coach, Clarence Spears, while driving through International Falls to meet another player, discovered Nagurski plowing a field by himself.

Beginning his college career in 1927, Nagurski spent the next three seasons gradually transitioning from guard and end to defensive tackle and fullback. Excelling at all four posts for the Golden Gophers, Nagurski established a fearsome reputation on both offense and defense, gaining All-America recognition three straight times. Particularly dominant as a senior in 1929, Nagurski performed so well on both sides of the ball that he became the only player ever to earn All-America honors at two positions in the same season.

Subsequently signed by George Halas for the then-princely sum of $5,000, Nagurski arrived in Chicago in 1930, with his 6'2", 225-pound frame making him easily the league's largest running back. Since the NFL did not begin keeping an official record of offensive statistics until 1932, the amount of yardage that Nagurski gained on the ground his first two years in the league remains a mystery. However, he clearly had an enormous impact on his new team, helping the Bears improve their record from 4-9-2 in 1929 to 9-4-1 in 1930, with his outstanding play earning him Second-Team All-Pro honors two straight times.

Nagurski then led the Bears to three consecutive division titles and a pair of NFL championships from 1932 to 1934, with the team compiling an overall record of 30-3-7. Gaining First-Team All-Pro recognition all three years, Nagurski established himself as the league's dominant player on both sides of the ball. After finishing second in the NFL with 533 yards rushing and leading the league with four rushing touchdowns in 1932, Nagurski gained a total of 1,119 yards on the ground over the course of the next two seasons. Although those numbers might not seem overly impressive, it must be considered that the George Halas Bears were not viewed as a collection of stars, but, rather, as a team whose members paid little attention to their individual statistics. Explaining during a 1984 interview with Paul Zimmerman of *Sports Illustrated* why he never posted huge rushing totals, Nagurski, who averaged fewer than 10 carries a game over the course of his career, said, "Halas stockpiled backs, and he believed in spreading it around. Plus, he wanted to keep me fresh for defense, where I'd put in a full afternoon. How many of today's 1,000-yard runners would like to spend half the game playing defense?"

Despite the relatively modest numbers that Nagurski compiled on offense, he gained general recognition as the premier running back of his time, with New York Giants head coach Steve Owen once saying, "How do I plan to stop Nagurski? With a shotgun as he's leaving the dressing room."

Instilling fear in his opponents with his destructive style of running, Nagurski made even the league's greatest players cringe at the thought of challenging him on the football field, with Giants Hall of Famer Mel Hein stating, "If you went at him low, he would stomp you to death. If you went at him high, he just knocked you down and ran over you."

Ernie Nevers of the Chicago Cardinals suggested, "Tackling Bronko was like trying to stop a freight train running downhill."

In discussing the manner in which he disposed of would-be tacklers, Nagurski said, "Just before they got to me, I'd knock 'em out of the way and keep running."

Bronko Nagurski intimidated his opponents with his bruising style of play.
Courtesy of RMYAuctions.com

Nagurski's biographer, Harold Rosenthal, wrote, "He probably broke more bones, legitimately, than any other player. Contact with him, either trying to stop him as a runner, or trying to block him as a lineman, was extremely costly. If he hit you right, you suffered a broken shoulder."

An enormous man, especially for the era in which he played, Nagurski had huge hands, powerful wrists, and an extremely thick neck, with Sid Luckman saying of his longtime teammate, "A monster. The neck, the hands. They measured him for a championship ring in 1943, when he made his comeback, and his ring size was 19½."

Playing at a time when the average defensive lineman weighed close to 220 pounds, Nagurski gradually increased his playing weight to 238 pounds over the course of his career, enabling him to often drag multiple tacklers with him. An outstanding blocker as well, Nagurski frequently cleared the way for the team's smaller running backs. In fact, on those occasions when Nagurski suffered an injury, instead of sitting on the bench, he sometimes assumed a spot on the offensive line. In addition to his size and strength, Nagurski possessed remarkable takeoff speed, accelerating rapidly when he first received the football.

Excelling on defense as well, Nagurski wreaked havoc on opposing offenses from his position on the defensive line, where the Bears often employed him as a ranging tackle or "Monster." Displaying the same aggressiveness on that side of the ball that he exhibited on offense, Nagurski delivered violent hits to opposing linemen and ball-carriers, making them extremely wary of his presence.

In discussing the totality of Nagurski's game, legendary sportswriter Grantland Rice claimed, "You could have played him at any position."

Insisting that Nagurski exceeded the two men generally accepted as the greatest football players of the first few decades of the 20th century, Rice added, "Eleven Bronko Nagurskis would have beaten 11 (Jim) Thorpes or 11 (Red) Granges."

Limited to only five games and 170 yards rushing by a back injury he sustained while delivering a block to an opposing defensive lineman, Nagurski failed to earn All-Pro honors for the first time in his career in 1935. In discussing the play that broke two of his vertebrae, Nagurski recalled, "I threw a cross-body block on an end—a stupid block—and I plowed into his knees with the small of my back."

Returning to top form in 1936, Nagurski gained All-Pro recognition by rushing for 529 yards, before helping the Bears advance to the NFL championship game the following year by gaining 343 yards on the ground. Nevertheless, Nagurski, who had spent the previous few years supplementing his income by wrestling in his spare time, chose to retire from football and make wrestling his full-time profession after he and George Halas reached an impasse on a new contract following the conclusion of the 1937 campaign. In explaining his decision years later, Nagurski said, "I wanted to go home anyway. I was tired of knocking myself out, going on the wrestling tour between games to make extra money."

Nagurski subsequently became World Heavyweight Champion three times between 1937 and 1941, before retiring from wrestling and returning to Minnesota to work on his farm. Nagurski remained in Minnesota until the Bears lured him out of retirement when a player shortage developed during World War II. Playing almost exclusively on the offensive and defensive lines in 1943, the 35-year-old Nagurski helped lead the Bears to the NFL title—their third with him serving as a member of the team. Retiring for good at season's end, Nagurski concluded his playing career with 2,778 yards rushing, 2,912 yards from scrimmage, 25 touchdowns, 474 yards passing, seven TD passes, and a rushing average of 4.4 yards per carry.

Following his retirement, Nagurski continued to work on his farm and wrestle until 1960, when his many physical ailments forced him to adopt a more sedentary lifestyle. Suffering from arthritis and aching knees that endured numerous operations, Nagurski ran a gas station in International Falls, Minnesota, before returning to Rainy River, Ontario, where he became a fishing guide. Nagurski remained at his place of birth until January 7, 1990, when he passed away two months after celebrating his 82nd birthday.

## CAREER HIGHLIGHTS

### Best Season

Nagurski posted the best numbers of his career in 1934, when he earned First-Team All-Pro honors for the third straight time by averaging 4.8 yards per carry and ranking among the league leaders with 586 yards rushing, 618 yards from scrimmage, seven touchdowns, and 44 points scored.

### Memorable Moments/Greatest Performances

Nagurski scored the first two touchdowns of his career during a 20–0 victory over the Minneapolis Red Jackets on October 5, 1930, scoring on runs of 8 and 2 yards.

Nagurski gave the Bears all the points they needed to defeat the Giants by a score of 12–0 on November 16, 1930, scoring the game's only two touchdowns on a pair of short runs.

Nagurski's 62-yard touchdown run highlighted a 26–13 win over the Chicago Cardinals on October 18, 1931.

Nagurski contributed to a 28–8 victory over the Giants on November 6, 1932, by completing a 55-yard touchdown pass to Red Grange.

Nagurski clinched a 9–0 win over the Packers on December 11, 1932, by recording a 56-yard touchdown run in the fourth quarter.

Nagurski led the Bears to a 17–14 win over the Portsmouth Spartans on November 26, 1933, by carrying the ball 18 times for 124 yards and one touchdown, which came on a game-winning 29-yard run in the fourth quarter, just moments after he committed a costly holding penalty on defense that enabled the Spartans to eventually take the lead. Angry with himself over his miscue, Nagurski returned the ensuing kickoff to the Chicago 45 yard line, after which he reportedly told his teammates in the huddle, "This is my fault. Give me the ball!" Playing like a man possessed, Nagurski subsequently proceeded to dole out punishment to the opposing defense until he ultimately recorded his 29-yard TD run in the closing moments.

Nagurski proved to be a huge factor in the Bears' 23–21 victory over the Giants in the 1933 NFL championship game, carrying the ball 13 times for 64 yards and throwing a pair of TD passes.

Nagurski had a hand in all three touchdowns the Bears scored during their 24–10 win over the Packers in the opening game of the 1934 regular season, throwing a 7-yard TD pass to Bill Hewitt and recording a pair of touchdown runs, the longest of which covered 40 yards.

Nagurski's 2-yard touchdown pass to Bill Hewitt late in the fourth quarter enabled the Bears to defeat the Detroit Lions by a score of 19–16 on November 29, 1934, with the victory clinching the Western Division title for Chicago.

Nagurski turned in the most memorable performance of his career nearly a decade later, with his extraordinary effort in the final game of the 1943 regular season enabling the Bears to clinch the Western Division title with a 35–24 victory over the Chicago Cardinals. After spending the entire season serving as a tackle on the offensive side of the ball, Nagurski returned to his more familiar position of fullback when the Bears found themselves trailing their arch-rivals by a score of 24–14 heading into the fourth quarter. Taking the game into his own hands, Nagurski ran for 84 yards and one touchdown in the final 15 minutes, leading the Bears to a come-from-behind win that earned them a berth in the NFL championship game. Looking back on his performance years later, Nagurski said, "That game gave me my greatest kick out of football."

### Notable Achievements

- Rushed for more than 500 yards four times.
- Led NFL with four rushing touchdowns in 1932.
- Finished second in NFL in rushing yards once, yards from scrimmage once, all-purpose yards once, and rushing average once.
- Finished third in NFL in rushing yards once and rushing touchdowns once.
- Led Bears in rushing four times.
- Ranks ninth in Bears history with 25 rushing touchdowns.
- Five-time division champion (1932, 1933, 1934, 1937, and 1943).
- Three-time NFL champion (1932, 1933, and 1943).

- Four-time First-Team All-Pro selection (1932, 1933, 1934, and 1936).
- Three-time Second-Team All-Pro selection (1930, 1931, and 1937).
- NFL 1930s All-Decade Team.
- #3 retired by Bears.
- Named to NFL's 75th Anniversary Team in 1994.
- Number 35 on the *Sporting News'* 1999 list of the 100 Greatest Players in NFL History.
- Number 19 on the NFL Network's 2010 list of the NFL's 100 Greatest Players.
- Elected to Pro Football Hall of Fame in 1963.

# 5

## MIKE SINGLETARY

The centerpiece and unquestioned leader of the Bears' defense for more than a decade, Mike Singletary spent 12 seasons in Chicago starring at middle linebacker, serving as team captain for squads that won six division titles, one NFC championship, and one Super Bowl. The second-leading tackler in franchise history, Singletary recorded more than 100 tackles 10 times, earning in the process 10 consecutive trips to the Pro Bowl, eight All-Pro nominations, and two NFL Defensive Player of the Year trophies. A member of the NFL 1980s All-Decade Team, Singletary also landed spots on the *Sporting News* and NFL Network's respective lists of the 100 Greatest Players in NFL History and a place in the Pro Football Hall of Fame.

Born in Houston, Texas, on October 9, 1958, Michael Singletary experienced considerable adversity during his formative years. The youngest of 10 children, Mike lost two of his brothers by the time he turned 12 years of age, with one dying of smoke inhalation and the other in an automobile accident. Further burdened by the divorce of his parents, Singletary recalled, "My mom needed me to be the man of the house. She said life is hard but it's what you make it. It's all about those who get off the ground and continue to do right and pray and keep God with you."

Developing a love for football at an early age, Singletary grew up rooting for the Dallas Cowboys, while honing his own skills as a middle linebacker and offensive guard in junior high school. Enjoying his play along the offensive line, Singletary recollected, "I really loved the trap play and getting the linebacker who had no clue where I was coming from. I liked using a low center of gravity at guard, and I carried that over to the way I played middle linebacker."

Continuing to develop his football skills at Houston's Evan E. Worthing High School, Singletary starred at middle linebacker for three seasons, expressing the satisfaction he derived from manning that post by saying, "It was the freedom to be able to make a big play anywhere at any time, as long as I was willing to hustle to get there. Being in the middle, I was able to see the ball and work on my vision and technique and mechanics. I was in a position where I could dictate where the defense was moving. I was going to put the defense in the best position."

After studying film of Singletary in action, Baylor University assistant coach Grant Teaff offered him an athletic scholarship, recalling, "I looked at it for exactly four minutes, shut off the projector, and said 'I'll take him.' On the first play, he smashed a runner up the middle. On the second play, he ranged to the sideline and knocked a guy out of bounds. On the third play, he got an interception."

Mike Singletary anchored the Bears' defense from his middle linebacker position for 12 seasons.
Courtesy of George A. Kitrinos

A four-year letterman at Baylor, Singletary recorded a school-record 662 tackles, with his exceptional play earning him All–Southwest Conference honors three times and All-America recognition in both his junior (1979) and senior (1980) years.

Selected by the Bears in the second round of the 1981 NFL Draft, with the 38th overall pick, Singletary arrived at his first pro training camp with defensive coordinator Buddy Ryan expecting great things from him. However, like any other rookie, Singletary found himself being treated harshly by Ryan, who referred to him only as "Number 50" during the early stages of his career. After slowly earning Ryan's trust, Singletary broke into the starting lineup by midseason, after which he went on to start all but two of the team's next 174 non-strike games.

Although the Bears compiled a losing record in each of his first two seasons, Singletary gradually emerged as a team leader during that time, calling all the signals on the defensive side of the ball, while influencing his teammates with the incredible focus and extraordinary level of intensity he displayed on the playing field. Nicknamed "Samurai Mike" for his aggressive style of play and passion for the game, the 6-foot, 230-pound

Singletary discussed the approach he took to his craft, saying, "Hitting people has always been my style . . . I'm not tall, but sometimes small things are the most dangerous. It's like a snake when it's coiled. You don't know when it'll strike, and whoosh, it's got you."

Making an extremely strong impression on Washington Redskins quarterback Joe Theismann, Singletary drew praise from his frequent foe, who said, "People say the eyes are the windows to the soul. Well, if you played opposite Mike Singletary, you saw everything that was going on in his soul because those eyes were just lit up—they never blinked."

Theismann continued, "Nobody was more prepared than Mike Singletary. I think two things make Mike Singletary unique—his intelligence and his passion for the game. Nobody played it with more passion than Mike Singletary . . . I can close my eyes today. I can see Richard Dent. I can see Mike Singletary. I can see Wilber Marshall. It was like chaos. Mike was the centerpiece of it all. Mike held it together."

Theismann then went on to call Singletary "an extremely bright guy," saying, "He had to be to play that kind of defense. God gives us athletic ability. What you do between your ears is what makes you a great player. That's the area where Mike really excelled. Being able to get people lined up, knowing how to flow, how to run under blocks if you need to, how to take on a big 300-pound guard, shed him, and go make a play. And the intuitive nature of reading plays."

After being named team captain in 1983, Singletary began a string of 10 straight seasons in which he recorded more than 100 tackles, leading the Bears in that category on eight separate occasions. In addition to gaining Pro Bowl recognition in each of those campaigns, Singletary earned All-Pro honors eight times, being named to the First Team seven times and the Second Team once. And, with the Bears fielding one of the league's top-ranked defenses throughout most of that period, Singletary received much of the credit, being accorded NFL Defensive Player of the Year honors in both 1985 and 1988.

As Singletary established himself as the focal point of the Bears' defense, he developed a symbiotic relationship with Buddy Ryan, with teammate Otis Wilson stating, "He knew exactly what was going on. That was Buddy's guy. He was really a coach on the field . . . Mike was a student of the game. He studied six, seven, eight hours of film."

Noting that Singletary's hard work paid off, Bears safety Gary Fencik claimed that the middle linebacker typically knew every play the opposing team intended to run, saying, "Singletary's calling out plays, and it's the actual play that they're going to run."

Fencik added, "The confidence that Buddy had that you had a middle linebacker who was completely prepared, who'd do anything that he wanted to do, was just tremendous trust. . . . He was always looking for ways to improve himself. He was very serious in that way."

Looking back on his unique relationship with Ryan, Singletary said, "I really didn't like Buddy for a long time. But he taught me about myself, made me reach for things I thought I never had. I never would have achieved what I have without Buddy."

Even though Singletary continued to excel at middle linebacker after Ryan left Chicago at the end of 1985 to become head coach of the Philadelphia Eagles, reserve defensive lineman Tyrone Keys maintained that his teammate never again shared the same level of trust with any of his other coaches, stating, "The number one thing was Singletary was able to make adjustments on the field when he was there with Buddy Ryan. After Buddy left, they had to stay in that same defense, and he wasn't allowed to make changes like that. When both Buddy and Mike were there, Buddy gave him the freedom to make the calls he saw fit."

Singletary remained in Chicago until 1992, announcing his retirement at season's end after earning his 10th consecutive Pro Bowl selection. Concluding his career with an unofficial total of 1,488 tackles (885 solo), Singletary ranks second only to Dick Butkus in that category in team annals. He also recorded 19 sacks, seven interceptions, and 12 fumble recoveries during his time in the Windy City. The Pro Football Hall of Fame subsequently wasted little time in opening its doors to Singletary, admitting him in 1998, the first time his name appeared on the ballot.

Unable to attain the same level of success as an NFL coach, Singletary has assumed several coaching positions around the league, including working as an assistant with the Baltimore Ravens, San Francisco 49ers, Minnesota Vikings, and Los Angeles Rams. He also spent two years serving as head coach of the 49ers, before being relieved of his duties following the conclusion of the 2010 campaign. After taking a brief break from football, Singletary became head coach of Trinity Christian Academy in Addison, Texas, on March 29, 2018. Less than two months later, he also assumed head coaching duties for the Memphis Express of the Alliance of American Football.

## CAREER HIGHLIGHTS

### Best Season

Singletary played his best ball for the Bears from 1984 to 1991, earning All-Pro honors in each of those eight seasons. Performing especially well in 1985 and 1988, Singletary gained recognition as the NFL Defensive Player of the Year following the conclusion of each of those campaigns. With the Bears winning the NFL championship in 1985 and Singletary recording three sacks, one interception, one forced fumble, three fumble recoveries, and an unofficial total of 161 tackles (109 solo), all while anchoring a defense that ranked first in the league against the run and third against the pass, we'll identify that as his finest all-around season.

### Memorable Moments/Greatest Performances

Singletary excelled in his third start as a pro, recording 10 tackles and forcing a fumble during a 16–13 overtime victory over the Kansas City Chiefs on November 8, 1981.

Singletary recorded the first interception of his career during a 35–24 win over the Denver Broncos in the final game of the 1981 regular season.

Singletary anchored a Chicago defense that recorded five sacks and allowed just 132 yards of total offense during a 27–0 shutout of the Tampa Bay Buccaneers on November 20, 1983.

Singletary helped lead the Bears to a convincing 34–14 victory over Tampa Bay in the 1984 regular-season opener by intercepting a pass and recording a sack.

Singletary followed that up in Week 2 by leading a Bears defense that created four turnovers and surrendered just 130 yards of total offense during a 27–0 win over the Denver Broncos.

Singletary earned NFC Defensive Player of the Week honors by recording an interception and a career-high three sacks during a 20–7 win over the Patriots on September 15, 1985.

Singletary led a stifling Bears defense that created four turnovers, recorded four sacks, and allowed just 106 yards of total offense during a 24–3 win over the Lions on November 10, 1985.

Excelling against the Giants in the divisional round of the 1985 playoffs, Singletary recorded a sack, recovered a fumble, and anchored a defense that allowed just 32 yards rushing and 181 yards of total offense during a 21–0 Bears victory.

In addition to serving as the focal point of a defense that surrendered just 7 yards rushing and 123 yards of total offense to the Patriots in Super Bowl XX, Singletary recovered two fumbles during the lopsided 46–10 victory.

Singletary recorded two of the nine sacks the Bears registered against New York quarterbacks Phil Simms and Jeff Rutledge during their convincing 34–19 win over the Giants in the 1987 regular-season opener.

Singletary earned NFC Defensive Player of the Week honors for the second and final time by recording a career-high 20 tackles, including 10 of the solo variety, during the Bears' 16–13 overtime victory over the Broncos on November 18, 1990.

### Notable Achievements

- Missed just two games entire career.
- Recorded more than 100 tackles 10 times.
- Led Bears in tackles eight times.
- Ranks second in Bears history with 1,488 career tackles.
- Six-time division champion (1984, 1985, 1986, 1987, 1988, and 1990).
- 1985 NFC champion.
- Super Bowl XX champion.
- Two-time NFC Defensive Player of the Week.
- Ten-time Pro Bowl selection (1983, 1984, 1985, 1986, 1987, 1988, 1989, 1990, 1991, and 1992).
- Seven-time First-Team All-Pro selection (1984, 1985, 1986, 1987, 1988, 1989, and 1991).
- 1990 Second-Team All-Pro selection.
- Nine-time First-Team All-NFC selection (1983, 1984, 1985, 1986, 1987, 1988, 1989, 1990, and 1991).
- Two-time NFL Defensive Player of the Year (1985 and 1988).
- NFL 1980s All-Decade Team.
- Pro Football Reference All-1980s First Team.
- Number 56 on the *Sporting News'* 1999 list of the 100 Greatest Players in NFL History.
- Number 57 on the NFL Network's 2010 list of the NFL's 100 Greatest Players.
- Elected to Pro Football Hall of Fame in 1998.

# 6

## — BILL GEORGE —

The heart and soul of the Bears' defense for more than a decade, Bill George spent 14 of his 15 NFL seasons in Chicago, during which time he pioneered the position of middle linebacker. After beginning his career as a middle guard on defense, George moved to middle linebacker in 1955, becoming in the process the first player to man that position on a full-time basis. Using his strength, quickness, aggressiveness, and intelligence to excel at his new post, George anchored Chicago's defense for the next 10 years, with his outstanding play earning him Pro Bowl and All-Pro honors eight times each. A key contributor to the Bears' 1963 NFL championship team, George also earned a spot on the NFL 1950s All-Decade Team, a number 49 ranking on the *Sporting News'* 1999 list of the 100 Greatest Players in NFL History, and a place in the Pro Football Hall of Fame.

Born some 50 miles south of Pittsburgh, in Waynesburg, Pennsylvania, on October 27, 1929, William J. George attended Waynesburg High School, where he excelled in football and wrestling. Spurning the numerous wrestling scholarship offers he received from other colleges, George instead elected to play football at Wake Forest University. Proving that he made the right decision, George went on to gain All-America recognition as a defensive tackle, becoming the first player in the school's history to be so honored.

Subsequently selected by the Bears in the second round of the 1951 NFL Draft, with the 23rd overall pick, George spent the 1951 campaign serving in the military, before beginning his career in pro football one year later. Earning a starting job immediately upon his arrival in Chicago, George spent his first three seasons playing middle guard in the Bears' traditional five-man defensive front, with his exceptional play at that post gaining him Pro Bowl recognition for the first of eight straight times in 1954.

As a middle guard, George's primary responsibility on passing downs was to bump the offensive center from a three-point stance and then drop

Bill George helped pioneer the position of middle linebacker.
Courtesy of MEARSonlineauctions.com

back into coverage. However, George took the first step toward altering his role during a 1954 meeting with the Eagles. Growing increasingly frustrated as Philadelphia's quarterback continued to complete several short passes just over his head, George told Bears defensive captain and left-side linebacker George Connor, "Hell, I could break up those passes if I didn't have to hit that offensive center first." With Connor responding, "What are you hitting him for, then? Why don't you go for the ball?", George began dropping into pass coverage immediately. After failing to catch the first pass thrown directly at him, George recorded the first interception of his career moments later. By successfully employing his new tactic throughout the remainder of the contest as well, George ended up providing the impetus for the creation of the 4-3 defense.

Although other teams began employing a similar defensive alignment shortly thereafter, George remained the standard-bearer at the middle linebacker position for years to come, earning First-Team All-Pro honors in each of the next seven seasons. Blessed with good size and strength, outstanding mobility, and the ability to read opposing offenses and make quick decisions, the 6'2", 237-pound George emerged as one of the league's premier players, with only Detroit's Joe Schmidt and New York's Sam Huff rivaling him as middle linebackers during that era. In discussing the many outstanding qualities that George possessed, Bears defensive coordinator Clark Shaughnessy said, "He is a rare physical specimen, both from the standpoint of power and agility. He's absolutely fearless on the field. He has a brilliant mind, an ability to size up a situation quickly and react to it, and, also, the ability to retain the complicated details of his job."

An extremely intelligent player, George became Shaughnessy's greatest pupil, developing such a complete understanding of defensive strategy that he eventually assumed responsibility for calling all the signals on that side of the ball. George also possessed a nasty on-field disposition, with Rick Reilly of *Sports Illustrated* calling him "the meanest Bear ever" many years later.

After performing at an extremely high level for nearly a decade, George suffered severe neck injuries in an automobile accident following the con-clusion of the 1961 campaign. Yet, even though he entered the 1962 season at somewhat less than 100 percent, George played well enough to lead the Bears to a record of 9-5 that represented their best mark in six years. Returning to top form the following year, George earned All-Pro honors for the eighth and final time in his career, with his exceptional play helping the Bears capture the NFL championship.

George, who missed just one game his first 12 years in the league, sub-sequently sustained severe knee damage during a 24–10 loss to the Dallas Cowboys on November 1, 1964, forcing him to sit out the season's final six contests. With Dick Butkus arriving in Chicago the following year, George assumed a backup role, appearing in only two games in 1965, before being released by the Bears at season's end. In his 14 years in the Windy City, George recorded 18 interceptions, amassed 144 interception-return yards, recovered 17 fumbles, and scored 26 points as a part-time kicker, successfully converting four of eight field goal attempts and 14 of 15 extra-point attempts.

After being released by the Bears, George signed with the Los Angeles Rams, for whom he started in 1966, before announcing his retirement at season's end. Returning to Chicago following his retirement, George spent three years serving as a member of Abe Gibron's coaching staff, before leaving the game for good when Gibron received his walking papers following the conclusion of the 1974 campaign. Elected to the Pro Football Hall of Fame that same year, George received the following words of praise from Gibron at his induction ceremony: "Bill George was the first great middle linebacker. He brought all the romance and charisma to the position. He was like having Clark Shaughnessy on the field. He called all the plays and had a special knack for it."

Unfortunately, George passed away just eight years later, dying tragically in a three-car automobile accident at only 52 years of age, on September 30, 1982. Upon learning of his passing, former Bears teammate Johnny Morris called him "the first classic middle linebacker" and said, "He was one of the most intense football players I ever saw. He was the backbone of the Bears defense for so many years. It's a real tragedy."

## BEARS CAREER HIGHLIGHTS

### Best Season

George earned First-Team All-Pro honors seven straight times from 1955 to 1961, with his career-high three interceptions and unofficial total of 11½ sacks in the last of those campaigns making that his finest all-around season.

### Memorable Moments/Greatest Performances

Manning the middle guard position, George anchored a Bears defense that allowed just 54 yards rushing and 139 yards of total offense during a 28–9 win over the Baltimore Colts on October 10, 1954.

In addition to performing well on the defensive side of the ball, George successfully converted field goal attempts of 15, 14, and 34 yards during a 29–7 victory over the Chicago Cardinals on December 5, 1954.

George led a Bears defense that created four turnovers and surrendered just 145 yards of total offense during a 24–10 win over the Packers on November 9, 1958.

Although the Bears lost to the Detroit Lions by a score of 16–15 on December 3, 1961, George intercepted two passes and recovered two fumbles, setting in the process a single-game franchise record for most takeaways.

George followed that up with another exceptional performance, helping to limit Jim Brown to only 62 yards rushing on 18 carries during a 17–14 win over the Browns on December 10, 1961.

George anchored a Bears defense that surrendered just 88 yards of total offense to the Rams during a 6–0 Chicago win on November 10, 1963.

George once again starred against the Rams on October 11, 1964, picking off two passes during a convincing 38–17 Bears victory.

## Notable Achievements

- Missed just one game in first 12 seasons, appearing in 149 out of 150 contests.
- Recorded 11½ sacks in 1961.
- Finished third in NFL in fumble recoveries twice.
- Tied for third in Bears history with 17 fumble recoveries.
- Two-time division champion (1956 and 1963).
- 1963 NFL champion.
- Eight-time Pro Bowl selection (1954, 1955, 1956, 1957, 1958, 1959, 1960, and 1961).
- Eight-time First-Team All-Pro selection (1955, 1956, 1957, 1958, 1959, 1960, 1961, and 1963).
- NFL 1950s All-Decade Team.
- Pro Football Reference All-1950s First Team.
- #61 retired by Bears.
- Number 49 on the *Sporting News'* 1999 list of the 100 Greatest Players in NFL History.
- Elected to Pro Football Hall of Fame in 1974.

# 7

## — SID LUCKMAN —

The first NFL quarterback to successfully run the T-formation, Sid Luckman helped revolutionize the pro game with his ability to move the football through the air. Rivaling Washington's Sammy Baugh as the league's finest passer for much of the 1940s, Luckman led all NFL signal-callers in passing yards, touchdown passes, and passer rating three times each, earning in the process three Pro Bowl selections, seven All-Pro nominations, one league MVP trophy, and a place on the NFL 1940s All-Decade Team. Luckman, who consistently placed near the top of the league rankings in every major passing category, also excelled on defense, recording 17 interceptions over the course of his career, with his outstanding all-around play leading the Bears to six division titles and four NFL championships. Elected to the Pro Football Hall of Fame in 1965, Luckman has also been honored by having his #42 retired by the Bears and being ranked as one of the 100 Greatest Players in NFL History by both the *Sporting News* and the NFL Network.

Born in Brooklyn, New York, on November 21, 1916, to Jewish parents who immigrated to the United States from Germany, Sidney Luckman learned how to throw a football at nearby Prospect Park, after first becoming interested in the game as a youngster when his father gave him a football as a gift. Developing into an excellent all-around athlete as a teenager, Luckman starred in both baseball and football while attending Erasmus Hall High School, with his skills on the gridiron earning him scholarship offers from several major colleges. Choosing to remain close to home, Luckman accepted a grant from New York's Columbia University, after which he enrolled at the New College for the Education of Teachers, an undergraduate school affiliated with the Teachers College at Columbia. Luckman subsequently spent the next three years there, before transferring to Columbia University when the New College closed in 1939.

Starring for weak Columbia teams as a triple-threat single-wing tailback, Luckman managed to excel even though he received very little support from his teammates, with head coach Lou Little later saying, "We would have had a very ordinary team, or less than that, without him." Although Luckman also punted, placekicked, and played brilliant defense for the Lions, he became known mostly for his exceptional passing ability, with sportswriter Jimmy Cannon stating, "You had to be there to realize how great Sid was because the statistics didn't measure his true worth to a team that didn't help him much. The defenders were in on him most of the time, but he got most of his passes away as he ran from his tacklers in a hurried ballet of evasion."

College official Red Frisell also expressed his admiration for Luckman when he said, "I worked behind Sid in six of his college games. In each of those games, he threw at least 30 passes, and, on every single one of them, he was knocked nearly out of his britches by some fast-charging opponent. Never once did I see him throw in fright or see him wince when he got his lumps. I never heard a word in protest about the beating he was taking. That brand of courage, coupled with his uncanny knack of hitting his target, put Luckman down in my book as the greatest forward passer I ever saw in the college ranks."

Extremely impressed with Luckman's play at the collegiate level, George Halas convinced the Pittsburgh Pirates (later the Steelers) to select him with the second overall pick of the 1939 NFL Draft and then trade him to the Bears. However, Luckman initially expressed no desire to turn pro, telling the Bears, "I have no intention of playing professional football. In fact, I have been advised against it. My plans are to enter the trucking business with my brothers."

Not one to give up easily, Halas, who envisioned making Luckman the centerpiece of a completely restructured offense in Chicago, persuaded the young quarterback to alter his plans by presenting him with a contract worth $5,500. Recalling years later the conversation that took place during the contract signing, Luckman revealed that Halas told him, "You and Jesus Christ are the only two people I would ever pay this to," to which he responded, "Thank you coach. You put me in great company."

Following Luckman's arrival in Chicago, Halas and assistant coach Clark Shaughnessy set about revamping the Bears' offense, which had previously been based in the single-wing formation that employed the quarterback primarily as a blocking back who rarely touched the ball. Hoping to make good use of the 6-foot, 200-pound Luckman's versatility, game-sense, and superior passing skills, Halas and Shaughnessy invented a rather complex scheme that built on the traditional T-formation, which other teams had used periodically through the years.

Sid Luckman led the Bears to six division titles and four NFL championships.
Courtesy of MEARSonlineauctions.com

Failing to fully grasp the many new concepts that included quick-hitting runs, fakes, and men in motion, Luckman struggled somewhat as a rookie, concluding the 1939 campaign with just 636 yards passing, five touchdown passes, four interceptions, and a 45.1 pass-completion percentage. Although Luckman posted only slightly better overall numbers the following year, he did an excellent job of directing Chicago's offense, with his solid play behind center earning him Pro Bowl and Second-Team All-Pro honors. More importantly, the Bears claimed the league championship with a lopsided 73–0 victory over Washington in the NFL title game, prompting other teams to subsequently adopt a similar philosophy on offense. Hoping to experience the same level of success, many other teams installed the T-formation, veering away from the single-wing attack that depended almost exclusively on running the football.

Establishing himself as arguably the NFL's finest signal-caller in 1941, Luckman gained First-Team All-Pro recognition for the first of four straight times by leading the league with a passer rating of 95.3 and a pass-completion percentage of 57.1, while also ranking among the leaders with 1,181 yards passing and nine TD passes. After another solid year in 1942, Luckman had the greatest season of his career in 1943, earning league MVP honors by leading all NFL quarterbacks with 2,194 yards passing, 28 touchdown passes, and a passer rating of 107.5. Also performing well on the defensive side of the ball, Luckman recorded four interceptions, which he returned for a total of 85 yards.

Choosing to enlist in the military immediately following the conclusion of the 1943 campaign, Luckman spent the next two years serving as an ensign with the US Merchant Marine. Stationed stateside during his tour of duty, Luckman, while unable to practice with the team, received permission to play for the Bears on game days until he received his discharge.

After being courted by the Chicago Rockets of the newly formed All-America Football Conference, Luckman returned to the Bears full-time in 1946, leading the league with 1,826 yards passing and 17 touchdown passes. He followed that up by tossing 24 TD passes and throwing for a career-high 2,712 yards in 1947, earning in the process First-Team All-Pro honors for the fifth and final time in his career.

Discussing years later his brief flirtation with the Rockets, who offered him a $25,000 contract to serve as their player/coach, Luckman said, "How could I possibly have taken it? How could I quit a club that had done so much for me?"

Luckman remained the Bears' starting quarterback for one more season, passing for 1,047 yards and 13 touchdowns in 1948, before assuming a backup role his last two years in the league. Announcing his retirement following the conclusion of the 1950 campaign, Luckman ended his career with 14,686 yards passing, 137 touchdown passes, 132 interceptions, a passer rating of 75.0, and a pass-completion percentage of 51.8. He also rushed for 204 yards and four touchdowns, intercepted 17 passes, which he returned for a total of 310 yards and two touchdowns, and amassed 107 yards returning punts. Luckman, who spent most of his time in Chicago serving as the Bears' primary punter, also punted for a total of 8,872 yards, averaging 38.6 yards per kick over the course of his career.

One of George Halas's favorite players, Luckman drew the following words of praise from his former head coach shortly after he retired: "Sid made himself a great quarterback. No one else did it for him. He worked hard, stayed up nights studying, and really learned the T. Sid wasn't built for quarterback. He was stocky, not fast, and not a great passer in the old tradition. But he was smart, and he was dedicated."

Longtime University of Illinois head coach Bob Zuppke also held Luckman in extremely high regard, once calling him, "the smartest football player I ever saw, and that goes for college or pro."

Following his playing days, Luckman returned to Columbia, where he spent several years serving as an assistant coach on offense. He also assumed a part-time position with the Bears, helping to tutor their young quarterbacks on the finer aspects of running the T-formation. However, Luckman never accepted a coaching salary from his former team, saying, "I can never repay the Bears for making my life a more enchanting life." A successful businessman as well, Luckman spent many years working in the packaging industry.

Elected to the College Football Hall of Fame in 1960, the Pro Football Hall of Fame in 1965, and the International Jewish Sports Hall of Fame in 1979, Luckman once said that he wanted three sentences on his tombstone: "He had it all. He did it all. He loved it all." Luckman lived until July 5, 1998, when he passed away at his home in Aventura, Florida, at the age of 81. Upon learning of his passing, Hall of Fame coach Marv Levy said, "Growing up in Chicago, I was a Chicago Bears fan, naturally, and Sid Luckman was their quarterback. You had to see Sid Luckman play in order to believe how good he was."

## CAREER HIGHLIGHTS

### Best Season

Although Luckman completed a higher percentage of his passes in 1941 and threw for more yards in 1947, he had easily the finest season of his career in 1943, earning NFL MVP honors by leading the league with 2,194 yards passing, 28 touchdown passes, a passer rating of 107.5, and a touchdown rate of 13.9 percent that remains the highest single-season mark in NFL history. Meanwhile, Luckman's 10.9 yards gained per pass attempt represents the second-highest figure ever posted by an NFL quarterback.

## Memorable Moments/Greatest Performances

Luckman threw the first touchdown pass of his career when he connected with Dick Plasman on a 68-yard scoring play during a 16–13 loss to the Giants on October 22, 1939.

Luckman threw an 85-yard touchdown pass to Bob Swisher during a 23–13 win over the Detroit Lions on November 12, 1939.

Luckman displayed his versatility in the 1939 regular-season finale, when he threw a pair of TD passes and recorded a 33-yard pick-six during a 48–7 trouncing of the Chicago Cardinals.

Luckman led the Bears to a 34–7 victory over the Pittsburgh Steelers on October 26, 1941, by completing a 45-yard touchdown pass to Ken Kavanaugh and a 56-yarder to Hampton Pool.

Luckman recorded the second pick-six of his career during a 38–7 win over the Packers on November 15, 1942, returning his interception of a Cecil Isbell pass 54 yards for a touchdown.

Luckman led the Bears to a 42–0 rout of the Detroit Lions the following week by throwing TD passes of 43 and 60 yards to Harry Clarke and Hugh Gallarneau, respectively.

Luckman torched the Detroit secondary again during a 27–21 win over the Lions on October 3, 1943, passing for 267 yards and three TDs, the longest of which went 64 yards to Bill Geyer.

Luckman continued to torment the Lions on October 31, 1943, passing for 241 yards and three TDs during a 35–14 win, with the longest of his scoring tosses going 51 yards to Dante Magnani.

Luckman turned in the finest performance of his career on Sid Luckman Day at New York's Polo Grounds, leading the Bears to a 56–7 mauling of the Giants on November 14, 1943, by completing 21 of 32 pass attempts for 433 yards and seven touchdowns. Luckman, who became the first quarterback in NFL history to pass for seven touchdowns and 400 yards in a game, completed three TD passes that covered more than 30 yards, with his scoring tosses including a 31-yarder to Connie Mack Berry, a 40-yarder to Hampton Pool, and a 62-yarder to Harry Clarke.

Luckman had another big day in the 1943 regular-season finale, throwing for 241 yards and four touchdowns during a 35–24 victory over the Chicago Cardinals.

Luckman led the Bears to a 21–7 win over the Boston Yanks on November 12, 1944, by passing for 258 yards and three TDs, which included a career-long 86-yard hookup with Ray McLean.

Although the Bears lost to Detroit by a score of 35–28 on November 11, 1945, Luckman starred in defeat, throwing for 279 yards and four TDs, three of which covered more than 30 yards.

Luckman helped the Bears forge a 28–28 tie with the Los Angeles Rams on October 13, 1946, by passing for 248 yards and three touchdowns, hitting Jim Keane from 40 yards out, and collaborating with Ray McLean on scoring plays that covered 39 and 48 yards.

Luckman led the Bears to a 40–7 rout of Philadelphia on October 12, 1947, by throwing for 314 yards and three TDs, which included connections of 74 and 70 yards with Ken Kavanaugh.

Luckman followed that up with a strong outing against Detroit, passing for 342 yards and three touchdowns during a 33–24 win over the Lions one week later.

An outstanding postseason performer, Luckman completed 9 of 12 pass attempts for 160 yards during the Bears' 37–9 win over the Giants in the 1941 NFL championship game.

Excelling against Washington in the 1943 NFL title game, Luckman led the Bears to a 41–21 triumph by passing for 286 yards and five touchdowns, the longest of which went 66 yards to Dante Magnani. Luckman also returned two punts for 32 yards and intercepted two passes during the contest, returning his picks a total of 39 yards.

Luckman also starred on both sides of the ball in the 1946 NFL title game, leading the Bears to a 24–14 win over the Giants by recording an interception, completing a 21-yard TD pass to Ken Kavanaugh, and putting his team ahead to stay early in the fourth quarter with a 19-yard TD run.

Even though Luckman completed just three of four pass attempts for 88 yards and one TD during the Bears' 73–0 dismantling of the Washington Redskins in the 1940 NFL championship game, he considered that contest to be the highlight of his career, saying years later, "It's the memory of a lifetime. Can you imagine anybody today winning a championship game, 73–0? That's what we did. It was like a miracle. . . . We beat a great football team. We beat one of the greatest football players who ever lived in Sammy Baugh. Nobody dreamed that could happen to the Redskins. He was probably one of the greatest athletes we ever had in our country." Luckman then added, "I think that game will be remembered as long as football is played."

**Notable Achievements**

- Passed for more than 2,000 yards twice, topping 2,500 yards once (2,712 in 1947).
- Threw more than 20 touchdown passes twice.
- Completed more than 50 percent of passes six times.
- Posted touchdown-to-interception ratio of better than 2–1 once.
- Posted passer rating above 90.0 three times, finishing with mark of 107.5 in 1943.
- Recorded four interceptions twice.
- Led NFL in passing yards three times, touchdown passes three times, completion percentage once, passer rating three times, and punting average once.
- Finished second in NFL in passes completed four times, passing yards once, touchdown passes once, passer rating twice, completion percentage three times, and interception-return yards once.
- Ranks among Bears career leaders with 1,744 pass attempts (3rd), 904 pass completions (4th), 14,686 passing yards (2nd), 137 touchdown passes (2nd), and 8,872 yards punting (11th).
- Holds share of NFL record with seven touchdown passes in one game (November 14, 1943, vs. Giants).
- Six-time division champion (1940, 1941, 1942, 1943, 1946, and 1950).
- Four-time NFL champion (1940, 1941, 1943, and 1946).
- 1943 NFL MVP.
- Three-time Pro Bowl selection (1940, 1941, and 1942).
- Five-time First-Team All-Pro selection (1941, 1942, 1943, 1944, and 1947).
- Two-time Second-Team All-Pro selection (1940 and 1946).
- NFL 1940s All-Decade Team.
- #42 retired by Bears.
- Number 39 on the *Sporting News'* 1999 list of the 100 Greatest Players in NFL History.
- Number 33 on the NFL Network's 2010 list of the NFL's 100 Greatest Players.
- Elected to Pro Football Hall of Fame in 1965.

# 8

## BRIAN URLACHER

**A**n extraordinary athlete who possessed great size, speed, and intelligence, Brian Urlacher continued the rich tradition of exceptional play at the middle linebacker position in Chicago, following in the footsteps of Bill George, Dick Butkus, and Mike Singletary. Serving as the anchor of the Bears' defense for more than a decade, Urlacher spent his entire 13-year NFL career in the Windy City, recording the third most tackles in franchise history. Leading the Bears to four division titles and one NFC championship, Urlacher earned eight Pro Bowl selections, five All-Pro nominations, and one NFL Defensive Player of the Year trophy, before being further honored following the conclusion of his playing career by being named to the NFL 2000s All-Decade Team and the Pro Football Hall of Fame.

Born in Pasco, Washington, on May 25, 1978, Brian Keith Urlacher grew up in Lovington, New Mexico, after moving there with his mother and two siblings at the age of seven following the separation of his parents. Developing a love for sports at an early age, Urlacher starred in football, basketball, and track at Lovington High School. Proving to be particularly proficient on the gridiron, Urlacher displayed his tremendous athleticism by playing several different positions, including running back, wide receiver, defensive back, and return specialist. While at Lovington, Urlacher also experienced a considerable growth spurt, sprouting five inches and adding nearly 60 pounds of muscle onto his frame after assistant coach Jamie Quinones introduced him to the weight room. A true force on the football field as a senior, Urlacher led the Wildcats to a perfect 14-0 record and the 3-A state championship by making 61 receptions and scoring 23 touchdowns, with 15 of those coming on pass receptions, six on punt and kickoff returns, and two on runs from scrimmage.

Yet, despite his outstanding play, Urlacher never received a scholarship offer from nearby Texas Tech University, where he hoped to continue his athletic career. With the only Division I-A schools expressing an interest in him being the University of New Mexico and New Mexico State University,

Urlacher chose to enroll at the former, where he spent the next four years playing for head coach Dennis Franchione and the New Mexico Lobos.

After serving as a backup linebacker his first two years in college, Urlacher assumed a far more prominent role after the coaching staff converted him into a "Lobo-Back" prior to the start of his junior year. Functioning very much like a combination linebacker/free safety, the 6'4", 235-pound Urlacher thrived at his new post, earning First-Team All–Mountain West honors by leading the nation with 178 tackles. Further

Brian Urlacher earned NFL Defensive Player of the Year honors in 2005.
Courtesy of Mike Morbeck

refining his pass coverage skills by working with defensive coordinator Bronco Mendenhall the following summer, Urlacher developed into one of the most dominant defensive players in all of college football, gaining conference Player of the Year and First-Team All-America recognition by recording 148 tackles, forcing five fumbles, and recovering three others. In all, Urlacher registered 442 tackles and 11 sacks, intercepted three passes, and forced 11 fumbles during his college career, while also catching six TD passes as a red zone receiver and returning five kicks for touchdowns as an occasional return man. Praising his former Lobos teammate for his exceptional play at the collegiate level, Sean Stein said, "I think he's the best football player I've ever seen."

Intrigued by Urlacher's unique skill set, the Bears made him the ninth overall pick of the 2000 NFL Draft, with the expectation of starting him at outside linebacker. However, after the rookie committed too many mental mistakes during the preseason, he found himself sitting on the bench behind the more experienced Roosevelt Colvin. Urlacher, though, returned to the starting lineup in Week 3, taking over at middle linebacker for an injured Barry Minter. Having learned from his earlier mistakes, Urlacher performed brilliantly the rest of the year, earning Pro Bowl and NFL Defensive Rookie of the Year honors by leading the team with 125 tackles (101 solo) and eight sacks, while also picking off two passes. Urlacher followed that up by recording a total of 267 tackles over the course of the next two seasons, with his stellar play gaining him Pro Bowl and First-Team All-Pro recognition both years.

Making an extremely favorable impression on players throughout the league during the early stages of his career, Urlacher drew praise from NFL veteran Bryan Robinson, who said, "He might be the fastest thing on two wheels at his position in the league."

Redskins vice president of football operations, Vinny Cerrato, stated, "He's a phenomenal athlete. He loves to play the game. In terms of tackling ability, he's one of the best."

San Diego Chargers defensive coordinator Dale Lindsey proclaimed, "Dick Butkus personifies what the Bears were and are. I think Brian Urlacher is a prototype of what people hope they will be in the future."

Patriots quarterback Tom Brady commented, "You watch him play, and he's all over the place."

Brady's New England teammate Damien Woody added, "He's a monster. He's as good as you're going to see."

In discussing his prize protégé, Bears head coach Dick Jauron stated, "Brian was born with certain physical tools, which you certainly can't teach, but his attitude is really what makes him special."

Blessed with outstanding speed, the 6'4" Urlacher, who spent most of his pro career playing at close to 260 pounds, did an exceptional job of tracking opposing ball-carriers from sideline to sideline, exhibiting extraordinary agility for a man his size, while also displaying tremendous determination. Extremely strong as well, Urlacher had the power to shed offensive linemen, with opponents claiming that he ranked among the league's hardest hitters. A natural fit for the middle linebacker position, Urlacher also proved to be an intelligent and instinctive player who used his feel for the game and knowledge of opposing offenses to read plays and align the Bears' defense accordingly.

After Urlacher earned his third straight trip to the Pro Bowl in 2003, he suffered a series of leg injuries that limited him to just nine games the following year. However, he returned with a vengeance in 2005, earning Pro Bowl, First-Team All-Pro, and NFL Defensive Player of the Year honors by recording 121 tackles and six sacks for a Bears team that captured its first division title in four years. Gaining Pro Bowl and First-Team All-Pro recognition once again in 2006, Urlacher helped lead the Bears to a regular season record of 13-3 and an eventual berth in the Super Bowl by registering 141 tackles and picking off three passes.

Peyton Manning, whose Indianapolis Colts defeated the Bears in Super Bowl XLI, gained a tremendous amount of respect for Urlacher during the contest, stating afterwards, "You need to know where Brian is . . . everything you hear about him is absolutely true."

Packers head coach Mike Sherman also had high praise for Urlacher, saying, "I think Urlacher is one of the all-time best players we've played against."

Meanwhile, veteran NFL quarterback Jon Kitna addressed the mental aspect of Urlacher's game when he said, "He's special because he's got size and speed, but also because of his football IQ, which is something that a lot of people are missing when they talk about Brian."

Gradually emerging as one of the Bears' team leaders during his time in Chicago, Urlacher often failed to receive credit for the wisdom he imparted to his teammates, and for the kindly manner with which he treated them. But those closest to the situation knew just how much he meant to the other players around him, with teammate Alex Brown stating, "Brian is the face of the Chicago Bears, and the way he handles that makes him special. We have 53 characters on this team, and he can relate to each one on a professional or personal level."

Bears cornerback Charles Tillman said of his longtime teammate, "He was one of the greatest teammates you could ever have. He made you feel like you were the star."

Former Bears head coach Lovie Smith described the hub of his team's defense as "The perfect leader," also suggesting, "With a guy like that, it doesn't matter what you're doing. Anything he's a part of is going to be better. To try and put it into a few words on exactly what he brought to the table—he brought everything. Anything you needed at the time—leadership, a confident voice—he just knew what to do."

Smith then added, "He was the best superstar you'll ever be around. He treated everyone like you're his best friend. Respectful to everybody. He did it all."

In discussing the leadership that he provided to his teammates, Urlacher said, "I felt like I led by example. I didn't have to say a lot. When I did, guys listened. I didn't feel like I had to be out there yelling and screaming at guys. I did that sometimes, mostly on game day. I just didn't feel like I needed to do that."

After recording more than 100 tackles for the seventh time in eight seasons in 2007, Urlacher underwent minor neck surgery to treat his arthritic back during the subsequent offseason. He then had a slightly subpar 2008 campaign, registering "only" 93 tackles, before missing virtually the entire 2009 season after dislocating his wrist during a Week 1 loss to the Green Bay Packers. Returning to action in 2010, Urlacher regained his earlier form, making the Pro Bowl in each of the next two seasons, before suffering through an injury-marred 2012 campaign that saw him miss the final four games with a pulled hamstring.

With Urlacher becoming an unrestricted free agent on March 12, 2013, the Bears announced one week later that they had failed to come to terms with him on a new contract, making him eligible to sign with any other team. Urlacher, who later belittled general manager Phil Emery's contract negotiations with him as "lip service," subsequently chose to announce his retirement, ending his career with 1,358 tackles (1,040 solo), 41½ sacks, 22 interceptions, 324 interception-return yards, 11 forced fumbles, 15 fumble recoveries, and five touchdowns. Although Urlacher told ESPN in 2015 that he still respected the Bears organization and front office, he also revealed that he had yet to speak with Emery, who the team replaced as GM following the conclusion of the 2014 campaign. After spending one year serving as an analyst for Fox Sports 1 on that network's *Fox Football Daily* program, Urlacher resigned from that role on September 16, 2014, to spend more time with his family.

## CAREER HIGHLIGHTS

### Best Season

Urlacher performed brilliantly for the Bears in 2001 and 2002, recording three interceptions, 116 tackles (89 solo), six sacks, two forced fumbles, and one touchdown in the first of those campaigns, before registering 4½ sacks, a career-high 151 tackles, and a league-leading 115 solo stops in the second. He also had a huge year in 2006, earning the last of his four First-Team All-Pro nominations by picking off three passes and making 141 tackles, including 92 of the solo variety. But Urlacher made his greatest overall impact in 2005, leading the Bears to the division title by recording 121 tackles (97 solo) and six sacks, with his exceptional play earning him NFL Defensive Player of the Year honors.

### Memorable Moments/Greatest Performances

In addition to recording the first sack of his career during a 14–7 loss to the Giants on September 17, 2000, Urlacher made 13 tackles, including 11 solo stops.

Urlacher starred in defeat once again the following week, recording a sack, 10 tackles, and his first interception as a pro during a 21–14 loss to the Detroit Lions on September 24, 2000.

Urlacher turned in a tremendous all-around effort during a 31–3 win over the Atlanta Falcons on October 7, 2001, earning NFC Defensive Player of the Week honors for the first of six times by intercepting a pass, recording a sack, and returning a fumble 90 yards for a touchdown. Commenting on Urlacher's exceptional performance years later, Greg Blache, Chicago's defensive coordinator at the time, stated, "We always knew he was good. The Atlanta game in 2001, that was like: 'He's here. He's arrived.' He had hit that groove and became that playmaker and game-changer. He was always good. He was always a great teammate. He was always a great leader. But that's the game when he hit his stride."

Urlacher excelled during a 27–24 win over the Tampa Bay Buccaneers on November 18, 2001, recording a sack, forcing a fumble, and making 14 tackles, with 10 of those being solo stops.

Urlacher earned NFC Special Teams Player of the Week honors by scoring what proved to be the game-winning touchdown of a 20–15 win over Washington on December 23, 2001, when he caught a 27-yard TD pass from Brad Maynard following a fake field goal attempt in the fourth quarter.

Urlacher led the Bears to a 14–13 victory over the Atlanta Falcons on September 15, 2002, by recording two sacks, recovering a fumble, and registering 12 tackles, with his outstanding performance gaining him recognition as NFC Defensive Player of the Week.

Urlacher earned that distinction again by registering two sacks and six tackles during a 23–13 win over the San Francisco 49ers on October 31, 2004.

Urlacher helped lead the Bears to a 24–14 victory over the Minnesota Vikings on December 5, 2004, by making eight tackles, recording 1½ sacks, and intercepting a pass, which he subsequently returned 42 yards.

Urlacher turned in arguably the finest all-around performance of his career during a 24–23 win over the Arizona Cardinals on October 16, 2006, helping the Bears overcome a 20-point deficit by forcing a fumble that teammate Charles Tillman returned for a touchdown and making 19 tackles, including 11 of the solo variety. Commenting on the manner with which Urlacher impacted the outcome of the game, teammate Devin Hester said, "We watched the film, and everybody was saying that he just turned into the Incredible Hulk the last four minutes of the game, just killing people and running over and tackling whoever had the ball."

Urlacher put the finishing touches on a 35–7 victory over the Packers on December 23, 2007, by returning an interception 85 yards for a touchdown in the fourth quarter.

Urlacher led the Bears to a 24–20 win over the Lions on December 5, 2010, by forcing one fumble and recording 17 tackles, with 10 of those being solo stops.

Although the Bears lost the 2010 NFC championship game to the Packers by a score of 21–14, Urlacher starred in defeat, recording 10 tackles, sacking Aaron Rodgers once, and picking off a Rodgers pass, which he returned 39 yards before being tripped up by the Green Bay quarterback.

Urlacher earned NFC Defensive Player of the Week honors by making 10 tackles, intercepting a pass, and recovering a fumble in the end zone for a touchdown during a 30–12 win over the Atlanta Falcons in the 2011 regular-season opener.

Urlacher earned that distinction for the final time by returning his interception of a Matt Hasselbeck pass 46 yards for a TD during a 51–20 rout of the Titans on November 4, 2012.

**Notable Achievements**

- Recorded more than 100 tackles nine times.
- Recorded five interceptions in 2007.
- Recorded eight sacks in 2000.
- Led NFL in solo tackles once and fumble-return yards once.
- Finished second in NFL in total tackles once and tackles for loss once.
- Led Bears in tackles eight times, sacks once, and interceptions once.
- Ranks among Bears career leaders with 1,358 tackles (3rd), 41½ sacks (8th), 22 interceptions (tied-11th), 324 interception-return yards (12th), 15 fumble recoveries (6th), and 182 games played (8th).
- Four-time division champion (2001, 2005, 2006, and 2010).
- 2006 NFC champion.
- Member of 2000 NFL All-Rookie Team.
- 2001 Week 15 NFC Special Teams Player of the Week.
- Six-time NFC Defensive Player of the Week.
- December 2010 NFC Defensive Player of the Month.
- Eight-time Pro Bowl selection (2000, 2001, 2002, 2003, 2005, 2006, 2010, and 2011).
- Four-time First-Team All-Pro selection (2001, 2002, 2005, and 2006).
- 2010 Second-Team All-Pro selection.
- Three-time First-Team All-NFC selection (2001, 2002, and 2005).
- 2000 NFL Defensive Rookie of the Year.
- 2005 NFL Defensive Player of the Year.
- NFL 2000s All-Decade Team.
- Pro Football Reference All-2000s First Team.
- Elected to Pro Football Hall of Fame in 2018.

# 9

# CLYDE "BULLDOG" TURNER

The NFL's premier center for most of his career, Clyde "Bulldog" Turner spent 13 seasons anchoring Chicago's offensive line, leading the Bears to six division titles and four league championships. Possessing the ideal combination of size and speed, Turner established himself as the finest blocking interior lineman of his era, opening holes for Chicago's talented stable of running backs, while also providing ample protection for quarterback Sid Luckman in the passing game. An outstanding defender as well, Turner excelled as a linebacker, with his brilliant all-around play earning him four Pro Bowl selections, eight All-Pro nominations, a spot on the NFL 1940s All-Decade Team, and a place in the Pro Football Hall of Fame.

Born in Plains, Texas, on March 10, 1919, Clyde Douglas Turner grew up some 165 miles southeast, in the town of Sweetwater, where he attended Newman High School. After graduating from Newman at the tender age of 16, Turner spent one year working in the cattle business, before enrolling at Hardin-Simmons University in Abilene, Texas. Assigning himself the moniker "Bulldog" while in college to draw attention to himself, Turner spent three years starring at center and linebacker for the Cowboys, gradually increasing his weight from 190 to 235 pounds. With Hardin-Simmons losing only three games over the course of those three seasons, Turner earned Associated Press Little All-America and *New York Sun* All-America honors in 1939, becoming in 1940 the first "small college" player to participate in the College All-Star Game.

Subsequently selected by the Bears with the seventh overall pick of the 1940 NFL Draft, Turner gave an early indication of what lay ahead for opposing defenders when he dominated the men that lined up against him during training camp to such an extent that they found themselves being chastised by the team's coaching staff. Complaining that they were being held by the 21-year-old rookie, Chicago's defensive linemen could only listen as the coaches admonished them by saying, "If we don't see it, the refs won't either."

Clyde "Bulldog" Turner proved to be the NFL's premier center for most of his career.
Courtesy of MEARSonlineauctions.com

Possessing tremendous self-confidence, Turner claimed many years later that he spent much of his career listening to such complaints, stating, "I was such a good blocker that the men they put in front of me—and some were stars who were supposed to be making a lot of tackles—would have their coaches saying, 'Why aren't you making any tackles?' They'd say, 'That bum Turner is holding.' Well, that wasn't true. I could handle anybody that they'd put in front of me."

Excelling in his first year as a pro, Turner helped lead the Bears to the NFL title, earning in the process Pro Bowl and Second-Team All-Pro honors. Surpassing New York Giants legend Mel Hein as the league's top center the following year, Turner gained First-Team All-Pro recognition for the first of seven times, with the Bears capturing the league championship once again. Continuing to excel in each of the next three seasons, Turner helped lead the Bears to two more division titles and another NFL championship.

Standing 6'1" and weighing 237 pounds, Turner possessed good size for a lineman of his day. But his quickness and explosion off the ball are the things that truly made him stand out on offense. Driving opponents out of his way like a bulldozer, Turner excelled as a downfield blocker, modeling much of his game after Mel Hein, who he studied carefully during the early stages of his career. Turner also proved to be the league's best long snapper, with Chicago's punters bragging that they always received the ball from him with the laces up. Extremely intelligent and versatile as well, Turner claimed, "I knew everybody's assignments, and I could play every position on the field."

Supporting his teammate's contention, George Connor stated, "Bulldog Turner was the best football player and smartest player I ever knew in my whole life. He could do everything."

Ed Sprinkle added, "Bulldog and Luckman were quite a combination. I don't know who did their job better."

Although Turner built much of his reputation on his extraordinary play at center, he proved to be nearly as proficient as a linebacker on defense, using his speed to chase down enemy ball-carriers and his ball-hawking skills to record 17 career interceptions, which he returned for a total of 298 yards and two touchdowns. A ferocious tackler, Turner attacked opposing runners the same way he drove into defensive linemen from his center position. Applying his superior knowledge of the game on that side of the ball as well, Turner, according to Ed Sprinkle, was "the smartest coach on the field during the games. He ran the defensive plays, knowing what to do even before the coaches did."

After starting every game for the Bears in each of the previous five seasons, Turner appeared in only two contests in 1945 after enlisting in the military. Inducted into the US Army Air Forces in January 1945, Turner spent most of the year serving as a physical training instructor, while also playing for the Second Air Force Superbombers football team in Colorado Springs, Colorado.

Returning to the Bears in 1946, Turner helped lead them to another NFL title, earning in the process First-Team All-Pro honors for the first of three straight times. Turner continued to star on both sides of the ball for the Bears through the end of the 1952 season, when he announced his retirement. Ending his career having appeared in every game for the Bears in 12 of his 13 NFL seasons, Turner proved to be one of the league's most durable players. A true 60-minute man, Turner rarely left the field of play, performing on offense, defense, and special teams as well. In addition to intercepting 17 passes over the course of his career, Turner recovered five fumbles, one of which he returned for a touchdown. An outstanding post-season performer, Turner picked off four passes in five NFL championship games.

After assuming the role of player-coach in 1952, Turner served the Bears as a full-time assistant in each of the next four seasons, before spending the next three years working as an assistant at Baylor University. He then briefly coached the New York Titans of the newly formed American Football League, leaving New York at the end of 1963. Turner subsequently moved back west to Texas, where he became a rancher. He later moved to Omaha, Nebraska, where he took a job as a manager for Interstate Steel Co. After surviving a stroke that he suffered while on a business trip to Chicago in 1974, Turner developed further health problems in his later years, including diabetes, cancer, and heart disease. He passed away at the age of 79 on October 30, 1998, following a lengthy battle with lung cancer. His #66 retired by the Bears following the conclusion of his playing career, Turner left behind him a legacy as one of the greatest center-linebackers ever to play in the NFL.

# CAREER HIGHLIGHTS

### Best Season

Turner had his finest all-around season for the Bears in 1942, when, in addition to leading the NFL with eight interceptions, he starred on the offensive side of the ball, with Jack Mahon of the International News Service writing that Turner "was in a class by himself at center this season."

### Memorable Moments/Greatest Performances

Performing brilliantly at center during Chicago's stunning 73–0 victory over Washington in the 1940 NFL championship game, Turner helped the Bears rush for 381 yards and amass 519 yards of total offense. Turner also intercepted a Sammy Baugh pass on defense, which he returned 24 yards for a touchdown.

Turner anchored a Bears defense that created six turnovers and surrendered just 93 yards of total offense to the Detroit Lions during a convincing 24–7 Chicago win on November 23, 1941.

Excelling on the other side of the ball the following week, Turner helped the Bears amass 523 yards of total offense during a 49–14 rout of the Philadelphia Eagles on November 30, 1941.

Turner recorded a sack and helped pave the way for Chicago running backs to gain 277 yards on the ground during a 33–14 win over the Packers in the Western Division tiebreaker playoff in 1941.

Turner contributed to a lopsided 41–14 victory over the Chicago Cardinals on October 11, 1942, by returning an interception 42 yards for a touchdown.

Turner set the tone for a 38–7 win over the Packers on November 15, 1942, by scoring the game's first points when he recovered a fumble, which he returned 42 yards for a touchdown.

Turner's only carry of his career turned out to be a memorable one, as he ran 48 yards for a touchdown during a 49–7 mauling of a combined Chicago Cardinals/Pittsburgh Steelers squad in the final game of the 1944 regular season.

During a 56–20 victory over the Washington Redskins on October 26, 1947, Turner picked off a Sammy Baugh pass, which he subsequently returned 96 yards for a touchdown, crossing the goal line with Baugh hanging on his back trying to bring him down. Turner later identified that play as the highlight of his career.

**Notable Achievements**

- Appeared in every game in 12 of 13 seasons, at one point appearing in 83 consecutive contests.
- Amassed more than 100 interception-return yards once (103 in 1947).
- Led NFL with eight interceptions in 1942.
- Finished second in NFL with 96 interception-return yards in 1942.
- Six-time division champion (1940, 1941, 1942, 1943, 1946, and 1950).
- Four-time NFL champion (1940, 1941, 1943, and 1946).
- Four-time Pro Bowl selection (1940, 1941, 1950, and 1951).
- Seven-time First-Team All-Pro selection (1941, 1942, 1943, 1944, 1946, 1947, and 1948).
- 1940 Second-Team All-Pro selection.
- NFL 1940s All-Decade Team.
- #66 retired by Bears.
- Elected to Pro Football Hall of Fame in 1966.

# 10

# MIKE DITKA

One of only two men to win an NFL title as a player, an assistant coach, and a head coach, Mike Ditka is perhaps remembered most by Bears fans for guiding the team to its last NFL championship in 1985. Prior to that, though, Ditka spent six seasons in Chicago establishing himself as one of the league's first great pass-receiving tight ends. Contributing greatly to the success the Bears experienced during the championship campaign of 1963, "Iron Mike," as he came to be known, led the team in receptions and receiving yards for the third straight time, doing so two years after he became the only tight end in franchise history to amass more than 1,000 receiving yards in a season. The NFL's Rookie of the Year in 1961, Ditka went on to record the sixth-most pass receptions, fifth-most receiving yards, and fourth-most TD catches in team annals over the course of the next five seasons, with his outstanding play earning him five Pro Bowl selections and six All-Pro nominations. Although Ditka failed to perform at the same lofty level after he left Chicago following the conclusion of the 1966 campaign, he later received the additional distinctions of being named to the NFL's 75th Anniversary Team and the NFL 100 All-Time Team, being included on the *Sporting News* and the NFL Network's respective lists of the 100 Greatest Players in NFL History, having his #89 retired by the Bears, and being inducted into the Pro Football Hall of Fame.

Born in the Pittsburgh-area town of Carnegie, Pennsylvania, on October 18, 1939, Michael Keller Dyczko grew up with his three younger siblings in nearby Aliquippa, where his mother raised the children while their father fought in the Pacific as a member of the US Marines during World War II. With the Ukrainian surname "Dyczko" proving to be difficult for others to pronounce, the family changed its name to "Ditka" before young Mike enrolled in elementary school.

Eventually developing into a three-sport star while attending Aliquippa High School, Ditka excelled in baseball, basketball, and football, prompting

Mike Ditka helped revolutionize the position of tight end.
Courtesy of RMYAuctions.com

several colleges to offer him an athletic scholarship, with his suitors including Notre Dame, Penn State, and the University of Pittsburgh. Finally
selecting the latter, Ditka spent three seasons at Pitt lettering in all three
sports, although he proved to be particularly proficient on the gridiron,
starring for the school as a tight end, linebacker, and punter. After leading
the Panthers in receptions three straight times and gaining consensus All-
America recognition in 1960, Ditka entered the 1961 NFL Draft, where
the Bears made him the fifth overall selection. Ditka subsequently chose to

sign with the Bears instead of the Houston Oilers, who also claimed him with the eighth overall pick of that year's AFL Draft.

Laying claim to the starting tight end job immediately upon his arrival in Chicago, Ditka ended up redefining the position with his pass-catching ability and unique blend of power and speed. While most NFL teams previously used their tight ends primarily as extra blockers, Ditka helped alter the mindset of coaches around the league by placing among the circuit leaders with 56 receptions, 1,076 receiving yards, and 12 TD catches, while also doing an exceptional job of blocking at the point of attack. In addition to gaining Pro Bowl, All-Pro, and NFL Rookie of the Year recognition with his fabulous performance, Ditka earned the respect and admiration of his teammates, with veteran Bears linebacker Bill George stating, "He is the best rookie I have ever seen. Eleven more of him and there would be no place for me on the team."

Ditka followed that up with three more outstanding seasons, posting the following numbers from 1962 to 1964:

| YEAR | REC | REC YD | TD REC |
|------|-----|--------|--------|
| 1962 | 58  | 904    | 5      |
| 1963 | 59  | 794    | 8      |
| 1964 | 75  | 897    | 5      |

Ranking among the NFL leaders in receptions all three years, Ditka finished as high as second in 1964, when only teammate Johnny Morris caught more passes. Ditka earned Pro Bowl and All-Pro honors all three years, gaining Second-Team All-Pro recognition in 1962, before being named to the First Team in each of the next two seasons.

In addition to establishing himself as one of the NFL's foremost pass-catchers his first few years in the league, Ditka became known as one of the circuit's most competitive and nastiest players, with Johnny Morris saying of his teammate, "Ditka was the epitome of the rough, tough, talented football player. He left many bruises on opposing players, and he could never conceive of giving less than 100 percent; it just wasn't in his nature."

Morris then added, "He was one of the first offensive intimidators. He would go after people like Ray Nitschke. He was the aggressor. There were so many times I'd see him throw a block, then immediately roll over and go for a second block. Most players, even the great ones, are satisfied after they do their job. Not him. He was never satisfied."

Bears quarterback Bill Wade commented, "Mike would catch the ball and look for people to hit. He would run over people. He would knock into them. He always liked to run short pass patterns and then run over everybody in his way. He was neat to have on the team because he was so spirited. He was a very, very tough football player. Ditka was in the mold of a real fighter on the football field and was a person who added a lot of spark to the Chicago Bear football team. He was what I would call a fighting Chicago Bear."

Looking back on the time he spent on the football field, Ditka said, "Those 60 minutes when I played, man those were special. I enjoyed the heck out of that. Wrigley Field, I enjoyed the mud, the slop, whatever, even people throwing beer on us when we lost going into the locker room. It was all good stuff. You turn around, give them a piece of your mind."

With Ditka's aggressive style of play beginning to take a physical toll on him and the Bears altering their offensive philosophy somewhat following the arrival of Gale Sayers in 1965, the talented tight end experienced a precipitous decline in offensive production, totaling just 68 receptions, 832 receiving yards, and four touchdowns from 1965 to 1966. Nevertheless, Ditka remained a huge asset to the team, particularly in the running game, with his exceptional blocking helping him earn another trip to the Pro Bowl and two more All-Pro selections. And, even in his somewhat diminished state, Ditka made an extremely favorable impression on Bears rookie linebacker Doug Buffone in 1966, with Buffone saying during an interview with Bleacher Report years later, "If Ditka played in today's game, he would catch 100 balls a season easily; he was that type of talent. In that era, you destroyed the tight end as he came off the line, absolutely destroyed him. There was none of this free release stuff you see now."

Despite his overall contributions to the team, Ditka began to wear out his welcome in Chicago in 1965, spending much of the next two seasons feuding with Bears owner and head coach George Halas. After angering Halas by publicly siding with backup quarterback Rudy Bukich over starting signal-caller Bill Wade, Ditka further infuriated his coach by expressing his dissatisfaction with his $25,000 salary, telling the media, "Halas throws nickels around like manhole covers." Having grown weary of the constant bickering, Halas elected to trade Ditka to the Philadelphia Eagles for quarterback Jack Concannon and a draft pick prior to the start of the 1967 campaign. During his six seasons in Chicago, Ditka caught 316 passes, amassed 4,503 receiving yards, and scored 36 touchdowns, with 34 of those coming on pass receptions and the other two on fumble recoveries. A true gamer, Ditka never missed a start in his six years with the Bears, appearing in 84 consecutive contests despite being plagued by numerous leg and foot injuries.

Ditka ended up spending two injury-marred seasons in Philadelphia, totaling just 39 receptions, 385 receiving yards, and four touchdowns, before joining the Dallas Cowboys in 1969. Assuming a part-time role in Dallas, Ditka caught only 72 passes for 924 yards and five touchdowns over the course of the next four seasons, although his leadership and outstanding blocking helped the Cowboys capture their first NFL championship in 1971. Choosing to retire at the end of 1972, Ditka concluded his playing career with 427 receptions, 5,812 receiving yards, and 45 touchdowns.

After retiring as an active player, Ditka spent nine seasons serving as an assistant under head coach Tom Landry in Dallas, with the Cowboys winning six division titles, three NFC championships, and one Super Bowl during that time. While working for the Cowboys, Ditka sent a letter to George Halas telling him that he hoped to one day return to the Bears as head coach "when he was ready." Taking Ditka up on his offer a few years later, Halas hired his former verbal sparring partner to be his team's head coach prior to the start of the 1982 season, after earlier dismissing Neill Armstrong from that position.

Ditka subsequently remained head man in Chicago for the next 11 years, winning NFL Coach of the Year honors twice by guiding the Bears to six division titles, three NFC championship game appearances, one Super Bowl victory, and an overall record of 106-62 from 1982 to 1992. During that time, Ditka became known as a tough, hard-nosed, no-nonsense disciplinarian who often clashed with his players and the members of the local media. Ditka's coaching reign came to an end after the Bears finished just 5-11 in 1992, with team president Mike McCaskey relieving him of his duties following the conclusion of the campaign. Commenting publicly on his dismissal for the first time several years later, Ditka told Fox Sports Network in 2005, "I was fired out of jealousy, plain and simple. I had become the Bears. The greatest moment of my life is when George Halas hired me. The lowest moment of my life was when a guy that shouldn't have been there fired me."

After leaving the Bears, Ditka took a broadcasting job with NBC, with whom he spent the next four years working as an analyst on *NFL Live* and as a color commentator for many other network broadcasts. Returning to the sidelines in 1997, Ditka served as head coach of the New Orleans Saints for three seasons, leading them to an overall record of 15-33, before being dismissed at the end of 1999. After being fired by the Saints, Ditka spent two years working as a studio analyst on *The NFL Today*. He is currently a commentator on ESPN's *NFL Live*, ESPN's *Sunday NFL Countdown*, and CBS Radio–Westwood One's *Monday Night Football* pregame show. Ditka, who recovered quickly from a heart attack he suffered in 1988, suffered a minor stroke at a suburban country club in Chicago in November 2012. He has since suffered a second heart attack, being stricken while playing golf in Naples, Florida, on November 23, 2018.

## BEARS CAREER HIGHLIGHTS

### Best Season

Ditka earned First-Team All-Pro honors in 1963 and 1964, concluding the second of those campaigns with 897 receiving yards and a career-high 75 receptions. However, he had his finest all-around season for the Bears in 1961, gaining recognition as the NFL Offensive Rookie of the Year by ranking among the league leaders with 56 receptions, 1,076 receiving yards, 12 touchdowns, and an average of 19.2 yards per catch.

### Memorable Moments/Greatest Performances

Ditka made a huge impact in just his second game as a pro, making five receptions for 130 yards and one touchdown during a 21–17 win over the Los Angeles Rams on September 23, 1961, with his TD coming on a 47-yard pass from Ed Brown.

Ditka contributed to a 31–17 victory over the Detroit Lions on October 8, 1961, by making five catches for 120 yards and one touchdown, which came on a 37-yard hookup with Bill Wade that tied the score at 17–17 early in the fourth quarter.

Ditka helped lead the Bears to a convincing 31–0 win over the San Francisco 49ers on October 22, 1961, by making four receptions for 107 yards and two touchdowns, the longest of which covered 47 yards.

Although Ditka made just one reception during a 16–14 loss to the Philadelphia Eagles on November 5, 1961, it went for a career-long 76-yard touchdown.

Ditka turned in an exceptional effort in a losing cause the following week, catching nine passes for 190 yards and three touchdowns during a 31–28 loss to the Packers on November 12, 1961, with the longest of his TD grabs covering 47 yards.

Ditka concluded the 1961 campaign in style, making eight receptions for 102 yards and two touchdowns during a 52–35 win over the Minnesota Vikings in the regular-season finale.

Ditka had a big game against Dallas on November 18, 1962, making seven receptions for 133 yards and one touchdown during a hard-fought 34–33 victory that the Bears won on a late field goal by Roger LeClerc.

Ditka also posted excellent numbers against Los Angeles on December 9, 1962, catching six passes for 155 yards and one touchdown during a 30–14 win over the Rams.

Ditka contributed to a 28–7 victory over the Vikings on September 22, 1963, by making eight receptions for 124 yards and two touchdowns, the longest of which covered 36 yards.

Ditka made a career-high four touchdown receptions during a 52–14 rout of the Rams on October 13, 1963, finishing the game with nine catches and 110 receiving yards.

Ditka had another huge game against Los Angeles on October 11, 1964, making six receptions, amassing 81 receiving yards, and scoring three touchdowns during a 38–17 Bears win, with the last of his TDs coming on a fumble recovery in the end zone.

Ditka made a career-high 13 receptions for 168 yards during a 27–20 loss to the Washington Redskins on October 25, 1964.

Ditka gave the Bears a 13–10 win over the Vikings on October 2, 1966, when he gathered in a 19-yard touchdown pass from Rudy Bukich late in the fourth quarter.

Ditka made what many people consider to be the defining play of his career late in the fourth quarter of a 17–17 tie with the Pittsburgh Steelers on November 24, 1963, just two days after the assassination of President John F. Kennedy, when he took a short pass from Bill Wade, broke several tackles, and ran 63 yards to set up the game-tying field goal. Teammate Rick Casares, who watched as Ditka avoided a tackle by John Reger and broke away from would-be tacklers Myron Pottios, Glenn Glass, and Clendon Thomas, before Thomas finally brought him down from behind some 35 yards later after being dragged for another 5 yards, later called the tight end's effort "the greatest run I ever saw." Ditka finished the game with seven receptions for 146 yards.

## Notable Achievements

- Surpassed 50 receptions four times, topping 70 catches once (75 in 1964).

- Surpassed 800 receiving yards three times, topping 1,000 yards once (1,076 in 1961).
- Scored 12 touchdowns in 1961.
- Played in every game for six straight seasons, appearing in 84 consecutive contests.
- Finished second in NFL in receptions once and touchdown catches once.
- Finished fourth in NFL in receiving yards once, touchdowns once, and yards per catch once.
- Led Bears in receptions and receiving yards three times each.
- Ranks among Bears career leaders with 316 receptions (6th), 4,503 receiving yards (5th), 34 touchdown receptions (4th), and 36 touchdowns (11th).
- 1963 division champion.
- 1963 NFL champion.
- 1961 NFL Offensive Rookie of the Year.
- Five-time Pro Bowl selection (1961, 1962, 1963, 1964, and 1965).
- Two-time First-Team All-Pro selection (1963 and 1964).
- Four-time Second-Team All-Pro selection (1961, 1962, 1965, and 1966).
- Five-time First-Team All-Western Conference selection (1961, 1962, 1963, 1964, and 1965).
- Pro Football Reference All-1960s First Team.
- #89 retired by Bears.
- Named to NFL's 75th Anniversary Team in 1994.
- Named to NFL 100 All-Time Team in 2019.
- Number 90 on the *Sporting News'* 1999 list of the 100 Greatest Players in NFL History.
- Number 59 on the NFL Network's 2010 list of the NFL's 100 Greatest Players.
- Elected to Pro Football Hall of Fame in 1988.

# 11

# DOUG ATKINS

The most physically dominating player of his era, Doug Atkins spent 12 seasons in Chicago establishing himself as one of the greatest pass-rushers in NFL history. Called "the most feared player I ever saw" by longtime Bears teammate Ed O'Bradovich, and "the most magnificent physical specimen I had ever seen" by Hall of Fame coach Weeb Ewbank, Atkins, who stood a towering 6'8" and weighed close to 275 pounds, used his size, tremendous strength, and exceptional athletic ability to overwhelm opposing offensive linemen from his right defensive end position. An eight-time Pro Bowl selection and six-time All-Pro, Atkins helped lead the Bears to two division titles and one NFL championship, with his exceptional play also earning him spots on the NFL 1960s All-Decade Team and the NFL 100 All-Time Team, as well as a place in the Pro Football Hall of Fame.

Born in Humboldt, Tennessee, on May 8, 1930, Douglas Leon Atkins had to learn how to fend for himself at a very young age. The son of a journeyman painter/carpenter who often squandered his money on alcohol, Atkins recalled, "My daddy worked for a while, then drank for a while. I soon realized that I needed to work in order to keep food on our table." Finding employment as a tomato packer at the age of 12, Atkins constructed crates out of plywood and then loaded the ripe produce on to boxcars, remembering, "It was very tough work, but I was making $50 a week, which was a small fortune for a young boy back in those times."

Atkins, who attended Humboldt High School, stood just 5'2" and weighed only 118 pounds as a freshman, causing him to be overlooked when he tried out for the school's football and basketball teams. However, after experiencing a growth spurt that left him standing 6'8" and weighing 195 pounds by the start of his senior year, Atkins went on to star for Humboldt High in both sports, enabling him to earn an athletic scholarship to the University of Tennessee.

After enrolling at Tennessee, Atkins initially intended to compete only on the hardwood, saying years later, "My scholarship actually was in basketball. Once I arrived on campus, I sort of put the football thing aside. That wasn't my real interest at that time." However, once head football coach Bob Neyland saw Atkins's rare combination of size and agility, he insisted that he play for him as well, with Atkins stating, "Coach reminded me that I had been recruited to play football and basketball, and that was exactly what I would be doing while I attended Tennessee. He said it was fine with him if I participated in other sports like basketball or track, but I had to be on the football field for every practice and every game."

Atkins ended up starting at defensive end for the Volunteers for three seasons, helping them capture the National Championship in 1951, before earning All-America honors as a senior the following year. An outstanding all-around athlete, Atkins also lettered in basketball and track and field, finishing runner-up in the high jump at the 1952 Southeastern Conference championships with a mark of 6'6".

Selected by the Cleveland Browns with the 11th overall pick of the 1953 NFL Draft, Atkins instead elected to play basketball for a professional team known as the Detroit Vagabond Kings, recalling, "The ironic thing was that I had just met a guy in a bar who traveled with a professional basketball team, the Detroit Vagabonds. That sounded like an appealing way of life

Doug Atkins proved to be one of the most physically dominating players in NFL history.
Courtesy of MEARSonlineauctions.com

to me. I asked him if he was taking on any additional players. He told me they'd just lost a fellow who had gotten married. The team offered $350 a month, a veritable fortune to me."

Atkins, though, eventually grew weary of the constant travel, prompting him to meet with Browns assistant coach Weeb Ewbank three months later. Recalling the events that transpired during their meeting, Atkins said, "We drank beer and talked football. He offered me $6,500 to play for the Browns. I finally got him up to $6,800. I signed for that money, two cheeseburgers, and eight beers. Today, I think the kids get $5 million signing bonuses."

Atkins ended up spending just two seasons in Cleveland before he grew dissatisfied with head coach Paul Brown's academic and extremely regimented approach to football, later saying, "We had to take tests. I cheated like hell to get through them. It was like college, but worse."

Acknowledging that the pairing of Atkins and Brown never had any chance of succeeding, George Halas stated, "I'm not at all surprised that Doug didn't get along with Paul Brown. Brown was a very straight fellow, a strict disciplinarian. Doug resented that from the first time they met. They were like oil and water."

Dealt to the Bears for a pair of draft picks following the conclusion of the 1954 campaign, Atkins spent his first two seasons in Chicago sharing playing time with Ed Sprinkle and Ed Meadows, before becoming the full-time starter at right defensive end in 1957. Blossoming into a star under the direction of George Halas, Atkins soon emerged as the NFL's top pass-rusher and most dominant defensive lineman, earning seven consecutive trips to the Pro Bowl and All-Pro honors in five of the next seven seasons.

Blessed with tremendous physical gifts, Atkins possessed great size, quickness, and agility, which, combined with his extraordinary strength and nasty temperament, made him the most feared defensive player in the league. In speaking of Atkins, former NFL offensive lineman Bill Curry said, "He looked like Michelangelo's David physically. That's what he looked like. Just huge. He was perfectly proportioned. He was symmetrical, but he was just so much bigger and stronger than any of the rest of us."

Hall of Fame quarterback Fran Tarkenton stated, "He is the strongest man in football, and, also, the biggest. When he rushes the passer with those oak tree arms of his way up in the air, he is 12 feet tall. And, if he gets to you, the whole world suddenly starts spinning."

Although Atkins thought nothing of leaping over opposing offensive linemen on his way to the quarterback, he usually preferred to go right through them, with Johnny Unitas claiming, "One of his favorite tricks was to throw a blocker at the quarterback."

Corroborating his teammate's statement, Colts offensive lineman Bob Vogel said, "Doug was so strong, he could throw me 10 feet."

Mike Ditka said of his longtime teammate, "He was just a vicious pass rusher. He'd take the tackle all the way back to the quarterback and knock them both down, things like that. He had a great wingspan. He just played the game hard. He played the game the way you were supposed to play it."

Also known for his fierce temper, Atkins developed a reputation as someone not to be trifled with, as Ditka suggested when he said, "He was one of the most physical guys that played the game ever. Nobody messed with Doug, believe me."

Bears offensive lineman Stan Jones expressed similar sentiments when he stated, "Doug was a man you never wanted to make angry."

Indeed, opposing players did everything within their power not to anger Atkins, with Bill Curry revealing a conversation that took place between himself and fellow Packers offensive lineman Bob Skoronski prior to Curry's first meeting with the Bears as a rookie: "Look, here's some things I want you to remember," Skoronski said. "Number 81 is Doug Atkins. He's 6'9" and he weighs 265 pounds. DON'T CUT HIM, and, if he falls down, help him up and say, 'nice play, Mr. Atkins.'"

"Well, I (Curry) started to laugh," Curry said, to which Skoronski responded, "Kid, this is not a joke, and I'm not kidding you now, because, if you cut him, on his knees, the first thing he's going to do is kill you, and then, he's going to kill me."

Baltimore Colts Hall of Fame offensive lineman Jim Parker, who Atkins claimed gave him more problems than any other tackle in the league, provided further testament to his frequent foe's mean streak when he said, "I considered myself the best tackle of this century, and I played against some mean ones, but I never met anyone meaner than Atkins. After my first meeting with him, I really wanted to quit pro football. He just beat the hell out of me. It was awful. Finally, my coaches convinced me not every pro player was like Atkins."

His temper not confined to the playing field, Atkins often clashed with the equally volatile George Halas, whose regimented ways grated on the huge defensive lineman's nerves. In discussing their primary point of contention, Halas said, "Doug resented discipline of any kind. He was way too casual about practice. He hated any kind of a routine. He thought he could get it all done on Sundays, which is not the way I work at all."

Revealing that Atkins took more liberties with Halas than any other member of the team, Ed O'Bradovich said, "He was the only one that would stand up to the old man. He'd tell the old man where to go and how fast to get there—and he meant it and didn't smile. Everybody else was, 'No, sir. Yes, sir.' Not Doug."

The relationship between the two men finally having run its course, Atkins requested a trade following the conclusion of the 1966 campaign, later revealing, "The biggest reason I got traded was that I wanted to get paid. I really retired after the 1966 Pro Bowl, but I changed my mind and played in 1966. I threatened to retire for good in 1967, and, during my talks with Coach Halas, I told him I wanted a raise. The most money I made with the Chicago Bears was in 1965, when Halas gave me a $5,000 bonus and paid me $25,000 that season. Before they kept records on quarterback sacks, I had two seasons in the 1960s where I had 20 or more sacks and still didn't get more money."

Atkins continued, "I'm going to tell you, the 'Old Papa Bear,' he was an ornery old cuss, and it got heated between us. He was 72 years old back then, but he was an aggressive old man, and he didn't back down. We had a love-hate relationship, to tell you the truth. He got to railing about me and, finally, he gave me a chance to talk, and I told him to trade me. Halas calmed down, and he told me to give him a week and he would see what he could do.

"Sure enough, I get a phone call from a sportswriter in Chicago, and he asked me how I felt about being traded to the New Orleans Saints. I told him I was ready to go, and I knew living in Louisiana was going to be a little easier finance-wise than living in Chicago. Coach Halas called me, and the conversation was short. He told me he traded me to the Saints, they would pay me what I wanted, and he told me he appreciated how well I played for him and his franchise, and he hung up the phone."

Atkins ended up spending three seasons in New Orleans, earning Second-Team All-Pro honors in 1968, even though he fractured his knee-cap during the latter stages of the campaign. Announcing his retirement one year later, Atkins drew praise from George Halas, who called him "the greatest defensive end I ever saw."

Ed O'Bradovich expressed similar feelings years later when he said, "He was the greatest defensive end to ever play the game. I would watch him pick up players and throw them around like he was plucking a chicken. . . . There were some great defensive ends in that era—Gino Marchetti with the Colts, Willie Davis with the Packers. But there was only one Doug Atkins. He high jumped 6-8 in college in 1951. The following year, the guy that won the Olympics jumped 6-8. He was like a gigantic hurdler. If an offensive lineman set up and took him on, he'd throw him like a rag doll. If he went down and tried to cut him, he'd jump over him. He was incredible."

Although the NFL did not begin keeping an official record of sacks until 1982, league historian John Turney writes, "Based on the number of sacks the Bears defense had, it is very likely that Atkins was in double digits in sacks from 1957 to 1963. *Pro Football Journal* writer/researcher Nick Webster can confirm that, from 1959 to 1962, he had at least 9½ sacks each season, with a few games each season missing film or play-by-plays. My research shows 12 sacks in 1963, 5 in 1964, 8½ in 1965, and 8 in 1966."

Turney continues, "Sadly, too many missing games will likely never reveal Atkins's true sack total, but, through our research, Webster and I can show 110½ confirmed sacks, all but a few from 1957 on. In a 1996 interview with Merlin Olsen, he told me that, if anyone may have challenged Deacon Jones's sack records, it would be Atkins, who Olsen and Jones studied on film. Olsen was particularly impressed with how Atkins would throw a tackle to the outside and take an inside route to the quarterback. Atkins told me, 'Hell, they were throwing themselves. I would take an outside charge and they'd be on their heels, and I'd step inside and throw them with their own backward momentum.'"

After retiring from the NFL, Atkins held several jobs, including working as an exterminator, as a pipe system manager, and selling caskets to funeral homes. He eventually retired to Knoxville, Tennessee, where he spent his final years suffering from Addison's disease, before dying of natural causes at the age of 85, on December 30, 2015.

Upon learning of his passing, Bears chairman George McCaskey said in a statement released by the team, "Doug Atkins is an all-time great who will be remembered as one of the pillars of the 1963 Championship Bears. He had a freakish combination of size and athletic ability and was as tough as anyone who ever stepped on a football field. Doug wasn't afraid to offer his opinion off the field as well, and he had a unique communication style when it came to interacting with Coach Halas. He embodied the spirit and commitment of what it means to be a Bear."

Looking back on his career some years earlier, Atkins said, "Football in a way was much like the work I knew in my early years. You had to toil and put in the time to earn results. I knew Coach Halas never felt I put in the time and effort in practice that he wanted me to, but, in my view, I did what was required. The results were there, and that is what counts."

## BEARS CAREER HIGHLIGHTS

### Best Season

Although Atkins likely got to opposing quarterbacks more times in a few other seasons, research reveals that he recorded an "unofficial" total of 12 sacks in 1963. With Atkins having earned his lone First-Team All-Pro nomination that year, we'll identify the 1963 campaign as the finest of his career.

### Memorable Moments/Greatest Performances

Atkins recorded four sacks during a 16–10 win over the Los Angeles Rams on November 3, 1957.

Atkins turned in another dominant performance against the Rams on October 9, 1960, anchoring a Chicago defense that registered seven sacks and allowed just 102 yards of total offense during a 34–27 Bears win, with the Rams scoring most of their points on three Chicago turnovers.

Atkins led a fierce Bears pass rush that recorded 12 sacks of Detroit quarterback Jim Ninowski during a 28–7 win over the Lions on November 20, 1960.

Atkins and his defensive mates also got to Fran Tarkenton 12 times during a 52–35 victory over the Vikings in the 1961 regular-season finale.

Atkins scored the only points of his career when he sacked Earl Morrall in the end zone for a safety during a 37–21 win over the Lions on September 29, 1963.

Atkins led a dominant Bears defense that recorded six sacks and six interceptions during a 52–14 rout of the Rams on October 13, 1963, with Atkins registering one of his three career picks during the contest.

Atkins recorded his second career interception during a 31–10 victory over the previously undefeated Packers on October 31, 1965.

## Notable Achievements

- Two-time division champion (1956 and 1963).
- 1963 NFL champion.
- Eight-time Pro Bowl selection (1957, 1958, 1959, 1960, 1961, 1962, 1963, and 1965).
- 1963 First-Team All-Pro selection.
- Five-time Second-Team All-Pro selection (1957, 1958, 1959, 1960, and 1965).
- Seven-time First-Team All–Western Conference selection (1958, 1959, 1960, 1961, 1962, 1963, and 1965).
- NFL 1960s All-Decade Team.
- Pro Football Reference All-1960s Second Team.
- Named to NFL 100 All-Time Team in 2019.
- Elected to Pro Football Hall of Fame in 1982.

# 12

## — STAN JONES —

versatile player who excelled at four different positions for the Bears, Stan Jones spent 12 of his 13 NFL seasons in Chicago, establishing himself as one of the greatest linemen in franchise history. Named to seven Pro Bowls and four All-Pro teams, Jones spent most of his career starring at guard on offense. However, after being moved to defensive tackle in 1962, he continued to perform well at that post the next few years, serving as a key member of the Bears' 1963 NFL championship team. Yet, Jones, who earned a spot on the Pro Football Reference All-1950s Second Team and a place in the Pro Football Hall of Fame, is perhaps remembered most for being the first athlete in any major sport to make weight training a central part of his workout regimen.

Born in Altoona, Pennsylvania, on November 24, 1931, Stanley Paul Jones grew up in the Harrisburg area, where he attended Lemoyne High School. First introduced to weights as a teenager, Jones gradually transformed himself from a skinny 140-pound boy into a strapping 200-plus-pound offensive lineman by the time he left Lemoyne High. Discussing years later the physical transformation that Jones underwent during that period in his life, his daughter, Sherrill, said:

> He was ahead of his time. In high school and college, his friends and teammates used to make fun of him because he was in the gym while they were out dancing and chasing girls. He first got hooked on weights because he grew up near York, Pennsylvania, where York Barbells were made. He figured that was the way to go. . . . He didn't consider himself a natural athlete, so he thought weight training would put him over the top. And it definitely did. He started out as a skinny pip-squeak, and, by the time he finished his career, he was one of the giants.

Stan Jones earned seven Pro Bowl selections and four All-Pro nominations during his time in Chicago.
Courtesy of RMYAuctions.com

After excelling as a two-way lineman in high school, Jones enrolled at the University of Maryland, where he continued to star on both sides of the ball at tackle. Performing especially well as a junior in 1953, Jones earned consensus All-America honors and won the Knute Rockne Memorial Award as the nation's outstanding lineman. In discussing the qualities that set Jones apart from other players who manned his position, Maryland head coach Jim Tatum stated, "He's so strong he can move an entire line out of the way on a block. I can't conceive of any player being stronger, and he is the most devastating blocker I ever saw."

Terrapins running back Chet Hanulak also marveled at his teammate's strength, saying, "Dick Modzelewski (Maryland's Outland Trophy winner in 1952) was a defensive tackle, shorter but heavier, and strong. During practices, Stan would do push-ups, at least 10 of them, with Dick on his shoulders."

Impressed with Jones's power and exceptional play at the collegiate level, the Bears selected him in the fifth round of the 1953 NFL Draft, with the 55th overall pick, even though he still had one year of eligibility left at Maryland. After earning All-America honors again as a senior, Jones joined the Bears in 1954, spending his first year in Chicago at right tackle, before being moved inside to guard the following year.

Playing either of the two guard positions for the next eight seasons, the 6'1", 255-pound Jones established himself as arguably the NFL's finest blocking interior lineman, earning seven Pro Bowl selections and four All-Pro nominations. Considered by many to be the league's strongest player, Jones, who excelled equally well in pass protection and run-blocking, later credited much of his success to his practice of lifting weights, stating, "If I hadn't lifted weights, I probably wouldn't have become a pro football player. It really helped me recover from the bruises after every game."

Jones also became known for his discipline and leadership, with Bears defensive tackle Fred Williams saying, "He was a leader, somebody you looked up to. And he could lift the side of a house."

Serving as the Bears' offensive captain for several seasons, Jones also drew praise from Maryland All-America quarterback Jack Scarbath, who said of his former Terrapins teammate, "He was always prepared, physically and mentally, for every game. He was always focused on his performance. He spent hours looking at films at a time when only the quarterbacks and defensive signal-callers put in that extra work. It was a work ethic that he carried into the pros."

After being named to the Pro Bowl as an offensive lineman in each of the previous seven seasons, Jones spent the 1962 campaign playing on both sides of the ball when Bears assistant coach George Allen asked him to help fortify the team's defensive line. Having lost some of his footspeed, Jones moved to defensive tackle full-time the following year, with his primary responsibility being to defend against the run. After spending three seasons at his new post, Jones asked George Halas to trade him to the Washington Redskins so that he might finish his career close to his home in Rockville, Maryland. Dealt to the Redskins following the conclusion of the 1966 campaign, Jones played right defensive tackle for the 'Skins for one season, before announcing his retirement at the end of the year.

After retiring as an active player, Jones embarked on a lengthy career in coaching that began with a five-year stint as defensive line and strength-and-conditioning coach for the Denver Broncos that lasted from 1967 to 1971. From Denver, he moved on to Buffalo (1972–1975), back to Denver (1976–1987), on to Cleveland (1988), and then on to New England (1991–1992), serving as d-line coach at each of those stops. Retiring to private life following the conclusion of the 1992 campaign, Jones remained away from the game for the next five years, before accepting an assistant coaching job with the Scottish Claymores of NFL Europe in 1998. Retiring for good at season's end, Jones eventually moved to Broomfield, Colorado, where he spent his final years. Jones passed away at the age of 78, on May 21, 2010, dying from complications of a stroke brought on by heart disease.

## BEARS CAREER HIGHLIGHTS

### Best Season

Jones had his finest season for the Bears in 1956, when he earned one of his three First-Team All-Pro selections by helping the Western Division champions average 30 points and more than 200 yards rushing a game.

## Memorable Moments/Greatest Performances

Jones helped the Bears rush for 406 yards and amass 504 yards of total offense during a 52–31 win over the Packers on November 6, 1955.

Jones helped pave the way for Chicago running backs to gain 308 yards on the ground during a 31–7 victory over the 49ers on October 14, 1956.

Jones and his line-mates dominated the line of scrimmage during a 38–21 win over the Lions in the 1956 regular-season finale, with the Bears rushing for 309 yards and amassing 446 yards of total offense.

Jones helped the Bears gain a season-high total of 273 yards on the ground during a 24–10 win over the Packers on November 9, 1958.

Jones's exceptional blocking helped the Bears amass 552 yards of total offense during a 52–35 victory over the Vikings in the final game of the 1961 regular season, with 205 of those yards coming on the ground.

With Jones having been moved to the defensive side of the ball prior to the start of the 1963 campaign, the Packers spent most of the regular-season opener trying to run right at him. Up to the challenge, Jones helped limit Jim Taylor and the rest of Green Bay's vaunted running attack to just 77 yards rushing during a 10–3 Bears win.

## Notable Achievements

- Missed just two games in first 11 seasons, appearing in 138 out of 140 contests.
- Two-time division champion (1956 and 1963).
- 1963 NFL champion.
- Seven-time Pro Bowl selection (1955, 1956, 1957, 1958, 1959, 1960, and 1961).
- Three-time First-Team All-Pro selection (1955, 1956, and 1959).
- 1960 Second-Team All-Pro selection.
- Pro Football Reference All-1950s Second Team.
- Elected to Pro Football Hall of Fame in 1991.

# 13

## DAN HAMPTON

Nicknamed "Danimal" for his ferocious style of play, Dan Hampton served as the cornerstone of a Bears defense that ranks among the greatest in NFL history. Known for his toughness and tenacity, Hampton persevered through 10 knee surgeries and numerous other injuries to establish himself as the most feared member of Chicago's famed "46 Defense," with his exceptional play helping the Bears win six division titles, one NFC championship, and one Super Bowl. Extremely versatile, Hampton starred at three different positions along the Bears' defensive front, earning in the process four Pro Bowl selections, five All-Pro nominations, recognition as the NFL Players Association's 1984 NFC Defensive Lineman of the Year, and eventual induction into the Pro Football Hall of Fame.

Born in Oklahoma City, Oklahoma, on September 19, 1957, Daniel Oliver Hampton migrated with his family to Jacksonville, Arkansas, as a youngster. After suffering a disabling fall from a tree that prevented him from competing in organized sports for much of his youth, Hampton spent his first three years at Jacksonville High School participating in band, playing the saxophone and five other instruments, before finally turning his attention to football as a senior. Despite his late start, Hampton performed so well on the gridiron that he received an athletic scholarship from the University of Arkansas.

Developing into one of the nation's top defensive linemen while in college, Hampton started for the Razorbacks for three seasons, making a total of 237 tackles, with 32 of those coming behind the line of scrimmage. Performing particularly well as a senior, Hampton earned All-America and Southwest Conference Defensive Player of the Year honors by recording 98 tackles, 18 of which went for a loss. First displaying his ability to play with pain during his time at Arkansas, Hampton played an entire game with three cracked ribs, recalling years later, "I didn't think about it during a play, but, as soon as the play was over, it felt like someone was sticking a knife in you."

Dan Hampton starred for the Bears at multiple positions along the defensive line.
Courtesy of MEARSonlineauctions.com

Mike Ditka, who later coached Hampton with the Bears, remembered scouting the big defensive lineman while serving as a member of the Dallas Cowboys coaching staff: "I watched Dan when he came out of Arkansas. I remember Coach Landry saying what a great football player he was going to be."

Selected by the Bears with the fourth overall pick of the 1979 NFL Draft, Hampton made an immediate impact his first year in the league, earning a spot on the NFL All-Rookie Team by making 70 tackles (48 solo), recording two sacks, and recovering two fumbles, while starting every game at left defensive end. Impressed with the 6'5", 265-pound Hampton's strong performance, Bears' veteran linebacker Doug Buffone stated, "He has size and ability; he keeps coming, and he plays hard. . . . Big, strong, fast. Hampton is right up there with the best of them."

Hampton followed that up by recording 73 tackles and a team-leading 11½ sacks in 1980, with his outstanding play gaining him Pro Bowl and First-Team All-NFC recognition. He subsequently recorded another 11½ sacks in 1981, before undergoing his first knee operation at season's end.

Moved inside to right defensive tackle in 1982, Hampton performed brilliantly during the strike-shortened campaign, earning Pro Bowl, Second-Team All-Pro, and NFC Defensive Player of the Year honors from *Pro Football Weekly* by recording 71 tackles and nine sacks in only nine games. Commenting on his teammate's exceptional play, fellow defensive tackle Jim Osborne said, "I've never seen a player with more ability. He amazes you and does it against the best."

Despite being slowed by injuries after being shifted to right defensive end the following year, Hampton had another solid season, recording five sacks in just 11 games. Moved back inside to tackle in 1984, Hampton had one of the most productive seasons of his career, gaining Pro Bowl, First-Team All-Pro, and NFLPA NFC Defensive Lineman of the Year recognition by recording 11½ sacks for the Bears' #1 ranked defense. Hampton subsequently spent the next several seasons splitting his time between left defensive end and right defensive tackle, performing exceptionally well at both posts. Named to another Pro Bowl and three more All-Pro teams, Hampton proved to be arguably the most important member of Chicago's vaunted defense, with his aggressive play forcing opposing offenses to assign him multiple blockers, freeing up other Bears defenders to make plays. In fact, between 1983 and 1990, the Bears won only 33 percent of the games that Hampton missed, allowing an average of 23 points per contest in the process. Meanwhile, they emerged victorious in 75 percent of the games that he played, surrendering an average of only 14 points in those contests.

Commenting on the level of intensity that Hampton brought to the Bears, Mike Singletary said, "Dan gets everybody revved up, walking around the locker room, mumbling, swearing at lockers and stuff. . . . On the field, he's hyped up, ready to go. Some guys need to hear somebody else fired up. Some guys can't reach in and turn it on. He's that guy who does it for everybody."

Former Baltimore Colts Hall of Fame defensive tackle Art Donovan addressed Hampton's on-field brilliance in his 1987 book, *Fatso*, when he called him "the best defensive lineman in the NFL" and "the closest thing to Gino Marchetti I've ever seen."

Bears teammate Otis Wilson also had high praise for Hampton, stating, "Dan was blessed with the perfect body to play defensive tackle or end. Plus, he had incredible footwork, which allowed him to get the leverage he wanted. . . . How did Hamp stay on the field with just an endless run of knee injuries, knee injuries that cost him over 20 games during his career? I'll give ya one word: guts. His mindset was ya gotta perform no matter how rotten you feel."

In discussing his ability to block out pain, Hampton said, "I grew up in the country, and it (ignoring pain) was something you did. If you got snake-bit or kicked by a horse, you didn't go to the doctor, you took care of it yourself . . . I hurt like everybody else. I lay in bed at night and I hurt. But, in the game, during a play, I don't. It's something I can block out. I get all the pain I want, but between the snap and the whistle, I just don't feel it. . . . Something that bothers this guy here doesn't bother me at all."

Hampton then added, "The mind controls the body. I couldn't imagine running a marathon, blocking out the pain for three hours. That's asinine."

Continuing to perform well during the second half of his career, Hampton recorded 10 sacks in 1986 and another 9½ in 1988, before missing most of the 1989 season with another knee injury. And, as his career progressed, Hampton assumed more of a leadership role on the club, stating, "There's a point after six or eight years when you go from being a recipient to a donor. Everybody does it. (Steve) McMichael does it. (Richard) Dent does it. . . . In a simplified way, when you get here, you're a little brother. When you leave here, you're a big brother. The trick is staying around long enough to be a big brother."

Hampton spent one more year in Chicago, retiring following the conclusion of the 1990 campaign with an unofficial total of 82 career sacks, which places him third in franchise history. After retiring as an active player, Hampton began a career in broadcasting, initially doing color commentary for NFL games on NBC during the early 1990s, before eventually becoming co-host of the syndicated Pro Football Weekly television show. Hampton also hosts the Bears postgame show on WGN Radio in Chicago and is involved in various charities that support children in the Chicago area and raise funds for retired NFL players in need.

Looking back on Hampton's playing career, Mike Ditka suggested, "A lot of times in football, it's not so much the stat, but *how* you play the game. If that's the measuring stick, then Dan Hampton played the game as well as anybody."

Claiming that his former teammate should be considered one of the all-time greats, Otis Wilson stated, "Hamp played outside, and he played defensive tackle. Warren Sapp doesn't deserve to be mentioned in comparison to Hampton. Hamp belongs in a conversation with Mean Joe Greene, Lee Roy Selmon, Reggie White, and Randy White."

## CAREER HIGHLIGHTS

### Best Season

Hampton arguably played his best ball for the Bears in 1982, when, despite the season being shortened to nine games by a players' strike, he recorded 71 tackles and nine sacks, with *Pro Football Weekly* subsequently naming him its NFL Defensive Player of the Year. But, with Hampton equaling his career-high of 11½ sacks in 1984 en route to earning First-Team All-Pro and NFL Players Association NFC Defensive Lineman of the Year honors, we'll identify that as his finest season.

### Memorable Moments/Greatest Performances

Hampton performed well in his first playoff appearance, sacking Ron Jaworski twice during Chicago's 27–17 loss to Philadelphia in the 1979 NFC wild card game.

Hampton had a huge game in just his second start at defensive tackle, recording a sack and 16 tackles (13 solo) during a 10–0 loss to the New Orleans Saints on September 19, 1982.

Hampton contributed to a 26–13 victory over the Patriots on December 5, 1982, by sacking New England quarterback Steve Grogan twice, beating Hall of Fame guard John Hannah both times. Following the contest, Hannah said, "It's not the first time I got my rear end handed to me, and it won't be the last."

Hampton recorded another two sacks during the Bears' 30–13 win over the Detroit Lions in the final game of the 1984 regular season.

Hampton followed that up with a strong performance against Washington in the divisional round of the 1984 playoffs, sacking Joe Theismann twice during a 23–19 Bears win.

Hampton contributed to the Bears' 46–10 manhandling of the Patriots in Super Bowl XX by recording a sack and recovering a fumble.

Hampton helped lead the Bears to a 12–10 win over the Packers on November 23, 1986, by recording 3½ sacks and scoring two points when he tackled running back Kenneth Davis in the end zone for a safety.

Hampton earned NFC Defensive Player of the Week honors by sacking Boomer Esiason twice during the Bears' 17–14 win over the Cincinnati Bengals in the 1989 regular-season opener.

**Notable Achievements**

- Recorded at least 10 sacks three times.
- Finished third in NFL with nine sacks in 1982.
- Led Bears in sacks twice.
- Ranks third in Bears history with 82 career sacks.
- Six-time division champion (1984, 1985, 1986, 1987, 1988, and 1990).
- 1985 NFC champion.
- Super Bowl XX champion.
- Member of 1979 NFL All-Rookie Team.
- 1989 Week 1 NFC Defensive Player of the Week.
- Four-time Pro Bowl selection (1980, 1982, 1984, and 1985).
- 1984 First-Team All-Pro selection.
- Four-time Second-Team All-Pro selection (1982, 1985, 1986, and 1988).
- Four-time First-Team All-NFC selection (1980, 1984, 1986, and 1988).
- Two-time Second-Team All-NFC selection (1982 and 1985).
- 1982 *Pro Football Weekly* NFL Defensive Player of the Year.
- 1984 NFL Players Association NFC Defensive Lineman of the Year.
- NFL 1980s All-Decade Team.
- Pro Football Reference All-1980s First Team.
- Elected to Pro Football Hall of Fame in 2002.

# 14

## — RICHARD DENT —

One of the premier pass-rushers of his time, Richard Dent contributed greatly to the success the Bears experienced on defense from 1984 to 1993 with his ability to apply pressure to opposing quarterbacks. Averaging just over 12 sacks per season during that 10-year stretch, Dent recorded a total of 124½ sacks as a member of the Bears, the highest figure in franchise history. Far from a one-dimensional player, Dent proved to be a stout run-defender as well, averaging 64 tackles and three forced fumbles per season, with his stellar all-around play helping the Bears win six division titles, one NFC championship, and one Super Bowl. A four-time Pro Bowler, four-time All-Pro, and one-time Super Bowl MVP, Dent later received the additional distinction of being inducted into the Pro Football Hall of Fame.

Born in Atlanta, Georgia, on December 13, 1960, Richard Lamar Dent grew up in poverty, forcing him to take jobs before he reached his teens. Reflecting back on his financial situation at the time, Dent said, "I had a bank account when I was 12. It wasn't much, but it felt like I was on a roll."

After graduating from J.C. Murphy High School, Dent enrolled at historically black Tennessee State University, where he spent four years playing defensive end for the Tigers. Gradually emerging as a force on defense during that time, Dent made an extremely favorable impression on Bears scout Bill Tobin, who called him "the best pure pass-rusher I'd seen in a long time." Nevertheless, Dent ended up lasting until the eighth round of the 1983 NFL Draft, where the Bears finally selected him with the 203rd overall pick.

While Dent's small college background contributed to his rather late selection, his lanky 6'5", 220-pound frame proved to be even more of a factor. Troubled by bad teeth, Dent had developed an eating disorder that made it difficult for him to chew food. But, with the Bears arranging for him to have his teeth fixed, Dent soon gained 20 pounds, before eventually reaching his normal playing weight of 265.

Used sparingly on defense as a rookie, Dent recorded just three sacks while serving as a backup to starting ends Dan Hampton and Mike Hartenstine. With Hampton moving inside to tackle the following year, Dent laid claim to the starting right defensive end job in Week 7, after which he went on to record a total of 17½ sacks that left him third in the league rankings. Dent also made 39 tackles and topped the circuit with four forced fumbles, earning in the process Pro Bowl and Second-Team All-Pro honors. He subsequently recorded a league-leading 17 sacks and seven forced fumbles for the NFL champion Bears in 1985, with his exceptional play gaining him Pro Bowl and First-Team All-Pro recognition. Dent continued to perform at an extremely high level in each of the next three seasons, helping the Bears capture three more division titles by amassing a total of 34½ sacks, while also averaging nearly 60 tackles per season.

Having established himself as one of the NFL's elite pass-rushers, Dent garnered praise from players and coaches throughout the league, with Los Angeles Rams tight end David Hill describing him as "Very physical, very fast off the ball—what else can I say about Richard Dent? Awesome."

Philadelphia Eagles head coach Ray Rhodes said, "He'll make the guy in front of him know he's in for a day's work."

Although Dent possessed good size and strength, he depended primarily on his speed and quickness to outmaneuver opposing offensive tackles, with former Redskins quarterback Joe Theismann commenting years later, "When you think of the Chicago Bears, you think of specific individuals that not only were game-changers, but were a part of something that changed the history of the game. . . . I think he was one of the most athletic, most dominant defensive ends to play the game. His quickness, his agility, and his tenacity were all things you had to take note of. Richard Dent, to me, was a defensive player that you had to pay the same kind of attention to that you did a Lawrence Taylor. I can't pay him any higher compliment than that."

In discussing the manner in which Dent affected the outcomes of games, former Bears teammate Tom Thayer noted, "You go look at any second- or third-and-long scenario, or anytime the Bears were ahead, and the other team was trying to pass to catch up. Richard was the biggest threat on the Bears defense. Look at how he performed in the big games. He was the Super Bowl MVP. You look at his performance in the playoffs and in the big games during the regular season throughout his career. But Richard was an every-game player. Big game or small game, he was always out there."

Jay Hilgenberg added, "He was a big-play guy. He had a knack for making huge plays, like when he flew over a blocker against the 49ers [to sack Joe Montana] or shook Craig James like a wet towel until he dropped the ball [in Super Bowl XX]."

Dent remained in Chicago for five more years, averaging 10½ sacks and 76 tackles per season from 1989 to 1993, although the Bears made the playoffs just once during that time. Performing especially well in 1990 and 1993, Dent gained Pro Bowl and Second-Team All-Pro recognition in the first of those campaigns by recording 12 sacks, 81 tackles, and a career-high three interceptions, before earning his final trip to the Pro Bowl three years later by recording 12½ sacks and 64 tackles. Electing to sign as a free

Richard Dent recorded more sacks than anyone else in franchise history.
Courtesy of SportsMemorabilia.com

agent with the San Francisco 49ers at the end of the 1993 season, Dent left Chicago with career totals of 124½ sacks, 641 tackles, 34 forced fumbles, 13 fumble recoveries, eight interceptions, and one touchdown.

Dent ended up spending just one season in San Francisco, starting only two games for the 49ers after breaking his leg. He subsequently returned to Chicago for one season, suffering through an injury-marred 1995 campaign in which he appeared in just three games, before splitting his final two seasons between the Indianapolis Colts and the Philadelphia Eagles. Choosing to announce his retirement after assuming a backup role in Philadelphia in 1997, Dent ended his playing career with 137½ sacks, 677 tackles, 37 forced fumbles, 13 fumble recoveries, and eight interceptions, with his 137½ sacks representing the third-highest total in NFL history at the time (he has since slipped to ninth).

Elected to the Pro Football Hall of Fame in 2011, Dent raised a few eyebrows by omitting any mention of Mike Ditka during his induction speech, with his public criticism of his former coach for the Bears' inability to repeat as Super Bowl champions causing a rift to develop between the two men. Feeling that Ditka mishandled the quarterback situation in Chicago some years earlier, Dent told the *Chicago Tribune*, "Well, we thought we were going to be king of the hill all the time. And we came back three years in a row and had home-field advantage. Our coach couldn't figure out the right quarterback to play. The disappointing part to me is that we only got one out of it. We should have been the first team ever to win three Super Bowls in a row. It was there in the taking, but we didn't manage that one position right."

Dent continued, "Mike didn't manage that quarterback position. Bringing Doug Flutie in and thinking that he's gonna come in and be on a team for three weeks and start him in a playoff game? Hell, I mean you're trying to change the name on the Super Bowl trophy to Mike Ditka from Vince Lombardi when you do something like that. We had won with [Mike] Tomczak and [Steve] Fuller. That's all we needed to do is stay with that plan."

Although Chicagoans may agree or disagree with Dent's assessment of the situation, the contributions that the former defensive end made to the Bears during his time in the Windy City are undeniable. In speaking of the overall impact that Dent made as a member of the team, Tampa Bay Buccaneers Hall of Fame linebacker Derrick Brooks said, "I don't think Richard was ever fully appreciated as being part of that dominant Bears team in 1985 because they had so many large personalities. But he was as good a pass-rusher as you'll find. During his prime years, he was the best at what he did."

## BEARS CAREER HIGHLIGHTS

### Best Season

Dent had a big year for the Bears in 1984, earning Pro Bowl and Second-Team All-Pro honors by finishing third in the NFL with a career-high 17½ sacks and leading the league with four fumble recoveries. He also performed extremely well in 1990, when, in addition to recording 12 sacks, he intercepted three passes, recovered two fumbles, and registered 81 tackles. But Dent had his finest all-around season in 1985, earning his lone First-Team All-Pro nomination by leading the NFL with 17 sacks and seven forced fumbles, while also recovering two fumbles and intercepting two passes, one of which he returned for a touchdown.

## Memorable Moments/Greatest Performances

Dent recorded the first sack of his career when he brought down Joe Montana behind the line of scrimmage during a 13–3 win over the 49ers on November 27, 1983.

Dent recorded two sacks in one game for the first time as a pro when he got to Steve Dils twice during a 19–13 win over the Vikings on December 11, 1983.

Dent topped that performance on October 21, 1984, sacking Steve DeBerg three times during a 44–9 blowout of the Tampa Bay Buccaneers.

Dent recorded 2½ of the 11 sacks the Bears registered against Archie Manning during a 16–7 win over the Vikings on October 28, 1984.

Dent earned NFC Defensive Player of the Week honors for the first time by recording 4½ of the nine sacks the Bears registered during a 17–6 win over the Raiders on November 4, 1984.

Dent excelled in his first playoff appearance, sacking Joe Theismann three times during the Bears' 23–19 win over Washington in the divisional round of the 1984 postseason tournament.

Dent helped lead the Bears to a 44–0 rout of the Cowboys on November 17, 1985, by recording two sacks and scoring the game's first points on a 1-yard interception return of a deflected pass.

Dent registered 3½ sacks and 6½ tackles during the Bears' 21–0 win over the Giants in the divisional round of the 1985 playoffs.

Dent earned Super Bowl XX MVP honors by recording 1½ sacks, forcing two fumbles, and blocking a pass during the Bears' lopsided 46–10 victory over the New England Patriots.

Dent recorded 4½ sacks during the Bears' 6–3 win over the Raiders in the 1987 regular-season finale, with his exceptional play earning him NFC Defensive Player of the Week honors.

Dent sacked Randall Cunningham three times during the Bears' 27–13 win over Philadelphia on October 2, 1989.

Dent recorded an interception and a sack during the Bears' 19–16 victory over Minnesota on September 23, 1990, gaining him recognition as the NFC Defensive Player of the Week.

Dent earned that distinction again by recording two sacks and applying constant pressure to Atlanta quarterback Chris Miller during a 30–24 win over the Falcons on November 11, 1990.

After registering 2½ sacks during the first meeting between the two teams earlier in the season, Dent earned NFC Defensive Player of the Week honors by recording three sacks and an interception during the Bears' 27–0 shutout of Tampa Bay on December 14, 1991.

Dent earned that distinction for the sixth and final time in his career by recording 2½ sacks and intercepting a pass during the Bears' 17–6 win over Philadelphia on October 10, 1993.

## Notable Achievements

- Recorded more than 10 sacks eight times, surpassing 15 sacks twice.
- Recorded more than 75 tackles four times.
- Led NFL in sacks once and forced fumbles twice.
- Finished second in NFL in sacks once and forced fumbles three times.
- Finished third in NFL in sacks once and forced fumbles once.
- Led Bears in sacks eight times.
- Holds Bears single-game record for most sacks (4½ twice).
- Holds Bears career record for most sacks (124½).
- Ranks among Bears career leaders with 34 forced fumbles (2nd), 13 fumble recoveries (tied-9th), and 641 solo tackles (10th).
- Six-time division champion (1984, 1985, 1986, 1987, 1988, and 1990).
- 1985 NFC champion.
- Super Bowl XX champion.
- Super Bowl XX MVP.
- Six-time NFC Defensive Player of the Week.
- Four-time Pro Bowl selection (1984, 1985, 1990, and 1993).
- 1985 First-Team All-Pro selection.
- Three-time Second-Team All-Pro selection (1984, 1988, and 1990).
- Five-time First-Team All-NFC selection (1984, 1985, 1988, 1990, and 1993).
- Elected to Pro Football Hall of Fame in 2011.

# 15

## — DAN FORTMANN —

Called "the perfect football player" and "the most important man on the Bear squad" by teammate Bob Snyder, Dan Fortmann spent his entire eight-year NFL career in Chicago, helping the Bears win five division titles and three league championships. Excelling as a guard on offense and a lineman/linebacker on defense, Fortmann gained All-Pro recognition in each of his eight seasons, with his superb all-around play also earning him spots on the NFL's 75th Anniversary All-Time Two-Way Team and the NFL 100 All-Time Team, as well as a place in the Pro Football Hall of Fame. Yet, prior to signing with the Bears, Fortmann had to think long and hard as to whether he should pursue a career in football or in medicine.

Born in Pearl River, New York, on April 11, 1916, Daniel John Fortmann attended Pearl River High School, where, in addition to starring in multiple sports, he earned class valedictorian honors. After enrolling at Colgate University at the tender age of 16, Fortmann continued to excel as both an athlete and a student, with head football coach Andrew Kerr later calling him "the best player I ever handled." Meanwhile, Fortmann received straight As as a pre-med student.

Having graduated with Phi Beta Kappa honors at only 19 years of age, Fortmann had a difficult decision to make when the Bears selected him in the ninth round of the first-ever NFL Draft in 1936, with the 78th overall pick. Uncertain as to whether he should go to medical school or play football, Fortmann heeded the advice of Bears head coach George Halas, who assured him he could do both. With Halas advancing funds to him for medical school, Fortmann enrolled at the University of Chicago, where he eventually obtained his degree in medicine. Meanwhile, Fortmann signed with the Bears in May 1936, making him, at 20 years of age, the youngest player ever to sign with an NFL team.

Looking back at the first few years of his playing career years later, Fortmann credited Halas with allowing him to pursue his dream of becoming a surgeon while also playing in the NFL, stating, "I was determined to go to medical school, but the academic quarters always overlapped with the start of football training camp. George Halas was very understanding. He allowed me to miss two weeks of camp each year while I finished up at school. . . . Normally, he didn't give anybody permission to miss practice. But he believed medical school was a tremendous ambition. It was almost as important to him as it was to me. Without Mr. Halas, I could never have prepared for my future."

Dan Fortmann earned a spot on the NFL 100 All-Time Team with his exceptional play on both sides of the ball.
Courtesy of RMYAuctions.com

While Fortmann completed his studies, he began to establish himself as one of the NFL's better all-around players almost as soon as he arrived in Chicago. Despite being the league's youngest player, and one of its smallest linemen, the 6-foot, 210-pound Fortmann earned All-Pro honors as a rookie, spending his first year in the league starting at right guard for the Bears. Continuing to perform well after being moved to the left side of Chicago's offensive line in 1937, Fortmann gained All-Pro recognition in each of the next seven seasons as well, with NFL coaches awarding him the second-highest point total of any player in the league in their voting for the 1939 All-Pro Team.

Excelling at one of the sport's most physically demanding positions despite his relative lack of size, Fortmann depended largely on his quickness and explosive charge to drive opposing linemen off the line of scrimmage. An outstanding blocker, Fortmann combined with the much larger Joe Stydahar to give the Bears a tremendous tandem on the left side of their offensive line. An exceptional leader as well, Fortmann called the line signals on offense and began serving as captain of the Bears during the championship campaign of 1940, with the United Press ranking him as the best lineman in the NFL at the end of the year and calling him "the heart and soul of the Bears' ground attack that rolled up a vast amount of yardage overland."

In addition to establishing himself as one of the league's best offensive linemen, Fortmann starred on defense, with his speed, quickness, and strength making him a deadly tackler and outstanding pass defender from his linebacker position. Using his intelligence to his advantage, Fortmann became an expert at diagnosing enemy plays, enabling him to bring down many an opposing ball-carrier near the line of scrimmage and intercept a total of eight passes over the course of his career.

After leading the Bears to the NFL title in two of the previous three seasons, Fortmann announced his retirement from football in January 1943. However, George Halas persuaded him to return for one more year, which resulted in another league championship for the Bears. Retiring for good shortly thereafter, Fortmann ended his playing career having missed just two games in his eight years in the league.

After briefly coaching linemen at the University of Pittsburgh following his retirement, Fortmann enlisted in the military in February 1945. He spent the next year serving in the Navy Medical Corps aboard a hospital ship in the South Pacific, before being discharged early in 1946. Fortmann, who earned his medical degree from the University of Chicago in 1940 and completed his surgical training in Pittsburgh, became a practicing physician at St. Joseph Medical Center in Burbank, California, following the war. He remained at that institution from 1947 until his retirement in 1984, being named the hospital's chief of staff in 1965. Fortmann also served as team doctor for the Los Angeles Rams from 1947 to 1963.

Sadly, Fortmann developed Alzheimer's disease later in life, forcing him to enter in 1988 the John Douglas French Center, a facility in Los Alamitos, California, that specializes in the care of Alzheimer's patients. Fortmann spent the remainder of his life there, losing his battle with the dreaded disease at the age of 79, on May 23, 1995.

## CAREER HIGHLIGHTS

### Best Season

Fortmann gained consensus First-Team All-Pro recognition six straight times from 1938 to 1943. The 1940 season, though, stood out above all others, with Fortmann being named the NFL's best offensive lineman by the United Press following the conclusion of the campaign.

### Memorable Moments/Greatest Performances

Fortmann starred on both sides of the ball during a 32–0 win over the Pittsburgh Pirates on October 2, 1939, helping the Bears amass a total of 441 yards on offense, while also limiting Pittsburgh to just 54 yards on defense.

Fortmann's exceptional blocking helped the Bears rush for 212 yards and accumulate 408 yards of total offense during a 44–7 rout of the Chicago Cardinals on October 15, 1939.

Fortmann and his line-mates dominated Philadelphia at the point of attack on November 19, 1939, with the Bears gaining 246 yards on the ground and amassing 531 yards of total offense during a 27–14 win over the Eagles.

Fortmann helped pave the way for Bear running backs to rush for a season-high 300 yards during a 16–7 win over the Brooklyn Dodgers on October 20, 1940.

Fortmann helped the Bears amass 613 yards of total offense during a 53–7 manhandling of the Chicago Cardinals on October 12, 1941.

Fortmann turned in an outstanding all-around performance against the Giants in the 1941 NFL championship game, recording an interception on defense and helping the Bears rush for 207 yards on offense during a convincing 37–9 win.

Fortmann scored the only touchdown of his career when he returned a fumble 69 yards for a TD during a 21–7 win over the Chicago Cardinals in the final game of the 1942 regular season.

**Notable Achievements**

- Missed just two games in eight seasons, appearing in 86 of 88 contests.
- Intercepted four passes in 1942.
- Five-time division champion (1937, 1940, 1941, 1942, and 1943).
- Three-time NFL champion (1940, 1941, and 1943).
- Three-time Pro Bowl selection (1940, 1941, and 1942).
- Six-time First-Team All-Pro selection (1938, 1939, 1940, 1941, 1942, and 1943).
- Two-time Second-Team All-Pro selection (1936 and 1937).
- 1940 UPI NFL Offensive Lineman of the Year.
- NFL 1930s All-Decade Team.
- Named to NFL's 75th Anniversary All-Time Two-Way Team in 1994.
- Named to NFL 100 All-Time Team in 2019.
- Elected to Pro Football Hall of Fame in 1965.

# 16

## — LANCE BRIGGS —

An outstanding outside linebacker who excelled against both the run and the pass, Lance Briggs spent his entire 12-year NFL career in Chicago serving as an integral member of Bears teams that won three division titles and one NFC championship. Although overshadowed much of the time by teammate Brian Urlacher, Briggs proved to be nearly as effective on the defensive side of the ball, recording more than 100 tackles on eight occasions, en route to registering the fifth most stops in franchise history. Excellent in pass coverage as well, Briggs recorded the second most touchdown interceptions in team annals, with his superb all-around play earning him seven trips to the Pro Bowl, three All-Pro selections, and one All-NFC nomination.

Born in Sacramento, California, on November 12, 1980, Lance Marrell Briggs attended Elk Grove High School, where he starred in football, prompting the University of Arizona to offer him an athletic scholarship. Continuing to excel on the gridiron in college, Briggs registered 308 tackles, 10½ sacks, 36 tackles for loss, three interceptions, five forced fumbles, and four fumble recoveries while playing strong-side linebacker for the Wildcats, earning in the process First-Team All–Pac-10 Conference honors twice.

Selected by the Bears in the third round of the 2003 NFL Draft, with the 68th overall pick, Briggs earned a starting job as a rookie, after which he went on to record 78 tackles and one interception, which he returned 45 yards for the first touchdown of his career. Improving upon his performance the following year, Briggs placed among the league leaders with 126 tackles and 102 solo stops, before earning First-Team All-Pro honors and the first of his seven consecutive trips to the Pro Bowl in 2005 by recording more than 100 tackles for the second of six straight times. Briggs followed that up by registering 109 solo stops for the NFC champion Bears in 2006, with that figure representing the second highest total in the league.

Spending most of his time at weak-side linebacker after playing on the strong side as a rookie, the 6'1", 244-pound Briggs did an exceptional job of defending against the run, using his speed, quickness, and instincts to often bring down opposing ball-carriers near the line of scrimmage. Briggs's greatest strength, though, may well have been his coverage skills, which enabled him to remain on the field in passing situations. In fact, Bears head coach Lovie Smith maintained that Briggs covered receivers, tight ends, and running backs coming out of the backfield better than his fourth cornerback or safety.

In discussing his teammate's ability to stay with opposing receivers, Brian Urlacher said, "He might not have had many picks and stuff like that, but the guy was always around the football."

Urlacher then added, "He was one of the best tacklers I've ever played with, if not the best. His instincts are unmatched by anybody."

When asked if Briggs was considered, in some ways, to be the Scottie Pippen to his Michael Jordan, Urlacher responded, "Unfairly, yeah, maybe. But I feel like I got that, too, playing next to him sometimes. Lance is a bad dude. He made so many plays that he shouldn't have made, that guys who—if they were out of position or not—weren't supposed to make the plays that he made. He did things that normal guys wouldn't do."

While Briggs excelled for the Bears on the playing field, he often proved to be a headache to team management due to his constant demands for more money. After the star linebacker became a free agent following the conclusion of the 2006 campaign, the Bears placed the franchise tag on him, guaranteeing him a salary of slightly more than $7.2 million for the 2007 season. Shortly thereafter, Briggs appeared on the *Mike North Morning Show*, where he vented his frustrations over being franchised. While Briggs stated that he appreciated his teammates, coaches, and the fans of Chicago, he also expressed his dissatisfaction with the organization, stating that he no longer wished to be a member of the team. Briggs again voiced his displeasure less than one week later during an interview with a Chicago radio station when he said, "I'll do everything that's within my power to not be with this organization." Briggs continued to express his unhappiness during a cellphone interview with Foxsports.com a few days later, announcing that he no longer considered himself a member of the Bears by proclaiming, "I am now prepared to sit out the year if the Bears don't trade me or release me. I've played my last snap for them. I'll never play another down for Chicago again." In explaining his demands, he said, "The Bears have shown I'm not in their long-term plans, so, if that's the case, I don't want to be here."

Despite his strong words, Briggs ultimately relented and played the 2007 season under the franchise tag. And, after rejecting an earlier trade proposal from the Washington Redskins, the Bears re-signed Briggs to a six-year, $36 million contract on March 1, 2008.

However, after earning three more Pro Bowl selections, Briggs again asked the Bears for a trade after the team refused to renegotiate his contract. Although Briggs ended up spending the 2011 season playing under the terms of his old deal, team management eventually gave him a one-year extension that made him a member of the team through the end of 2014.

Lance Briggs recorded more than 100 tackles in a season eight times.
Courtesy of Mike Morbeck

Unfortunately, after missing just four games his first 10 years in the league, Briggs fractured his shoulder during a 45–41 loss to the Washington Redskins in Week 7 of the 2013 campaign, forcing him to sit out the next seven contests. Hampered by injuries the following season as well, Briggs appeared in only eight games, making just 35 tackles, before announcing his retirement on September 9, 2015, when he failed to receive any offers following the expiration of his contract. Over the course of his 12 seasons in Chicago, Briggs recorded 1,174 tackles (936 solo) and 15 sacks, forced 16 fumbles, recovered seven others, and intercepted 16 passes, five of which he returned for touchdowns. He also scored a sixth TD on a fumble return.

Paying tribute to his longtime teammate during his own 2018 Pro Football Hall of Fame acceptance speech, Brian Urlacher said, "He elevated not only my game, but the entire defense—his enthusiasm was contagious." Urlacher then spoke to Briggs directly, saying, "We'll be back here in a couple years for your induction."

Since retiring as an active player, Briggs has served as a studio analyst for Comcast SportsNet Chicago's pre- and postgame Bears coverage. He also hosts *The Lance Briggs Show* on that same station. Sharing a large part of himself with his audience during a March 2017 broadcast, Briggs revealed that he has begun to display many of the symptoms associated with degenerative brain disease. Stating that his love for football outweighed the risks he knew he took by playing the game, Briggs suggested that he expected one day to experience some form of short-term memory loss, difficulty thinking, and motor impairment, telling his listeners:

> I enjoyed every minute of football. I didn't feel like I was in the game until I got a good pop. Either I got popped or I popped somebody. You're not supposed to be doing the things we're doing to our bodies . . . CTE affects guys in a different way, and you start seeing it even in the practice of football. You get worried. I get concerned for myself. And even though I've never had any suicidal thoughts, or anything like that, for it to happen to some great men, and great football players, I know that I can't separate myself from that crowd.

## CAREER HIGHLIGHTS

### Best Season

Briggs gained First-Team All-Pro recognition for the only time in his career in 2005, when, in addition to recording 107 tackles (83 solo), he forced one fumble, recovered two others, registered two sacks, and picked off two passes, one of which he returned for a touchdown. But Briggs posted slightly better overall numbers the following year, earning Second-Team All-Pro honors for one of two times in 2006 by intercepting two passes, recording one sack, and establishing career-high marks with 130 tackles, 109 solo stops, and four forced fumbles.

### Memorable Moments/Greatest Performances

Briggs recorded the first interception of his career during a 34–21 loss to the Packers on December 7, 2003, subsequently returning the ball 45 yards for a touchdown.

Briggs recorded a season-high 14 tackles during a 19–17 overtime victory over the Tennessee Titans on November 14, 2004, that the Bears won when Adewale Ogunleye and Alex Brown sacked Billy Volek in the end zone in OT.

Although the Bears lost to the Lions by a score of 19–13 on December 26, 2004, Briggs starred in defeat, recording 11 tackles, ½ sack, and an interception, which he returned 38 yards for a TD.

Briggs helped lead the Bears to a 24–23 win over the Arizona Cardinals on October 16, 2006, by making 15 tackles, including 13 of the solo variety.

Although the Bears suffered a 29–17 defeat at the hands of the Indianapolis Colts in Super Bowl XLI, Briggs turned in an outstanding effort, recording a game-high 13 tackles, with 11 of those being solo stops.

Briggs and the Bears gained a measure of revenge against the Colts in the 2008 regular-season opener, with Briggs returning a fumble 21 yards for a touchdown during a 29–13 Chicago win.

Briggs earned NFC Defensive Player of the Week honors for the first of two times by recording an interception, a sack, and seven tackles during a 25–19 win over Seattle on September 27, 2009.

Briggs earned that distinction again by recording an interception and six tackles during a 24–18 win over the Tampa Bay Buccaneers on October 23, 2011.

Briggs highlighted a 34–18 victory over the Dallas Cowboys on October 1, 2012, by returning his interception of a Tony Romo pass 74 yards for a touchdown.

Briggs lit the scoreboard again the following week, returning his interception of a Blaine Gabbert pass 36 yards for a touchdown during a 41–3 rout of the Jacksonville Jaguars on October 7, 2012.

## Notable Achievements

- Recorded more than 100 tackles eight times.
- Amassed 110 interception-return yards in 2012.
- Finished second in NFL with 109 solo tackles in 2006.
- Finished third in NFL with 102 solo tackles in 2004.
- Led Bears in tackles six times.
- Ranks among Bears career leaders with 1,174 tackles (5th), 16 forced fumbles (tied-3rd), and 5 touchdown interceptions (2nd).
- Three-time division champion (2005, 2006, and 2010).
- 2006 NFC champion.
- Two-time NFC Defensive Player of the Week.
- Seven-time Pro Bowl selection (2005, 2006, 2007, 2008, 2009, 2010, and 2011).
- 2005 First-Team All-Pro selection.
- Two-time Second-Team All-Pro selection (2006 and 2009).
- 2005 First-Team All-NFC selection.

# 17

## — GEORGE CONNOR —

An All-Pro at three different positions, George Connor spent his entire eight-year NFL career in Chicago, excelling as an offensive tackle, defensive tackle, and linebacker. After beginning his career as a lineman, Connor eventually established himself as one of the sport's first big, mobile linebackers, helping to define that position for future generations of Bears greats. Earning four trips to the Pro Bowl and six All-Pro nominations with his outstanding all-around play, Connor later received the additional distinctions of being named to the NFL's 75th Anniversary All-Time Two-Way Team and being elected to the Pro Football Hall of Fame.

Born in Chicago, Illinois, on January 21, 1925, George Leo Connor weighed less than three pounds when his mother gave birth to him two months prematurely. Not expected to survive infancy, Connor did so with the help of his mother, a nurse who fed him hourly with an eyedropper filled with boiled cabbage juice for the first year of his life. Growing up somewhat undersized, Connor entered Chicago's De La Salle High School as a 5'4", 135-pound freshman. Nevertheless, he ended up making the school's football team, performing well enough to earn a scholarship to the College of the Holy Cross.

Growing to a robust 6'3" and 240 pounds while in college, Connor excelled as a lineman on both sides of the ball for Holy Cross, gaining recognition as a Second-Team All-American and the outstanding football player in New England as a sophomore in 1943. After spending the next two years serving in the US Navy during World War II, Connor, who the New York Giants selected with the fifth overall pick of the 1946 NFL Draft, transferred to the University of Notre Dame to be closer to his ill father. Continuing his outstanding play at Notre Dame, Connor helped lead the Fighting Irish to consecutive National Championships in 1946 and 1947, earning in the process consensus All-America honors both years, and being named the first winner of the Outland Trophy as college football's best interior lineman in the first of those campaigns. Singing the praises of Connor years later, Notre Dame head coach Frank Leahy said, "In the line, we never coached a player superior defensively to tackle George Connor."

Choosing to sign a guaranteed three-year $39,000 contract with the Bears following his graduation, Connor entered the NFL as one of the league's highest paid linemen. Proving to be well worth the investment, Connor, after being named Second-Team All-Pro in 1949, earned Pro Bowl and First-Team All-Pro honors four straight times from 1950 to 1953.

An excellent blocker, Connor anchored the Bears' offensive line from his left tackle position his first six years in the league, before playing exclusively on defense his final two seasons. But, while Connor began his career as a tackle on defense, he spent his last several seasons in Chicago playing linebacker, receiving his first exposure to that position during a 1949 contest with the Philadelphia Eagles.

With the Bears having a difficult time containing Eagles fullback Steve Van Buren, head coach George Halas consulted with assistant Hunk Anderson to devise a method of slowing down Philadelphia's potent running attack. After several minutes, Anderson suggested to Halas, "Why don't we put in a big man like Connor back as a linebacker? They won't be able to run over him like they do the lighter guys. Besides, he's one of our most aggressive guys, and that's the best kind to play linebacker."

The plan worked, as Connor held Van Buren in check the rest of the way, with the Bears handing the Eagles their only loss of the season. Looking back years later at Anderson's innovative idea, Connor said, "Most teams had never seen it before. Blockers didn't really know how to handle me out there off the line of scrimmage. And all the fans were looking at me because the newspapers made such a big thing about it with diagrams and all. Now, everyone plays it."

George Connor earned All-Pro honors at three different positions.
Courtesy of RMYAuctions.com

As a result, even though Connor proved to be one of the league's top offensive linemen for most of his career, he is remembered far more for the impact he made on the pro football world as a linebacker. Yet, George Halas viewed Connor simply as an exceptional football player, stating on one occasion, "We always set high standards for George Connor, and he exceeded them."

Ed Sprinkle also had high praise for his longtime teammate, saying, "George typified what the Bears were back then—tough and hard-nosed."

Meanwhile, in speaking of Connor—a handsome man with a well-developed physique—legendary sportswriter Grantland Rice referred to him as "the closest thing to a Greek God since Apollo."

Certainly, Connor's size and strength contributed greatly to the success he experienced on the football field. But he also possessed great intelligence and superb instincts, enabling him to analyze his opponent and diagnose offensive plays before they began.

Although Connor sustained a knee injury that limited him to just nine games in 1954, he continued to perform well at linebacker until his troublesome knee forced him to announce his retirement during training camp in 1956. With the NFL failing to keep an official record of most defensive statistics until years later, it is not known how many sacks or tackles Connor recorded during his eight years in the league. However, he has been officially credited with seven interceptions, 66 interception-return yards, 10 fumble recoveries, and one defensive touchdown. Connor also made five receptions for 89 yards on offense.

Following his retirement, Connor remained in the Chicago area, working at different times as a manufacturers' representative, an assistant coach, a broadcaster, and a master of ceremonies for numerous charity events. He lived until March 31, 2003, passing away at the age of 78 after a long illness.

Speaking of Connor many years earlier at the latter's Hall of Fame induction ceremony, George Halas said, "It would be difficult for me to go on record as saying where he excelled. I would rather have had three like him, but I feel fortunate to have had one Connor for eight seasons."

## CAREER HIGHLIGHTS

### Best Season

Connor earned Pro Bowl and consensus First-Team All-Pro honors four straight times from 1950 to 1953, playing his best ball for the Bears in the last of those campaigns, when he gained First-Team recognition from multiple wire services on both offense and defense.

## Memorable Moments/Greatest Performances

Connor helped the Bears rush for 324 yards and amass 455 yards of total offense during a 35–21 win over the Lions on November 5, 1950.

Connor's strong blocking at the point of attack helped the Bears amass 452 yards of total offense during a 24–21 win over the New York Yanks on October 14, 1951, with 311 of those yards coming on the ground.

Connor and his line-mates once again dominated the Yanks at the line of scrimmage on December 9, 1951, with the Bears rushing for 336 yards and accumulating 485 yards of total offense during a convincing 45–21 victory.

Connor scored the only touchdown of his career when he returned a fumble 48 yards for a TD during a 21–20 win over the Lions on December 4, 1955.

Yet, perhaps the most memorable play of Connor's career took place during a 52–31 victory over the Packers at Wrigley Field on November 6, 1955, when he brought down Green Bay kick returner Veryl Switzer with a devastating tackle. Recalling the hit, which resulted in Switzer's helmet flying in one direction, the ball in another, and Bears linebacker Bill George recovering the fumble deep in Green Bay territory, leading to a Chicago touchdown, Connor later said, "After five minutes, there was a roar from the crowd. I asked Johnny Lujack what happened, and he said, 'Switzer just got up.'"

## Notable Achievements

- Finished third in NFL with 53 fumble-return yards in 1955.
- 1950 division champion.
- Four-time Pro Bowl selection (1950, 1951, 1952, and 1953).
- Four-time First-Team All-Pro selection (1950, 1951, 1952, and 1953).
- Two-time Second-Team All-Pro selection (1949 and 1955).
- NFL 1940s All-Decade Team.
- Pro Football Reference All-1950s Second Team.
- Named to NFL's 75th Anniversary All-Time Two-Way Team in 1994.
- Elected to Pro Football Hall of Fame in 1975.

# 18

## MATT FORTE

One of only five players in NFL history to surpass 1,200 yards from scrimmage in each of his first eight seasons, Matt Forte proved to be the league's best all-purpose back for much of his career, which he spent primarily with the Bears. Starring in the Chicago offensive backfield from 2008 to 2015, the versatile Forte amassed more yards from scrimmage than any other NFL player during that time, while also making more receptions and accumulating more receiving yards than any other running back in the league. A strong and elusive runner, Forte gained more than 1,000 yards on the ground five times, ending his time in the Windy City with the second most rushing yards in franchise history. An outstanding pass receiver as well, Forte made at least 50 receptions six times, with his 102 catches in 2014 setting a new NFL record for running backs that has since been broken. Earning a pair of Pro Bowl selections with his stellar all-around play, Forte left Chicago as one of the franchise's all-time leaders in virtually every major offensive category, before spending his final two seasons with the New York Jets.

Born in Lake Charles, Louisiana, on December 10, 1985, Matthew Garrett Forte grew up some 300 miles east, in the city of Slidell, where he starred in football and track while attending Slidell High School. A two-year letterman on the gridiron, Forte performed especially well as a senior, earning All-Metro honors and recognition as the St. Tammany Parish Player of the Year and the District 5-5A Offensive MVP by rushing for 1,375 yards, gaining another 253 yards on 18 pass receptions, and scoring 25 touchdowns. A standout sprinter as well, Forte competed in the 100- and 200-meter events, posting personal-best times of 10.68 seconds in the 100 and 22.10 seconds in the 200.

Choosing to remain close to home following his graduation from Slidell High, Forte accepted an athletic scholarship from Tulane University in New Orleans, where he spent the next four years excelling at running back for the Green Wave. After amassing 2,741 yards from scrimmage and scoring 21 touchdowns over the course of his first three seasons, Forte exploded in his senior year, earning Third-Team All-America honors by rushing for 2,127 yards and scoring 23 touchdowns.

Subsequently selected by the Bears in the second round of the 2008 NFL Draft, with the 44th overall pick, Forte received rave reviews from general manager Jerry Angelo, who gushed, "What he gives us is a big back, a three-down back. He has enough speed to get to the outside. And he has the ability to make people miss at the second level. And those were the two areas where we never really could find any consistency, which made us an easy team to defend."

Matt Forte amassed more yards from scrimmage than any other NFL player during his time in Chicago.
Courtesy of Chris Usalis

Replacing Cedric Benson as Chicago's primary running threat in his first season, Forte quickly established himself as one of the league's better all-around backs, earning a spot on the NFL All-Rookie Team by rushing for 1,238 yards and eight touchdowns, making 63 receptions for 477 yards and four TDs, and finishing third in the league with 1,715 yards from scrimmage. Performing well once again in 2009, Forte gained 929 yards on the ground, made 57 receptions for 471 yards, scored four touchdowns, and amassed 1,400 yards from scrimmage, before beginning an exceptional six-year run during which he posted the following numbers:

| YEAR | RUSH YD | REC | REC YD | YD FROM SCRIMMAGE | TD |
|------|---------|-----|--------|-------------------|-----|
| 2010 | 1,069 | 51 | 547 | 1,616 | 9 |
| 2011 | 997 | 52 | 490 | 1,487 | 4 |
| 2012 | 1,094 | 44 | 340 | 1,434 | 6 |
| 2013 | 1,339 | 74 | 594 | 1,933 | 12 |
| 2014 | 1,038 | 102 | 808 | 1,846 | 10 |
| 2015 | 898 | 44 | 389 | 1,287 | 7 |

Despite missing the final four games of the 2011 season with a sprained MCL, Forte earned Pro Bowl honors for the first of two times. He also missed one game in 2012 and three others in 2015. Gaining Pro Bowl recognition once again in 2013, Forte placed near the top of the league rankings in yards rushing, yards from scrimmage, and touchdowns, before ranking among the league leaders in receptions and yards from scrimmage the following year. In addition to setting a new single-season NFL record for running backs by making 102 catches in 2014, Forte amassed more receiving yards in one season than any other back in team annals.

An extremely hard worker who put a lot of pressure on himself, Forte made a strong impression on Bears head coach Marc Trestman, who said during the latter stages of the 2014 campaign, "It's very clear Matt is hyper-competitive in his preparation. We have to try to slow him down at times. Mike Clark, our strength coach, has to just say, 'Don't come in today. Just rest.' Because he's a guy who's going to try to outwork you every single day during the season and in the offseason. That's clearly apparent."

Quarterback Jay Cutler added, "He's a workhorse every day. He doesn't change. He's the same guy in the building whether it's Sunday or whether it's Thursday late in the season. He's a consummate professional. And I think guys, now more than before, have really taken notice to his approach to the game, his approach to taking care of himself on and off the field. If you're a young guy in the locker room, Matt Forte is a guy you want to watch and try to emulate."

Preferring to focus on the physical skills displayed by the speedy, 6'1", 221-pound Forte, Bears offensive coordinator Adam Gase said, "I feel lucky to be around a guy who is at an elite level in all three phases of a running back. I've never been around that in my career. I know it hasn't been that long, but he's probably one of the best who has been able to do that in this game."

Patriots head coach Bill Belichick also expressed his admiration for Forte's varied skill set, stating, "Forte is a great back. He's exceptional in the running game and the passing game. He really does everything well. He breaks tackles with his strength and his balance, and he avoids guys with his quickness and his vision. He's a very smart, instinctive player who puts himself in a good position to get the ball or get into spaces where the defense has fewer players, whether it be runs or passes."

Assuming more of a role of leadership following the departures of Lance Briggs and Charles Tillman at the end of 2014, Forte subsequently became a team captain, admitting that his new title meant a great deal to him when he said, "I've always led by example, but now I've gotten that much more of an opportunity to be a vocal leader. I've become a leader in both what I do and what I say."

Ironically, the 2015 campaign ended up being Forte's last in Chicago, with new Bears general manager Ryan Pace announcing on February 12, 2016: "We recently met with Matt to inform him we will not extend a contract offer for the 2016 season. These decisions are never easy, especially given what Matt has meant to our team and community. We have a tremendous amount of respect for him. Matt is one of the all-time great Bears and did an exceptional job for us on and off the field last season. He was a tremendous teammate. We thank him for his professionalism and wish him the very best as he continues his career."

Leaving the Bears with career totals of 8,602 yards rushing, 487 receptions, 4,116 receiving yards, 12,718 yards from scrimmage, and 64 touchdowns, Forte ranks extremely high in team annals in all five categories.

Choosing to sign with the Jets as a free agent, Forte spent the next two seasons in New York rushing for a total of 1,194 yards, amassing 1,750 yards from scrimmage, and scoring 11 touchdowns, before announcing his retirement after injuring his knee during the 2017 campaign. Making his decision known to the public in a statement to Sports Spectrum, Forte said, "For the past 10 years, I've been blessed to play professionally a game that I've loved since I was six years old. But, after much prayer and reflection, I've decided to retire from the NFL. . . . It's time for the workhorse to finally rest in his stable."

Forte continued, "To all of my many coaches and teachers over the years, thank you for your dedication and commitment to my growth and success as a person and player. . . . I had played as long as I actually wanted to play, and, through a lot of prayer and talking to my wife and family and everyone, I decided to call it a career and move on to bigger and better things. A decade is a long time, but, in the grand scheme of things, there's a lot of life ahead of me."

Forte then delivered a special message to the fans of Chicago, saying, "To all Chicago Bears fans, you're truly the best fans in all of professional sports. Thank you for embracing my family and me from day one! The roar of the crowd at Soldier Field as I'd break a run or make a big catch will forever be ingrained in my mind."

Shortly after Forte announced his retirement, he joined NBC Sports Chicago, where he serves as a game day studio analyst and appears on a variety of the station's other programs during the NFL season.

## BEARS CAREER HIGHLIGHTS

### Best Season

Forte had several outstanding seasons for the Bears, with the 2008, 2010, 2011, and 2014 campaigns all ranking among the finest of his career. But he posted his best overall numbers as a member of the Bears in 2013, when he earned one of his two Pro Bowl selections by placing near the top of the league rankings with 1,339 yards rushing, 1,933 yards from scrimmage, nine rushing touchdowns, and 12 TDs, while averaging 4.6 yards per carry, which represented the second-highest mark of his career (he averaged 4.9 yards per carry in 2011).

### Memorable Moments/Greatest Performances

Forte excelled in his first game as a pro, contributing to a 29–13 victory over the Indianapolis Colts in the 2008 regular-season opener by rushing for 123 yards and scoring a touchdown on a 50-yard first-quarter run.

Forte helped lead the Bears to a 27–3 win over the St. Louis Rams on November 23, 2008, by rushing for 139 yards and two touchdowns, the longest of which covered 47 yards.

Forte rushed for a season-high 121 yards and one touchdown during a 48–24 win over the Lions on October 4, 2009, with his TD run covering 37 yards.

Forte had another big game against Detroit in the 2010 regular-season opener, earning NFC Offensive Player of the Week honors by rushing for 50 yards, making seven receptions for a career-high 151 yards, and scoring twice during a 19–14 win. Scoring the Bears' only two touchdowns of the contest, Forte collaborated with Jay Cutler on an 89-yard scoring play in the second quarter, before scoring the game-winning TD when he hauled in a 28-yard pass from Cutler with just 1:32 left in regulation.

Forte led the Bears to a 23–6 win over the Carolina Panthers on October 10, 2010, by rushing for a season-high 166 yards and scoring two touchdowns, which came on runs of 18 and 68 yards.

Forte turned in another outstanding performance against Carolina on October 2, 2011, carrying the ball 25 times for a career-high 205 yards and one touchdown during a 34–29 Bears win.

Forte helped lead the Bears to a 24–18 victory over Tampa Bay on October 23, 2011, by gaining 145 yards on the ground and scoring a touchdown on a 32-yard run.

Although the Bears lost to Washington by a score of 45–41 on October 20, 2013, Forte rushed for 91 yards and three touchdowns during the contest, with his longest TD run covering 50 yards.

Forte led the Bears to a 27–20 win over the Packers on November 4, 2013, by carrying the ball 24 times for 125 yards and one touchdown.

Forte starred during a 33–28 loss to the Packers in the final game of the 2013 regular season, rushing for 110 yards, gaining another 47 yards on four pass receptions, and scoring three touchdowns, with two of those coming on the ground and another through the air.

Forte gave the Bears a dramatic 18–7 victory over the Chiefs on October 11, 2015, when he collaborated with Jay Cutler on a 7-yard scoring play with just 18 seconds left in regulation. He finished the game with 71 yards rushing, five catches for 38 yards, and that one touchdown.

### Notable Achievements

- Rushed for more than 1,000 yards five times, topping 900 yards on two other occasions.
- Surpassed 50 receptions six times and 500 receiving yards three times.
- Amassed more than 1,000 yards from scrimmage eight times, topping 1,500 yards four times.
- Scored at least 10 touchdowns three times.
- Set NFL record for running backs (since broken) by making 102 receptions in 2014.
- Finished second in NFL with 1,339 yards rushing in 2013.
- Finished third in NFL in yards from scrimmage three times.
- Finished fourth in NFL in receptions once and all-purpose yards once.
- Led Bears in rushing eight times and receptions four times.
- Ranks among Bears career leaders with 8,602 yards rushing (2nd), 487 receptions (2nd), 4,116 receiving yards (7th), 12,718 yards from scrimmage (2nd), 12,718 all-purpose yards (2nd), 45 rushing touchdowns (4th), 64 touchdowns (3rd), and 396 points (9th).
- 2010 division champion.
- Member of 2008 NFL All-Rookie Team.
- 2010 Week 1 NFC Offensive Player of the Week.
- Two-time Pro Bowl selection (2011 and 2013).

# 19

## — RED GRANGE —

A legendary figure in the history of American sports, Red Grange joined baseball's Babe Ruth, boxing's Jack Dempsey, golf's Bobby Jones, and tennis's Bill Tilden in ushering in what became known as the "Golden Age of Sports" during the 1920s. A star halfback at the University of Illinois from 1923 to 1925, Grange established himself as college football's greatest player, mesmerizing fans with his extraordinary running ability. Continuing to build upon his reputation after leaving Illinois, Grange signed with the Chicago Bears in 1925, joining them on a lengthy barnstorming tour that helped legitimize professional football. With Grange's mere presence causing fans to turn out in droves, the star running back saved the fledgling National Football League, with many writers claiming that it likely would have collapsed without him. In discussing the tremendous impact that Grange had on the NFL, Steve Hirdt of the Elias Sports Bureau said during a 1980s interview, "Grange was the greatest open-field runner of his time. . . . But his place among the greatest players in NFL history has to do more with the stability that he brought to the league."

Grange ended up spending parts of seven seasons in Chicago, helping to lead the Bears to three division titles and two NFL championships, with his outstanding play earning him three All-Pro selections and a spot on the NFL 1920s All-Decade Team. And, even though a knee injury Grange suffered during the early stages of his career prevented him from ever reaching the same level of greatness as a pro that he attained in college, his impact on the Bears franchise and the NFL as a whole earned him numerous honors following his playing days, with the Bears retiring his #77, the Pro Football Hall of Fame including him in its initial set of inductees, and both the *Sporting News* and the NFL Network awarding him a spot on their respective lists of the 100 Greatest Players in NFL History.

Born in Forksville, Pennsylvania, on June 13, 1903, Harold Edward Grange moved with his family to the Chicago suburb of Wheaton, Illinois, at the age of five. Excelling in multiple sports during his four years at Wheaton High School, Grange earned 16 varsity letters in football, baseball, basketball, and track, scoring 75 touchdowns and 532 points on the gridiron, while also winning the state championship in both the long jump and 100-yard dash as a junior in 1921. Extremely busy away from the playing field as well, Grange spent his summers working as an iceman, developing the strength in his upper body by lifting 50- and 100-pound bags of ice for more than eight hours a day.

After accepting a scholarship from the University of Illinois, Grange initially considered competing in just baseball, basketball, and track, before finally agreeing to play football as well. Proving to be particularly proficient on the gridiron, Grange scored three touchdowns in his very first game, with one of those coming on a 66-yard punt return. Concluding his first year at Illinois with 1,260 yards rushing, 12 touchdowns, and a rushing average of 5.6 yards per carry, Grange led the Illini to an undefeated record and the National Championship. He followed that up by scoring 13 touchdowns and gaining 1,164 yards on the ground in 1924, with his magnificent performance against previously undefeated Michigan on October 18 of that year gaining him legendary status. After returning the opening kickoff 95 yards for a touchdown, Grange scored three more times in the first 12 minutes of the contest, with his TD runs of 67, 56, and 44 yards giving him more touchdowns than the Wolverines had allowed in the previous two seasons. Grange later added an 11-yard touchdown run and a 20-yard TD pass, in leading Illinois to a 39–14 win that ended Michigan's 20-game unbeaten streak. In one of the greatest individual performances ever, Grange accounted for all six Illinois touchdowns, amassed 402 yards of total offense, and intercepted two passes on defense.

Grange had another huge game the following year, leading Illinois to a 24–2 upset win over the University of Pennsylvania by scoring three touchdowns and rushing for a career-high 237 yards through ankle-deep mud. With Grange's blinding speed and elusive running style earning him the nickname "The Galloping Ghost," legendary writer Damon Runyon suggested, "This man Red Grange of Illinois is three or four men rolled into one for football purposes. He is Jack Dempsey, Babe Ruth, Al Jolson, Paavo Nurmi, and Man o' War. Put together, they spell Grange."

Although Grange, at 5'11" and 175 pounds, lacked great size, he possessed exceptional speed and outstanding moves in the open field that made him a threat to go the distance any time he touched the football. In discussing his philosophy as a runner, Grange said, "If you have the football and 11 guys are after you, if you're smart, you'll run."

Announcing the day after the final game of his junior year that he had decided to turn pro, Grange signed with the Bears almost immediately, becoming in the process the first player to leave college early to pursue a career in professional football. Agreeing to participate in a 19-game barnstorming tour that included both NFL and exhibition games, Grange became easily the league's highest-paid player, with the terms of his new contract stipulating that he was to receive a guaranteed $3,000 per game and a share of the gate receipts that ended up amounting to $100,000, during an era when most players earned less than $100 per game.

Grange's decision to forgo his final year of college in order to play professionally shocked the collegiate world, with the star running back saying years later, "When I came into pro football during the 1920s, it was a nothing game. I took quite a beating in the press and from the different schools in joining pro football. Probably, I would have been thought more of had I joined the Capone mob in Chicago instead of professional football."

But, while many criticized Grange for his decision, his participation in the 67-day tour brought pro football into the national consciousness and likely saved the NFL. In one game out east, 65,000 fans packed into New York's Polo Grounds to watch the Bears defeat the Giants by a score of 19–7. In addition to helping the Bears financially, the profits from that contest may well have prevented the Giants from going out of business. Meanwhile, the overwhelming media presence at each game caused Grange's notoriety to increase dramatically, making him even more of a household name.

Seeking an even larger share of the pot the following year, Grange and his agent, theater owner and promoter C. C. Pyle, demanded an ownership interest in the Bears. After having their proposal rejected by George Halas, Pyle established the American Football League, which lasted just one season. Awarded an NFL franchise of his own in 1927, Pyle founded the New York Yankees football franchise, which remained in existence for three years. Competing for the Yankees only in 1927, Grange appeared in 13 games, before a knee injury he sustained during a meeting with his former team brought his days as a dominant runner to an end.

The signing of Red Grange by George Halas helped legitimize pro football.
Courtesy of the Library of Congress

Facing the Bears in Chicago on October 16, 1927, Grange caught a short pass and twisted his knee when his cleat dug into the turf following a hit by George Trafton. Although Grange remained an effective player for several more years, he lost much of his speed and agility, commenting years later, "After it happened, I was just another halfback."

After sitting out the entire 1928 campaign, Grange returned to the Bears in 1929, spending the next six seasons serving as a member of their offensive backfield, while also doing an outstanding job at defensive back. Although the NFL did not begin keeping an official record of most offensive statistics until 1932, Grange scored a total of 15 touchdowns the previous two seasons, earning in the process First-Team All-Pro honors each year. Grange also gained Second-Team All-Pro recognition in 1932, when he led the NFL with seven touchdowns and ranked among the league leaders with 11 receptions, 168 receiving yards, and 42 points scored.

Choosing to announce his retirement following the conclusion of the 1934 campaign, Grange ended his pro career with official totals of 569 yards rushing, 857 yards from scrimmage, and 32 touchdowns, compiling virtually all those numbers as a member of the Bears. Leaving the game at only 31 years of age, Grange later explained his decision to retire when he did by saying, "Every football player knows when his time is up. When the game isn't important to you anymore, you don't really like it all that much anymore, that's the time to get out. I got out when it started to be a drudge. I didn't like to practice anymore. It was a much bigger labor than it had been. The things I'd been able to do, I simply couldn't do anymore."

After retiring as an active player, Grange briefly coached for the Bears, before becoming the first well-known athlete to begin a career in broadcasting, spending more than 30 years announcing football games on radio and television. Stricken with Parkinson's disease later in life, Grange spent his final years living in Lake Wales, Florida, where he died of pneumonia at the age of 87 on January 28, 1991.

Named to the Football Writers Association of America's all-time All-America team at a 100th anniversary celebration of college football in 1969, Grange received the additional distinction of being ranked #1 on ESPN's 2008 list of the Top 25 Players in College Football History. Yet, despite the many honors that others bestowed upon him through the years, Grange remained a humble man, stating on one occasion, "They built my accomplishments way out of proportion. I never got the idea that I was a tremendous big shot. I could carry a football well, but there are a lot of doctors and teachers and engineers who could do their thing better than I."

Although the offensive numbers that Grange compiled during his relatively brief professional career are not particularly impressive, he has remained one of football's greatest legends through the years, with Steve Hirdt saying during that 1980s interview, "He was so big, even 50 years after he last carried the ball, his name still resounds in the sports world. It evokes an era when the films that were made of football games weren't of great quality. They had sort of a ghost-like look to them; you weren't quite sure of who was who until one guy would emerge from the pack, running away from everybody else for a touchdown 'Oh, that's Grange. That's Grange right there.'"

Meanwhile, Bob Zuppke, who coached Grange at Illinois, stated, "I will never have another Grange, but neither will anyone else. They can argue all they like about the greatest football player who ever lived, but I was satisfied I had him when I had Red Grange."

## BEARS CAREER HIGHLIGHTS

### Best Season

Grange earned First-Team All-Pro honors in both 1930 and 1931, scoring a total of 15 touchdowns over the course of those two seasons. Nevertheless, Grange played his best ball for the Bears in 1925, when, fully healthy for the only time as a professional, he accounted for at least 401 total yards and three touchdowns in his five official league games. Furthermore, Grange made his greatest overall impact on the NFL that year, helping to bring credibility to the pro game.

### Memorable Moments/Greatest Performances

Grange performed extremely well in his pro debut, running for 96 yards and intercepting a pass during a scoreless tie with the Chicago Cardinals on November 26, 1925.

Grange led the Bears to a 14–7 win over the Frankford Yellow Jackets on December 5, 1925, by scoring both Chicago touchdowns on a pair of 1-yard runs.

Grange clinched a 19–7 victory over the Giants the very next day by returning an interception 35 yards for a touchdown in the fourth quarter. In addition to his pick-six, Grange carried the ball 11 times for 53 yards, made a 23-yard reception, and completed two passes for 32 yards.

Grange put the finishing touches on a 27–0 win over the Minneapolis Red Jackets on October 27, 1929, by hitting his brother, Gardie, with a 16-yard touchdown pass in the fourth quarter.

Grange closed out the scoring of a 20–0 victory over the Red Jackets on October 5, 1930, by hauling in a 30-yard TD pass from Joey Sternaman in the third quarter.

Grange contributed to a 32–6 win over the Chicago Cardinals on October 19, 1930, by scoring a pair of touchdowns on runs that covered 38 and 15 yards.

Grange also lit the scoreboard twice during a 20–7 victory over the Red Jackets on November 2, 1930, scoring on a 25-yard pass from Laurie Walquist and a 14-yard run.

Grange accounted for both touchdowns the Bears scored during a 13–6 win over the Frankford Yellow Jackets on November 22, 1930, scoring on runs that covered 51 and 78 yards.

Grange threw a pair of touchdown passes to Luke Johnsos during a 21–0 win over the Green Bay Packers on December 7, 1930, connecting with Johnsos from 21 and 30 yards out.

Grange provided most of the offensive firepower when the Bears defeated the Chicago Cardinals by a score of 26–13 on October 18, 1931, scoring three touchdowns, with his TDs coming on a 17-yard pass reception and runs of 35 and 10 yards.

Grange again crossed the goal line three times during a 28–8 win over the Giants on November 6, 1932, with his scores coming on a 7-yard run, a 17-yard pass from Keith Molesworth, and a 55-yard hookup with Bronko Nagurski.

Grange scored the only touchdown of a 9–0 win over the Portsmouth Spartans on December 18, 1932, that gave the Bears the NFL championship when he gathered in a short pass from Bronko Nagurski.

Grange made his most memorable play as a member of the Bears in the 1933 NFL championship game, when, after recording a key interception earlier in the contest, he preserved a 23–21 win over the Giants by making a touchdown-saving tackle of Red Badgro on the game's final play. Describing the events that transpired in the game's closing moments after he hauled in a pass and headed for the Chicago end zone, Badgro recalled some 60 years later, "If I had gotten by Red Grange, I would have scored. Grange had me around the middle . . . his arms were around the ball, and I couldn't get rid of it. If I get by him, we win the game . . . I wish I had the ball again."

**Notable Achievements**

- Intercepted seven passes in 1934.
- Led NFL with seven touchdowns in 1932.
- Finished second in NFL in rushing touchdowns once, touchdown receptions once, and points scored once.
- Three-time division champion (1932, 1933, and 1934).
- Two-time NFL champion (1932 and 1933).
- Two-time First-Team All-Pro selection (1930 and 1931).
- 1932 Second-Team All-Pro selection.
- NFL 1920s All-Decade Team.
- #77 retired by Bears.
- Number 80 on the *Sporting News'* 1999 list of the 100 Greatest Players in NFL History.
- Number 48 on the NFL Network's 2010 list of the NFL's 100 Greatest Players.
- Elected to Pro Football Hall of Fame in 1963.

# 20

## JAY HILGENBERG

The unsung hero of Chicago's offense for much of the 1980s, Jay Hilgenberg anchored the Bears' offensive line from his center position for nine seasons, helping to pave the way for a rushing attack that consistently ranked among the league's best. Serving as captain of some of the finest offensive lines in franchise history, Hilgenberg proved to be the most durable member of the unit, appearing in 163 out of a possible 165 contests during his 11 years in Chicago, while starting all but two non-strike games from 1984 to 1991. A key contributor to the success the Bears experienced during that time, Hilgenberg helped lead them to six division titles, one NFC championship, and one Super Bowl win, with his exceptional play earning him four All-Pro selections and seven consecutive Pro Bowl and First-Team All-NFC nominations. Amazingly, Hilgenberg accomplished all he did after entering the NFL as an undrafted free agent.

Born in Iowa City, Iowa, on March 21, 1959, Jay Walter Hilgenberg seemed destined for a career in football from the time he first entered the world. The son of All-America University of Iowa center Jerry Hilgenberg and the nephew of Minnesota Vikings linebacker Wally Hilgenberg, young Jay grew up around football, before making a name for himself as a wrestler and gridiron star at Iowa City High School. Continuing to follow in his father's footsteps, Hilgenberg excelled at center while attending the University of Iowa, even though he remained somewhat undersized at 6'2" and close to 230 pounds.

Subsequently bypassed by all 28 teams in the 1981 NFL Draft due to concerns over his size, Hilgenberg ended up signing with the Bears as a free agent. He then spent his first two seasons in Chicago serving as a backup offensive lineman and playing on special teams, while gradually adding more than 30 pounds of bulk onto his frame until he reached his eventual playing weight of 265 pounds. Finally given an opportunity to start midway through the 1983 campaign, Hilgenberg replaced Dan Neal at center for the season's final eight games, performing so well at that post that he remained there for the next eight years.

After helping the Bears finish first in the NFL in rushing for the first of four straight times in 1983, Hilgenberg served as the centerpiece of a unit that enabled Walter Payton to amass 1,684 yards on the ground the following year. Either Payton or Neal Anderson rushed for more than 1,000 yards in each of the next six seasons as well, with Hilgenberg's outstanding blocking at the point of attack proving to be critical to the success of both men. Also excelling in pass protection, Hilgenberg did a superb job of blocking up front for quarterbacks Jim McMahon, Steve Fuller, Mike Tomczak, and Jim Harbaugh throughout the period.

Jay Hilgenberg appeared in 163 out of a possible 165 games during his time in Chicago. Courtesy of MEARSonlineauctions .com

Perhaps the most overlooked aspect of Hilgenberg's game, though, was his ability as a long-snapper, with former teammate Steve McMichael saying, "Jay could deep-snap better than anybody. Because of that, popping his arms back that way, his elbows are terrible now. Can't straighten his arms out at all. I feel sorry for him for that, but I know he'd do it all over again. . . . He had a great career, especially for a guy who was a free agent out of Iowa, making the Pro Bowl seven straight years for the Bears."

In addition to being named to the Pro Bowl seven consecutive times from 1985 to 1991, Hilgenberg gained First-Team All-NFC recognition in each of those campaigns. He also received All-Pro honors four times, being named to the First Team in 1988 and 1989, and the Second Team in both 1986 and 1990.

The 1991 season proved to be Hilgenberg's last in Chicago since he ended up leaving the Windy City during the subsequent offseason following a lengthy holdout. Miffed that the Bears offered him less money than first-round draft pick Stan Thomas, Hilgenberg refused to sign for less than $1 million. Unwilling to meet his disgruntled center's demands, team president Mike McCaskey instead traded him to the Cleveland Browns for a conditional draft pick. Hilgenberg spent one year in Cleveland, starting all 16 games for the Browns at center in 1992, before joining the New Orleans Saints the following year. After appearing in nine games with the

Saints in 1993, Hilgenberg announced his retirement in April 1994 after undergoing a successful angioplasty to remove a blockage near his heart discovered during a routine examination. Commenting on his situation at the time, Hilgenberg said, "I wasn't angry; I was more scared. I wanted to see my daughter grow up. I wanted to be there for her. I don't think I really got angry at all, maybe a little bit. I've been working out real hard. I wanted to play another year, but that's not going to happen now. There's no decision. I've played long enough. I'm happy with that, won a Super Bowl and everything. It's been nice."

Returning to Chicago following his retirement, Hilgenberg eventually landed a position as game analyst for WBBM-AM Radio in Chicago and the Bears Radio Network—one he continues to hold.

## BEARS CAREER HIGHLIGHTS

### Best Season

Hilgenberg earned First-Team All-Pro honors in both 1988 and 1989, with the second of those campaigns proving to be the finest of his career. Anchoring the Chicago offensive line from his center position, Hilgenberg helped the Bears place near the top of the league rankings in yards rushing (2,287) and rushing average (4.4 yards per carry).

### Memorable Moments/Greatest Performances

Hilgenberg's superb blocking at the point of attack helped the Bears rush for 302 yards and amass 406 yards of total offense during a 27–0 win over the Broncos on September 9, 1984.

Hilgenberg helped pave the way for Chicago running backs to gain 229 yards on the ground during a lopsided 34–3 victory over the Vikings on November 25, 1984, with the Bears amassing 399 yards of total offense during the contest.

Hilgenberg helped the Bears rush for a season-high 250 yards during a 24–3 win over the Lions on November 10, 1985.

Hilgenberg and his line-mates dominated the Tampa Bay defense at the point of attack on December 7, 1986, with the Bears gaining 245 yards on the ground and amassing 432 yards of total offense during a 48–14 rout of the Bucs.

Hilgenberg and his cohorts once again controlled the line of scrimmage during a 34–7 victory over the Dolphins in the 1988 regular-season opener, with the Bears rushing for 262 yards and accumulating a total of 427 yards on offense during the win.

## Notable Achievements:

- Missed just two non-strike games in 11 seasons, appearing in 163 of 165 contests.
- Six-time division champion (1984, 1985, 1986, 1987, 1988, and 1990).
- 1985 NFC champion.
- Super Bowl XX champion.
- Seven-time Pro Bowl selection (1985, 1986, 1987, 1988, 1989, 1990, and 1991).
- Two-time First-Team All-Pro selection (1988 and 1989).
- Two-time Second-Team All-Pro selection (1986 and 1990).
- Seven-time First-Team All-NFC selection (1985, 1986, 1987, 1988, 1989, 1990, and 1991).

# 21

# JOE FORTUNATO

S pending his entire 12-year NFL career in the Windy City, Joe Fortunato joined Bill George and Larry Morris in forming one of the greatest linebacking trios in Bears history. Excelling on the left side of Chicago's defense for most of those 12 seasons, Fortunato ranked among the finest outside linebackers of his time, earning five trips to the Pro Bowl and four All-Pro nominations. Equally effective against the run and the pass, Fortunato recovered 22 fumbles and intercepted 16 passes, with his fumble recoveries tying him with Hall of Fame defensive end Andy Robustelli for the most in NFL history at the time of his retirement. An extremely durable player, Fortunato missed just one game his entire career, with his many contributions to the Bears earning him a spot on the NFL 1950s All-Decade Team. Fortunato accomplished all he did even though he arrived in Chicago at the rather advanced age of 25 after playing one year in the Canadian Football League and spending two years in the US Army.

Born in the steel mill town of Mingo Junction, Ohio, on March 28, 1930, Joseph Francis Fortunato worked in his grandparents' grocery store as a child and the steel mill as a teenager, before attending Mingo Junction High School, where he starred in football, basketball, and baseball. After earning All–Ohio Valley Athletic Conference honors for his outstanding play on the gridiron, Fortunato enrolled at Virginia Military Institute, where he remained briefly until transferring to Mississippi State University when VMI's head coach accepted the Bulldogs' head-coaching job.

Excelling on both sides of the ball for Mississippi State from 1950 to 1952, Fortunato starred at fullback and linebacker, recording 11 interceptions on defense as a sophomore in 1950, before gaining First-Team All-America recognition in his junior year. Performing extremely well once again as a senior, Fortunato earned honorable mention All-America honors by rushing for 779 yards and cementing himself as one of the nation's top linebackers.

Speaking years later of his former college teammate, Bobby Collins said, "The thing you should know about Joe as a football player is that he had the speed to run people down and then the size and strength to cause a lot of damage after he got there. He was a great, great football player."

Although the Bears selected Fortunato in the seventh round of the 1952 NFL Draft, with the 80th overall pick, they had to wait three years to acquire his services, since, after competing in the Canadian Football League for one year, he spent the next two years at Fort Benning, Georgia, serving his country as a member of the US Army. Finally joining the Bears in 1955, Fortunato immediately laid claim to the starting left-linebacker job, which he retained for virtually his entire career (he also spent two seasons at right-outside linebacker).

Establishing himself before long as one of the team's top players, Fortunato picked off two passes, recovered two fumbles, and scored one touchdown in 1956, before earning Pro Bowl honors for the first of five times two years later. A leader both on the field and in the locker room, Fortunato soon became team captain, taking over the defensive signal-calling when George Allen replaced Clark Shaughnessy as the Bears defensive coordinator late in 1962.

Earning Pro Bowl and All-Pro honors four straight times from 1962 to 1965, Fortunato excelled in pass coverage and did an outstanding job of defending against the run, proving himself to be one of the league's surest tacklers. A playmaker who possessed both speed and power, the 6'1", 225-pound Fortunato recorded a total of 38 takeaways over the course of his career—a figure that places him sixth in franchise history. Clearly the leader of the Bears by 1965, Fortunato spent his final two years in Chicago mentoring a young Dick Butkus, with longtime friend Tony Byrne, who spent many years serving as mayor of Natchez, Mississippi, the town to which Fortunato retired following the conclusion of his playing career, stating, "Joe would never tell you this, but he was so respected by his teammates and coaches. He was the Bears captain. When they drafted a young linebacker named Dick Butkus, they assigned him to be Joe's roommate. They wanted Dick Butkus to learn from the best."

After suffering a knee injury in 1966, Fortunato lost his starting job to second-year linebacker Doug Buffone early the following year, prompting him to announce his retirement. Looking back years later on the manner with which Fortunato helped prepare him for the starting assignment, Buffone told the *Chicago Sun-Times*, "I learned from Joe Fortunato. I knew exactly what I had to do."

Remaining with the Bears for another two years after he retired as an active player, Fortunato spent the 1967 campaign serving as the team's linebacker coach, before assuming the role of defensive coordinator in 1968. Leaving the organization in 1969 following a staff shakeup under new head coach Jim Dooley, Fortunato received the following words of praise from George Halas, who said at the time: "He was not only an unselfish team player and one of the great corner linebackers, but also a gentleman and genuine credit to pro football and the Bears."

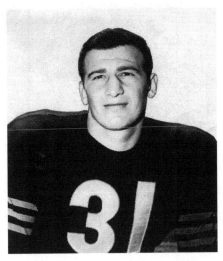

Joe Fortunato ranks second in franchise history with 22 fumble recoveries.
Courtesy of MEARSonlineauctions.com

Later named one of the NFL's 300 greatest players, Fortunato co-owned Big Joe Oil Company in Natchez, Mississippi, after he left football. Sadly, Fortunato developed Alzheimer's later in life, finally losing his battle with the dreaded disease at the age of 87, on November 6, 2017. Following his passing, Bears chairman George H. McCaskey issued a statement that read: "Joe Fortunato was not only a great player for the Chicago Bears, including being a part of our 1963 championship at Wrigley Field, he was a key figure in one of the greatest linebacker trios in Bears history alongside Hall of Famer Bill George and Larry Morris."

Paying tribute to his longtime friend and fellow Natchez resident, Tony Byrne said, "Joe was a whole lot more than a great athlete or football player. He was a great man, a warm, giving friend who loved people and loved this town. He did a whole lot for a whole lot of people. He is most known as a great Chicago Bear, but, in life, he was as gentle as a Teddy Bear."

Meanwhile, Bobby Collins said of his former college teammate, "If you didn't know Joe and you just sat down to talk to him, you'd never suspect he was this great football star, feared by his opponents. He was just a friendly, generous guy. He'd rather talk about you than about himself."

## CAREER HIGHLIGHTS

### Best Season

Fortunato made his greatest overall impact in Chicago during the championship campaign of 1963, when, in addition to intercepting two passes and recovering three fumbles, he served as a catalyst for a dominant Bears defense that led the NFL with 36 interceptions and surrendered just 144 points to the opposition.

### Memorable Moments/Greatest Performances

Fortunato scored the first of his three career touchdowns in the final game of the 1956 regular season, when he recorded a 27-yard pick-six during a 38–21 win over the Detroit Lions.

Fortunato crossed the opponent's goal line again on October 27, 1957, when he recorded a 1-yard TD run during a 21–17 loss to the San Francisco 49ers.

Fortunato contributed to a 35–15 victory over the Baltimore Colts on October 21, 1962, by intercepting a Johnny Unitas pass, which he subsequently returned 36 yards.

Fortunato scored the final touchdown of his career when he returned a fumble 24 yards for a TD during a 27–17 win over the Colts on October 9, 1966.

### Notable Achievements

- Missed just one game entire career.
- Ranks second in Bears history with 22 fumble recoveries.
- Two-time division champion (1956 and 1963).
- 1963 NFL champion.
- Five-time Pro Bowl selection (1958, 1962, 1963, 1964, and 1965).
- Three-time First-Team All-Pro selection (1963, 1964, and 1965).
- 1962 Second-Team All-Pro selection.
- NFL 1950s All-Decade Team.
- Pro Football Reference All-1960s Second Team.
- Named to NFL 100 All-Time Team in 2019.

# 22

## — DEVIN HESTER —

One of the greatest return men in NFL history, Devin Hester spent eight years in Chicago, amassing more yards on special teams than any other player in franchise history. The NFL's all-time leader in punt-return touchdowns, return touchdowns, and non-offensive touchdowns, Hester did most of his damage while playing for the Bears, scoring 19 times on special teams, while also amassing the third most all-purpose yards in team annals. A productive wide receiver as well, Hester surpassed 50 receptions and 500 receiving yards twice each, with his contributions on offense and special teams earning him three trips to the Pro Bowl, four All-Pro nominations, a spot on the NFL 2000s All-Decade Team, and a place on the NFL 100 All-Time Team.

Born in Riviera Beach, Florida, on November 4, 1982, Devin Devorris Hester suffered through a difficult childhood that saw his parents separate when he was a toddler, his mother sustain a serious injury in a car accident before he became a teenager, and his father die of cancer just two years later. Turning to sports as a way of escaping his depression, Hester established himself as a star athlete at Suncoast High School, excelling in track as a sprinter and long jumper, while also earning accolades for his performance on the gridiron, where he played cornerback, wide receiver, running back, and return specialist. Named the top high school prospect in Florida by SuperPrep.com, Hester received the additional distinction of being named to *Parade* magazine's All-America team.

After fielding offers from several colleges, Hester chose to enroll at the University of Miami, where he continued to excel in both track and football. In addition to capturing the 2004 Big East Indoor long jump title with a leap of 7.37 meters, Hester competed in the 60- and 100-meter events, posting personal best times of 6.77 seconds and 10.62 seconds, respectively. Hester also played for the Miami Hurricanes football team from 2003 to 2005, during which time he gradually transitioned from wide receiver to return specialist and defensive back. Nicknamed "Hurricane Hester" by his fans and teammates, Hester displayed an ability to score from anywhere on the field, returning six kicks for touchdowns, including a 98-yard kickoff return against Florida as a freshman and an 81-yard punt return against Duke as a junior. Hester, though, played his best ball for the Hurricanes in his sophomore year, earning First-Team All-America honors as a kick returner by scoring four touchdowns on special teams.

Selected by the Bears in the second round of the 2006 NFL Draft, with the 57th overall pick, Hester subsequently found his selection being criticized by the members of the local media, who maintained that the Bears should have spent their early picks on offensive prospects instead. In response, Hester stated, "Whenever I got a shot, the team that selected me, I just promised myself that I would give them something that they wouldn't regret. . . . The Chicago Bears drafted me, and I'm going to make sure they're not second-guessing themselves about that."

Although the Bears originally drafted Hester as a cornerback, they employed him exclusively as a return man his first year in the league, with the former Hurricane earning a spot on the NFL All-Rookie Team and gaining Pro Bowl and First-Team All-Pro recognition by scoring six touchdowns and amassing 1,128 yards on special teams, leading the NFL with 600 punt-return yards, and placing second in the circuit with an average of 12.8 yards per punt return. With Hester's exceptional play helping the Bears capture the NFC championship, Indianapolis Colts head coach Tony Dungy expressed his concerns prior to Super Bowl XLI over the explosive rookie's ability to go the distance any time he touched the football, stating, "Devin Hester is a weapon, he is a nuclear weapon. So, you are never quite comfortable when your enemy has a nuclear weapon. . . . He can score from anywhere on the field at any time, and that is not a good feeling."

Proving Dungy prophetic, Hester became the only player in Super Bowl history to return the opening kickoff for a touchdown when he gave the Bears an early 7–0 lead over the Colts by sprinting 92 yards after fielding Adam Vinatieri's kick at the Chicago 8 yard line.

Hester followed up his brilliant rookie campaign with a similarly impressive performance in 2007, once again earning Pro Bowl and First-Team All-Pro honors by scoring six touchdowns on special teams, finishing second in the league with 651 punt-return yards and an average of 15.5 yards per punt return, and amassing 1,876 all-purpose yards, with 299 of those yards coming on 20 pass receptions as a part-time receiver.

Accorded more playing time on offense in each of the next two seasons, Hester caught a total of 108 passes for 1,422 yards and six touchdowns, which, combined with the 60 yards he gained on the ground and the 1,220

Devin Hester scored more touchdowns on special teams than any other player in NFL history.
Courtesy of Mike Morbeck

yards he amassed on special teams, gave him a total of 2,702 all-purpose yards. Yet, the 5'11", 190-pound speedster never seemed totally comfortable at wide receiver, often lining up at the wrong spot and failing to run the proper route. Furthermore, Hester's production on special teams fell off somewhat, as he failed to return a kick for a touchdown in either 2008 or 2009. Commenting on Hester's diminished performance in that area following the conclusion of the 2008 campaign, Bears head coach Lovie Smith stated, "I know his returns dropped off a little bit this year, but his plate was full there for a while. We think we have a happy medium now for him as a punt returner and continuing to develop as a wide receiver."

Although Hester continued to assume the same dual role from 2010 to 2012, he saw increasingly less time at wide receiver, enabling him to focus primarily on the strongest part of his game. Having one of his finest all-around seasons in 2010, Hester earned Pro Bowl and First-Team All-Pro honors for the third time by leading the NFL with 564 punt-return yards and an average of 17.1 yards per return, returning three punts for touchdowns, making 40 receptions for 475 yards and four touchdowns, and amassing 1,496 all-purpose yards. He also performed extremely well the following year, gaining Second-Team All-Pro recognition by accumulating 1,540 all-purpose yards, averaging a league-leading 16.2 yards per punt return, and scoring four touchdowns, with three of those coming on returns.

Playing exclusively on special teams in 2013, Hester amassed 1,692 all-purpose yards and led the NFL with a career-high 1,436 kickoff-return yards. Yet, despite his outstanding play, the Bears chose not to re-sign him during the subsequent offseason, with general manager Phil Emery saying in a prepared statement on March 6, 2014:

> For the past eight seasons, we have been honored to have Devin Hester as a part of our organization. While Devin has redefined the pinnacle standard of the return position in the NFL, the memories and contributions he has given us cannot be measured by stats or numbers. . . . Not only is Devin a special player, he is also an exceptional person. He is a great teammate, husband and father. Devin represented the organization off-the-field as well as he did on it. When his career is over, he will always be a welcome member of the Bears family. We thank him for his dedication and wish him and his family all the best.

Expressing his appreciation to the fans of Chicago following Emery's announcement, Hester posted on his Facebook page: "To all my Chicago people . . . I can't thank you all enough for my time in Chicago. I've always said I wanted to retire a Chicago Bear, but sometimes things don't work out the way we would like. Chicago will always hold a special place in my heart, and, if I am fortunate enough to break the return record, we will have all broken it together . . . no matter where I am. Thank you again and God Bless."

Leaving Chicago with career totals of 3,241 punt-return yards, 5,504 kickoff-return yards, and 19 touchdowns on special teams, Hester ranks first in franchise history in each of those categories. He also made 217 receptions for 2,807 yards and 14 touchdowns, gained 80 yards on the ground, and amassed 11,632 all-purpose yards, which represents the third-highest figure in team annals.

Hester subsequently signed with the Atlanta Falcons, with whom he spent the next two seasons, earning his fourth trip to the Pro Bowl in 2014 by amassing 1,908 all-purpose yards and leading the league with 1,128 kickoff-return yards. After suffering through an injury-marred 2015 campaign, Hester split the 2016 season between the Baltimore Ravens and Seattle Seahawks, before announcing his retirement prior to the start of the ensuing campaign. Hester later signed a one-day contract with the Bears that allowed him to officially retire as a member of the team.

## BEARS CAREER HIGHLIGHTS

### Best Season

Hester posted his best receiving totals in 2008 and 2009, surpassing 50 receptions and 650 receiving yards in each of those campaigns. Meanwhile, he performed brilliantly on special teams in 2006, 2010, 2011, and 2013. But Hester made his greatest overall impact in 2007, earning one of his three First-Team All-Pro nominations by amassing 1,874 all-purpose yards and scoring a career-high eight touchdowns, with four of those coming on punt returns and another two on kickoff returns.

### Memorable Moments/Greatest Performances

Hester scored the first touchdown of his career in his first game as a pro, returning a punt 84 yards for a TD during a 26–0 win over the Packers in the 2006 regular-season opener.

Hester completed a memorable fourth-quarter comeback by the Bears that saw them overcome a 20-point deficit to the Arizona Cardinals on

October 16, 2006, by returning a punt 83 yards for a touchdown with 2:58 remaining in regulation. Hester's return, which gave the Bears a 24–23 victory, highlighted a magnificent afternoon in which he recorded a single-game franchise record 152 punt-return yards.

Hester scored the longest touchdown in franchise history during a 38–20 win over the Giants on November 12, 2006, when he returned a missed field goal 108 yards for a TD.

Hester scored the first points of a 23–13 victory over the Vikings on December 3, 2006, when he returned a punt 45 yards for a touchdown early in the second quarter.

Hester displayed his explosiveness during a 42–27 Monday night win over the St. Louis Rams on December 11, 2006, scoring on kickoff returns of 94 and 96 yards.

Although the Bears ended up losing Super Bowl XLI to the Indianapolis Colts by a score of 29–17, Hester made history when he returned the opening kickoff 92 yards for a touchdown.

Hester contributed to a 20–10 victory over the Kansas City Chiefs on September 16, 2007, by returning a punt 73 yards for a touchdown.

Hester scored again on special teams two weeks later, when he returned a kickoff 97 yards for a touchdown during a 37–27 loss to the Detroit Lions on September 30, 2007.

Hester displayed his versatility during a 34–31 loss to Minnesota on October 14, 2007, by returning a punt 89 yards for a touchdown and tying the score at 31–31 with just 1:38 left in regulation when he collaborated with Brian Griese on an 81-yard touchdown reception. Unfortunately, the Vikings won the game moments later when Ryan Longwell kicked a 55-yard field goal as time expired.

Hester helped lead the Bears to a 37–34 overtime victory over the Denver Broncos on November 25, 2007, by returning a punt 75 yards for a touchdown and scoring again on an 88-yard kickoff return. The Bears ended up winning the game on a 39-yard field goal by Robbie Gould less than four minutes into the overtime session.

Hester proved to be the difference in a 33–25 win over the New Orleans Saints in the 2007 regular-season finale, gathering in a 55-yard TD pass from Kyle Orton and returning a punt 64 yards for a touchdown.

Hester gave the Bears a 25–19 win over the Seattle Seahawks on September 27, 2009, when he caught a 36-yard touchdown pass from Jay Cutler with 1:52 remaining in the fourth quarter. He finished the game with five catches for 76 yards and that one TD.

Exactly one year later, on September 27, 2010, Hester returned a punt 62 yards for a touchdown during a 20–17 win over the Packers.

Hester scored again on special teams a few weeks later when he returned a punt 89 yards for a touchdown during a 23–20 loss to the Seattle Seahawks on October 17, 2010.

Hester turned in a memorable performance against the Vikings on December 20, 2010, leading the Bears to a 40–14 victory by making a 15-yard TD reception, returning a punt 64 yards for a touchdown, and nearly scoring a third time on a 79-yard kickoff return.

Hester contributed to a 34–29 victory over the Carolina Panthers on October 2, 2011, by returning a punt 69 yards for a touchdown and helping to set up another score by returning a kickoff 73 yards.

Hester continued to torment the Vikings on October 16, 2011, scoring on a 98-yard kickoff return and making five receptions for 91 yards and one touchdown during a 39–10 Bears win.

Hester scored another touchdown on special teams when he returned a punt 82 yards for a TD during a 37–13 win over the Lions on November 13, 2011.

Hester scored his last points as a member of the Bears during a 45–41 loss to the Redskins on October 20, 2013, when he returned a punt 81 yards for a touchdown.

## Notable Achievements

- Surpassed 50 receptions, 500 receiving yards, and 700 yards from scrimmage twice each.
- Amassed more than 1,000 all-purpose yards eight times, topping 1,500 yards four times.
- Led NFL in kickoff-return yards once, punt-return yards twice, kickoff-return touchdowns twice, punt-return touchdowns three times, non-offensive touchdowns three times, and punt-return average twice.
- Finished second in NFL in punt-return yards once, punt-return touchdowns twice, non-offensive touchdowns once, and punt-return average twice.
- Led Bears in receiving yards twice.
- Holds NFL career records for most punt-return touchdowns (14), return touchdowns (19), and non-offensive touchdowns (20).
- Ranks among NFL career leaders with 3,695 punt-return yards (3rd), 7,333 kickoff-return yards (11th), 11,028 punt- and kickoff-return

yards (8th), five kickoff-return touchdowns (9th), and 11.7-yard punt-return average (9th).

- Holds Bears career records for most punt-return yards (3,241) and kickoff-return yards (5,504).
- Ranks third in Bears history with 11,632 all-purpose yards.
- Two-time division champion (2006 and 2010).
- 2006 NFC champion.
- Member of 2006 NFL All-Rookie Team.
- 13-time NFC Special Teams Player of the Week.
- Three-time NFC Special Teams Player of the Month.
- Three-time Pro Bowl selection (2006, 2007, and 2010).
- Three-time First-Team All-Pro selection (2006, 2007, and 2010).
- 2011 Second-Team All-Pro selection.
- NFL 2000s All-Decade Team.
- Named to NFL 100 All-Time Team in 2019.

# 23

## CHARLES TILLMAN

Arguably the finest defensive back in Bears history, Charles "Peanut" Tillman spent 12 of his 13 NFL seasons in Chicago, establishing a reputation as one of the league's most opportunistic players. In addition to recording the third most interceptions in team annals, Tillman amassed more interception-return yards, scored more defensive touchdowns, and forced more fumbles than any other player ever to don a Bears uniform, with his practice of stripping or "punching" the ball away from opposing players eventually becoming known as the "Peanut Punch." The NFL's single-game record holder for most forced fumbles, Tillman also holds the Bears' single-season mark in that category, with his franchise-record 10 forced fumbles and three touchdown interceptions in 2012 earning him one of his two trips to the Pro Bowl and his lone All-Pro nomination. Excelling at both cornerback positions at different times during his stay in the Windy City, Tillman proved to be a significant contributor to Bears teams that won three division titles and one NFC championship.

Born in Chicago, Illinois, on February 23, 1981, Charles Tillman lived a nomadic existence as a youngster, traveling around the world with his father, a sergeant in the US Army. After attending 11 different schools, Tillman eventually graduated from Copperas Cove High School in Texas, where he earned All-District 8-5A honors twice as a wide receiver. Offered an athletic scholarship by the University of Louisiana at Lafayette, Tillman spent four years starting at left cornerback for the Ragin' Cajuns football team, with his excellent play at that post prompting the Bears to select him in the second round of the 2003 NFL Draft, with the 35th overall pick.

Earning a starting job immediately upon his arrival in Chicago, Tillman had an outstanding rookie season, leading the Bears with four interceptions, while also finishing second on the team with 83 tackles. Meanwhile, Tillman, whose aunt nicknamed him "Peanut" due to the strange configuration of his body during infancy, had his unusual moniker made known to the rest of the team by safety Mike Brown after the latter met him during training camp.

Plagued by injuries in 2004, Tillman appeared in only eight games, limiting him to just 39 tackles and no picks. However, he rebounded in 2005 to begin an exceptional eight-year run during which he established himself as one of the NFL's finest all-around cornerbacks. Missing a total of only six contests during that time, Tillman recorded five interceptions and more than 90 tackles three times each, while also forcing a total of 36 fumbles.

An outstanding cover corner, Tillman did an excellent job of blanketing opposing wide receivers from his left cornerback position, before moving to the right side of Chicago's defense in 2010. The 6'2", 210-pound Tillman also proved to be a sure tackler who delivered many jarring hits to enemy ball-carriers. Tillman, though, built his reputation largely on his ability to create turnovers, with his 36 interceptions and 42 forced fumbles as a member of the Bears clearly exhibiting his proficiency in that area. And, once Tillman got his hands on the football, he knew what to do with it, amassing a total of 675 interception-return yards and scoring nine touchdowns on defense during his time in Chicago.

Charles Tillman holds franchise records for most interception-return yards, forced fumbles, and touchdowns scored on defense.
Courtesy of Jeffrey Beall

Although Tillman spent his first several years in the league playing at a high level, he consistently found himself being overlooked for postseason honors, with other standout corners such as Champ Bailey, Ronde Barber, Nnamdi Asomugha, Asante Samuel, and Darrelle Revis being recognized instead. However, Tillman finally received his just due in 2011, when he earned his first Pro Bowl selection by recording a career-high 99 tackles and returning two of his three interceptions for touchdowns. Tillman followed that up with a banner year, gaining Pro Bowl and consensus First-Team All-Pro recognition in 2012 by making 86 tackles, leading the league with 10 forced fumbles, and recording another three interceptions, all of which he returned for touchdowns.

Unfortunately, Tillman subsequently tore his right triceps midway through the 2013 campaign, preventing him from ever again performing at an elite level. After undergoing season-ending surgery in mid-November, Tillman spent the rest of the year on injured reserve, before missing almost the entire 2014 season after reinjuring his triceps during a 28–20 win over San Francisco in Week 2. With the 34-year-old Tillman becoming a free agent at season's end, the Bears chose not to re-sign him, leaving him to ink a one-year deal with the Carolina Panthers. In addition to his 36 interceptions, 675 interception-return yards, 42 forced fumbles, and nine defensive touchdowns, Tillman left Chicago with career totals of 856 tackles (737 solo), 11 fumble recoveries, and three sacks.

Tillman ended up spending just one season in Carolina, before announcing his retirement after tearing his ACL during the latter stages of the 2015 campaign. Making his decision known to the public on July 18, 2016, via a three-minute YouTube video, Tillman signed a one-day contract with the Bears a few days later that enabled him to officially retire as a member of the team. Paying tribute to Tillman during the retirement ceremony, Bears chairman George McCaskey said:

> Every once in a while, a player comes along with uncommon ability and tenacity on the field, and unsurpassed compassion and charitable spirit off the field, the kind that makes us grateful as fans and proud as an organization. Charles Tillman was such a player and is such a person. . . . For 12 seasons, he made life miserable for Bears opponents, revolutionizing his position and adding "Peanut Punch" to the football vernacular. In the community, in countless hospital rooms, he counseled the worried parents with a "been there" perspective and a sympathetic ear and offered them hope. He also supported the brave men and women who defend our great country.

A noted philanthropist, Tillman, who created The Charles Tillman Cornerstone Foundation in 2005 after he learned that his second-youngest daughter needed to undergo a heart transplant following a diagnosis of dilated cardiomyopathy, has continued his charitable work in retirement. In addition to helping to improve the lives of critically and chronically ill children in the Chicago area through his foundation, Tillman has done a considerable amount of work with the USO, including organizing an international tour to Iraq and a second to Germany in April 2015. Tillman, who graduated from the University of Louisiana with a bachelor's degree in criminal justice, more recently became involved in law enforcement. After training with federal agents at the FBI Training Academy in Quantico, Virginia, in 2017, Tillman began a two-year probationary period in February 2018 that should lead to him becoming a fully instated FBI agent.

## BEARS CAREER HIGHLIGHTS

### Best Season

Tillman had a big year for the Bears in 2005, recording five interceptions, which he returned for a total of 172 yards and one touchdown, forcing four fumbles, and registering 93 tackles, including 82 of the solo variety. He also performed extremely well in 2010 and 2011, intercepting five passes, amassing 127 interception-return yards, recording 82 tackles, forcing four fumbles, and recovering three others in the first of those campaigns, before picking off three passes, scoring two touchdowns, and registering a career-high 99 tackles (82 solo) in the second. However, Tillman made his greatest overall impact in 2012, earning consensus First-Team All-Pro honors by recording three interceptions, all of which he returned for touchdowns, making 86 tackles (74 solo), and leading the NFL with 10 forced fumbles, with his 13 takeaways setting a single-season franchise record.

### Memorable Moments/Greatest Performances

Tillman contributed to a 24–16 victory over the Detroit Lions on October 26, 2003, by recording eight solo tackles and the first interception of his career, which he subsequently returned 32 yards to help set up a Bears touchdown.

Tillman helped preserve a 13–10 victory over the Minnesota Vikings on December 14, 2003, by intercepting a Daunte Culpepper pass intended for Randy Moss in the end zone with just 1:02 left in regulation. Describing his game-saving play years later, Tillman recalled, "Randy Moss was notorious for going up and just catching balls; picking it off and catching it at its highest point. It was backside, he was the only receiver backside, I was a rookie—you do the math. I knew the ball was coming to him. So, I just knew that I had to be more physical than him. And, yeah, I came down with the ball. . . . It showed the world I could play with anybody."

Tillman gave the Bears a 19–13 win over the Lions on October 30, 2005, when he picked off a Jeff Garcia pass and returned the ball 22 yards for a touchdown with 8:43 left in overtime, earning in the process NFC Defensive Player of the Week honors for the first of three times.

Tillman turned in a tremendous all-around effort during a 19–7 victory over the Packers on December 4, 2005, recording a sack and seven tackles, forcing a fumble, recovering another, and intercepting a pass in the Chicago end zone in the waning moments of the first half and subsequently returning the ball 95 yards to the Green Bay 12 yard line, to set up a Robbie Gould 25-yard field goal.

In an October 16, 2006, meeting with the Cardinals that the Bears went on to win by a score of 24–23, Tillman put them within six points of Arizona with five minutes remaining in the fourth quarter when he returned a fumble 40 yards for a touchdown.

Tillman contributed to a 34–7 win over the Lions on October 5, 2008, by returning an interception 26 yards for a touchdown.

Tillman put the finishing touches on a 30–6 victory over the Cleveland Browns on November 1, 2009, when he closed out the scoring in the fourth quarter with a 21-yard pick-six.

Although the Bears lost to the Eagles by a score of 24–20 on November 22, 2009, Tillman recorded seven tackles and forced three fumbles, two of which the Bears recovered.

Tillman helped the Bears record a 37–13 victory over the Lions on November 13, 2011, by returning his interception of a Matthew Stafford pass 44 yards for a touchdown.

Tillman lit the scoreboard again in the 2011 regular-season finale, when he returned an interception 22 yards for a touchdown during a 17–13 win over the Minnesota Vikings.

Tillman crossed the opponent's goal line again on October 1, 2012, when he returned his interception of a Tony Romo pass 25 yards for a touchdown during a 34–18 win over Dallas.

Tillman earned NFC Defensive Player of the Week honors by recording a 36-yard pick-six during a 41–3 rout of the Jacksonville Jaguars on October 7, 2012.

Tillman earned that distinction again two weeks later by recording eight solo tackles and forcing two fumbles during a 13–7 win over the Lions on October 22, 2012.

Tillman helped lead the Bears to a lopsided 51–20 victory over the Tennessee Titans on November 4, 2012, by recording nine solo tackles and setting an NFL record by forcing four fumbles, three of which the Bears recovered.

Tillman scored the last of his nine career touchdowns when he returned an interception 10 yards for a TD during a 28–13 win over the Arizona Cardinals on December 23, 2012.

## Notable Achievements

- Recorded five interceptions three times.
- Amassed more than 100 interception-return yards twice.
- Forced 10 fumbles in 2012.
- Surpassed 80 tackles seven times.
- Led NFL in touchdown interceptions twice and forced fumbles once.
- Finished second in NFL in forced fumbles once.
- Finished third in NFL in interception-return yards once.
- Led Bears in interceptions three times.
- Holds NFL single-game record for most forced fumbles (4 vs. Tennessee on November 4, 2012).
- Holds Bears single-season record for most forced fumbles (10 in 2012).
- Holds Bears career records for most interception-return yards (675), touchdown interceptions (8), defensive touchdowns scored (9), and forced fumbles (42).
- Ranks among Bears career leaders with 36 interceptions (3rd) and 856 tackles (8th).
- Ranks sixth in NFL history with 44 career forced fumbles.
- Three-time division champion (2005, 2006, and 2010).
- 2006 NFC champion.
- Three-time NFC Defensive Player of the Week.
- October 2012 NFC Defensive Player of the Month.
- 2013 NFL Man of the Year.
- Two-time Pro Bowl selection (2011 and 2012).
- 2012 First-Team All-Pro selection.

# 24

# ED SPRINKLE

**I**dentified by George Halas as "the greatest pass-rusher I've ever seen," Ed Sprinkle spent his entire 12-year NFL career in Chicago, becoming one of the very first players to gain notoriety for his ability to apply pressure to opposing quarterbacks. Indeed, Sprinkle did such an exceptional job of pressuring opposing signal-callers that, after spending the first half of his career playing both offense and defense, he served the Bears almost exclusively as a defensive end his last several years in the league. Contributing greatly to whatever success the Bears experienced during that time, Sprinkle helped lead them to two division titles and one NFL championship, earning in the process four Pro Bowl selections, four All-Pro nominations, and a spot on the NFL 1940s All-Decade Team.

Born in Bradshaw, Texas, on September 3, 1923, Edward Alexander Sprinkle grew up in nearby Tuscola, where he attended sparsely populated Tuscola High School, whose senior class the year he graduated included just 13 students. Encouraged by his mother to attend college, Sprinkle enrolled at Hardin-Simmons University in Abilene, where he began his career in football. Recalling years later the influence his mother had on his decision to further his education, Sprinkle said, "She wanted to make sure I went to college. It was a good thing for me, otherwise I'd have ended up working on a farm."

After earning All–Border Conference honors while attending college in Abilene, Sprinkle transferred to the Naval Academy following his junior year when Hardin-Simmons cancelled its athletic program due to the nation's involvement in World War II. Although Sprinkle seriously considered pursuing a career in the military during his time at Annapolis, his love for football eventually won out, with Sprinkle later saying, "I was interested in professional football because of Bulldog Turner. He went to Hardin-Simmons, where I went. I met Bulldog, and I was going to try to make it with Bulldog's help."

Signing with the Bears as an undrafted free agent in 1944, Sprinkle spent his first two seasons in Chicago playing end on defense and assuming the role of a backup guard on offense. Shifted to end (or wide receiver) on offense prior to the start of the 1946 season, Sprinkle later explained the move by stating, "I wasn't big enough to play guard. I weighed 210 pounds."

Although Sprinkle never developed into anything more than an average offensive player, making 32 receptions, amassing 451 receiving yards, and catching seven touchdown passes during his career, he truly excelled on defense, gradually developing into the league's top pass-rusher, with his quickness and determination often forcing opposing teams to double-team him. Since the NFL did not keep an official record of defensive statistics such as sacks and tackles until years after Sprinkle retired, it is not known how many times he brought down opposing quarterbacks behind the line of scrimmage over the course of his career. But Sprinkle built a reputation second to none in terms of his ability to rush the passer, with Rams linebacker Don Paul saying, "Ed Sprinkle was probably, in his day, the most feared pass-rusher in football."

A hard-nosed and extremely aggressive player referred to by many as "the meanest man in pro football," the 6'1", 210-pound Sprinkle proved to be a menace to opposing offenses, delivering harmful hits to blockers, running backs, and quarterbacks alike. Acquiring the nickname "The Claw" from his infamous clothesline tackling technique, Sprinkle frequently dispensed with his opponent by delivering a powerful left forearm to his neck or head area, later revealing, "They were going to put me at left end. I said, 'I want to be a right end because I could reach over with my left arm.' I am left-handed."

Sprinkle's aggressive style of play caused many of his opponents to accuse him of being a dirty player, with Hall of Fame quarterback Norm Van Brocklin stating, "Ed Sprinkle was a 190-pound rattlesnake. He was the meanest guy in the world. . . . When he came in, he used to club you across the head with that left hand, early or late. He always had my eyes watery all the time. He always clubbed me with that thing across the face. Your eyes would start watering."

Pittsburgh Steelers defensive tackle Ernie Stautner noted, "Ed Sprinkle was tough, fast, and you really had to watch out for him. You couldn't turn your back on him, or he'd club you."

San Francisco 49ers running back Hugh McElhenny added, "Sprinkle would drive you 10 yards out of bounds, and the official would be taking the ball away from you, but Sprinkle would still be choking you."

Fellow 49er Bill "Tiger" Johnson commented, "Ed Sprinkle was kind of a Jekyll and Hyde. Off the field, a wonderful guy. On the field, his character did change. He was a punishing football player."

And Doug Buffone, who joined the Bears more than a decade after Sprinkle played his last game for the team, said, "I didn't play with him, but you heard about him as a player when you came into the league and played for the Bears. He RUINED people."

Yet, there were those who spoke out on Sprinkle's behalf, with 49ers coach Red Hickey suggesting, "He was just short of being dirty. He always got there just in time to hurt you. But it was in time that it was legal."

Ed Sprinkle came to be known as "the meanest man in pro football" during his time in Chicago.
Public domain, photographer unknown

Meanwhile, Bears teammate Johnny Lujack offered, "Sprinkle never liked to lose. Sprinkle was not a dirty football player, as a lot of people think he was, but he wanted to give you the impression that he was. And that gave him the edge."

Although Sprinkle admitted, "I'd hit anybody on any play, as hard as I could hit them," he took exception to claims made that he played outside the rules of the game, stating, "I guess I got the reputation for being a dirty player, but I never played dirty. I just played hard football. I didn't bite anyone, or kick anyone, or any of that stuff that goes along with being a dirty player. I did put players out of the game with hard hits, but I don't think that's playing dirty."

Sprinkle then added, "We were meaner in the 1950s because there were fewer positions, and we fought harder for them. It was a different era."

And, as for being called "the meanest man in pro football," Sprinkle defended himself thusly: "I was about as aggressive as any football player that walked on the field. If I had an opportunity to hit someone, I hit them. I had a reputation with my teammates and George Halas as being the roughest player the Bears ever had. That doesn't make me mean or dirty."

After earning Pro Bowl and All-Pro honors four times each from 1949 to 1954, Sprinkle assumed a backup role on defense in 1955, surrendering his starting job to Doug Atkins. Choosing to announce his retirement at season's end, Sprinkle, in addition to the offensive numbers mentioned earlier, concluded his playing career with four interceptions, 55 interception-return yards, 12 fumble recoveries, and two touchdowns on defense. He also scored one touchdown on special teams.

After retiring as an active player, Sprinkle worked as an engineer at Inland Steel, before opening a bowling alley and his own tile and carpet shop. He also spent one year serving as an assistant coach with the New York Titans of the newly formed American Football League during the early 1960s. Sprinkle lived until the age of 90, dying of natural causes on July 28, 2014.

## CAREER HIGHLIGHTS

### Best Season

Although Sprinkle posted his best offensive numbers in 1946 and 1948, he made his greatest overall impact on defense in 1952, earning one of his two official All-Pro nominations from the Associated Press.

### Memorable Moments/Greatest Performances

Sprinkle scored the first touchdown of his career when he gathered in a 34-yard pass from Sid Luckman during a 21–14 win over the Philadelphia Eagles on October 20, 1946.

Sprinkle scored what proved to be the game-winning touchdown of a 10–7 victory over the Packers on November 3, 1946, when he returned a fumble 30 yards for a TD.

Wreaking havoc on defense during the Bears' 24–14 win over the Giants in the 1946 NFL championship game, Sprinkle forced two New York running backs to leave the contest with injuries (George Franck with a separated shoulder and Frank Reagan with a broken nose). Sprinkle also broke the nose of quarterback Frank Filchock, causing him to lose the football, which Bears defensive back Dante Magnani subsequently grabbed out of the air and returned 19 yards for a touchdown.

Sprinkle made two touchdown receptions during a lopsided 45–7 victory over the Packers in the 1948 regular-season opener, the longest of which came on a 34-yard connection with rookie quarterback Bobby Layne.

Although the Bears lost to the Cleveland Browns by a score of 42–21 on November 25, 1951, Sprinkle made perhaps the most memorable play of the game, when, after separating quarterback Otto Graham from the football with one of his patented pass rushes, he recovered the loose pigskin and returned it 55 yards for a touchdown.

Despite being used almost exclusively on defense in 1952, Sprinkle gave the Bears a 24–23 win over the Detroit Lions on November 23 of that year, when he gathered in a 2-yard TD pass from George Blanda in the fourth quarter.

Sprinkle scored the last of his 10 career touchdowns during a 35–28 loss to the 49ers on October 18, 1953, when he returned a blocked punt 21 yards for a TD.

### Notable Achievements

- Finished second in NFL in fumble-return yards twice.
- Two-time division champion (1946 and 1950).
- 1946 NFL champion.
- Four-time Pro Bowl selection (1950, 1951, 1952, and 1954).
- Four-time Second-Team All-Pro selection (1949, 1951, 1952, and 1954).
- NFL 1940s All-Decade Team.

# 25

## GARY FENCIK

Nicknamed "Hit-Man" for the ferocity with which he tackled opposing ball-carriers, Gary Fencik spent his entire 12-year NFL career in Chicago excelling at both safety positions. A member of Bears teams that won four division titles, one NFC championship, and one Super Bowl, Fencik combined at different times with Doug Plank and Dave Duerson to form the hardest-hitting safety tandem in the NFL, recording more than 100 tackles four times, en route to making the sixth-most stops in franchise history. An outstanding ball-hawk as well, Fencik picked off more passes and registered more takeaways than anyone else in team annals, with his excellent all-around play earning him two trips to the Pro Bowl, two All-Pro selections, and six All-NFC nominations.

Born in Chicago, Illinois, on June 11, 1954, John Gary Fencik attended Barrington High School in the northwest suburb of Barrington, where he excelled both in the classroom and on the football field. Continuing to star on the gridiron at Yale University, Fencik spent his college career playing wide receiver, performing well enough at that post to be selected by the Miami Dolphins in the 10th round of the 1976 NFL Draft, with the 281st overall pick.

Moved to defensive back by the Dolphins at his first pro training camp, Fencik ruptured his left lung while making a tackle against the New Orleans Saints during a scrimmage at Lockhart Stadium, forcing him to miss the next several weeks. Unable to learn Miami's defensive schemes or make much of an impression upon his return to the team, Fencik found himself being released by the Dolphins on Labor Day, after which the Bears swooped in and signed him as a free agent. Looking back at the events that transpired at the time, Fencik said, "I didn't really have time to develop my craft down there. But it was a good experience. Just the wrong place, wrong time. Fortunately, though, they were the ones who decided to draft me as a defensive back. So, if it hadn't been for a great scout in the Dolphin organization, I'd probably be a real young professional making a lot of money with a secure job the rest of my life."

Fencik spent his first season in Chicago serving mostly on special teams while learning how to play the safety position from young veteran Doug Plank. Having learned his lessons well, Fencik joined his mentor in the Bears' starting defensive backfield the following year, with Plank moving to free safety to accommodate his pupil, who laid claim to the starting strong safety job. Performing well in his first full season at his new post, Fencik placed among the Bears leaders in both tackles and interceptions, with his four picks tying Plank for second on the team. After intercepting another four passes in 1978, Fencik earned First-Team All-NFC honors for the first of three times in 1979 by ranking among the league leaders with six picks. He subsequently gained Pro Bowl recognition in each of the next two seasons, with his team-leading six interceptions, 121 interception-return yards, and 135 tackles in 1981 also earning him All-Pro honors for the first of two times.

Crediting much of his success to Plank, who developed a reputation as one of the league's hardest hitters during his career, Fencik said years later, "Coming to the Chicago Bears, there's one person I owe my career to, and that's Doug Plank. Doug was the star of the defense when I got here, and he taught me

Gary Fencik recorded more interceptions than anyone else in franchise history. Courtesy of PristineAuction.com

basically how to play safety. And that was to play with absolute abandon, and I became a much more physical player."

Fencik's physicality became such that he and Plank become known as the "Hitmen," with the duo developing into the most feared and intimidating safety tandem in the league. In discussing Fencik's ability to deliver jarring hits to opposing ball-carriers, Buddy Ryan stated, "Gary Fencik was probably the best open-field tackler, and he was also able to deliver a blow, as well as get the guy down. Gary was a guy that put 'em down."

Ryan also stressed that the 6'1", 194-pound Fencik developed into an outstanding player despite his physical limitations, saying, "When the Good Lord passed out all that ability, he didn't give Gary his full share, but he gave him a full share of something inside that made him a great player."

Fencik, himself, admitted, "If you have speed and strength, and you have the size, that's the best situation you can have. I never seemed to have any of those."

But Fencik added, "I think that the mental and assimilating part of the game is knowing where you have to be and how you're going to get there, and it's not always the fastest guy, but the guy who thinks the smartest and plays the most intelligently, and that was certainly one of the strong points, hopefully, of my game because I used my talents to the utmost. I really studied hard, and I think you can get really great tendencies, but you have to be football smart on the field, and, if I hadn't been, I certainly wouldn't have played as long as I did."

Fencik continued, "I was lucky because I worked for most of my career in a system that you had to be smart, and, with Buddy Ryan, we did a lot of different things that demanded a lot from you in terms of smarts on the field, and that played into the strength of my game."

Former Lions quarterback Eric Hipple discussed the cerebral part of Fencik's game when he said, "What made that defense fun to play against was Gary Fencik back there at safety. He just ran that whole thing. He was smart. He was checking in and checking out of plays just like a quarterback would. So, you're trying to play this chess game with him, trying to figure him out. That's what made the game fun. What made it un-fun was when they came free."

Moving to free safety after Plank retired following the conclusion of the 1982 campaign, Fencik spent the next five years at that post, serving as the Bears' defensive captain throughout the period. Performing particularly well in 1984 and 1985, Fencik recorded a total of 10 interceptions, with his outstanding play earning him All-NFC honors both years and Second-Team All-Pro recognition in 1985. Choosing to announce his retirement after assuming a backup role in 1987, Fencik ended his playing career with 38 interceptions, 488 interception-return yards, 1,102 tackles, 13 fumble recoveries, two sacks, and one touchdown, with his 38 picks and 51 take-aways both representing franchise records.

Fencik, who obtained his MBA in finance from Northwestern University while still playing for the Bears, did a little broadcasting work after retiring as an active player, before beginning an extremely successful career in the financial sector. In discussing the path he ultimately chose to pursue, Fencik said, "One of the benefits of going to Yale is that I had roommates, classmates, even teammates who were going to med school, law school, or business school, so I never stopped thinking about what I was going to do after football."

After working as a color commentator on Bears radio broadcasts from 1990 to 1993, Fencik accepted a position with Wells Fargo, where he spent the next few years running their Chicago investment office. He also later worked for UBS, before joining Adams Street Partners, where he currently is a full partner.

## CAREER HIGHLIGHTS

### Best Season

Although Fencik also performed extremely well for the Bears in 1979, 1984, and 1985, gaining All-NFC recognition in each of those campaigns, he had the finest all-around season of his career in 1981, when he earned First-Team All-Pro honors for the only time by recording 135 tackles, intercepting six passes, which he returned for a total of 121 yards and one touchdown, and successfully defensing 17 pass attempts.

### Memorable Moments/Greatest Performances

Fencik recorded the first interception of his career during a 24–23 win over the Los Angeles Rams on October 10, 1977.

Fencik helped the Bears record a 14–10 victory over Washington in the final game of the 1978 regular season by making a key interception, which he subsequently returned 59 yards.

Fencik picked off two passes in one game for the first time as a pro during a 35–7 win over the Detroit Lions on November 4, 1979.

Fencik scored the only points of his career during a 35–24 win over Denver in the 1981 regular-season finale, when he returned his interception of a Craig Morton pass 69 yards for a TD.

Fencik earned NFC Defensive Player of the Week honors by intercepting two passes during a 34–14 win over Tampa Bay in the 1984 regular-season opener, returning one of those 61 yards.

Fencik helped lead the Bears to a 17–6 win over the Los Angeles Raiders on November 4, 1984, by recording a pair of interceptions.

Although the Bears lost the 1984 NFC championship game to the 49ers by a score of 23–0, Fencik picked off Joe Montana twice during the contest.

### Notable Achievements

- Recorded at least five interceptions four times.
- Amassed more than 100 interception-return yards twice.
- Recorded more than 100 tackles four times.
- Led Bears in interceptions four times and tackles three times.
- Holds Bears career records for most interceptions (38) and most takeaways (51).
- Ranks among Bears career leaders with 488 interception-return yards (3rd), 1,102 tackles (6th), and 13 fumble recoveries (tied-9th).
- Four-time division champion (1984, 1985, 1986, and 1987).
- 1985 NFC champion.
- Super Bowl XX champion.
- 1984 Week 1 NFC Defensive Player of the Week.
- Two-time Pro Bowl selection (1980 and 1981).
- 1981 First-Team All-Pro selection.
- 1985 Second-Team All-Pro selection.
- Three-time First-Team All-NFC selection (1979, 1980, and 1981).
- Three-time Second-Team All-NFC selection (1982, 1984, and 1985).
- Pro Football Reference All-1980s Second Team.

# 26

# BILL HEWITT

One of the finest two-way ends of his era, Bill Hewitt starred on both sides of the ball for the Bears for five seasons, helping them win three division titles and two NFL championships. An outstanding receiver on offense and dominant run-stuffer on defense, Hewitt gained All-Pro recognition four times while playing for the Bears, with his exceptional all-around play eventually earning him spots on the NFL's 75th Anniversary All-Time Two-Way Team and the NFL 100 All-Time Team, as well as a place in the Pro Football Hall of Fame. Yet, Hewitt is largely remembered for being the last player to compete in the NFL without wearing a helmet.

Born in Bay City, Michigan, on October 8, 1909, William Ernest Hewitt attended Bay City Central High School, where he didn't play football until his senior year. After enrolling at the University of Michigan, Hewitt lettered in football for three seasons, emerging as an elite player as a senior in 1931, after missing most of the previous year with a broken ankle. Starting four games at left end (wide receiver) and five games at fullback, Hewitt earned team MVP and First-Team All–Big Ten honors by gaining 446 yards on 118 rushing attempts.

With the NFL Draft having not yet been instituted, Hewitt signed with the Bears as a free agent following his graduation from Michigan, beginning his professional career with them in 1932. Performing well his first year in Chicago, the 5'9", 190-pound Hewitt earned Second-Team All-Pro honors by making seven receptions for 77 yards and rushing for 29 yards and one touchdown on offense, while also doing an outstanding job on defense, with his strong play helping the Bears capture the NFL title for the first of two straight times. Establishing himself as one of the league's top players the following year, Hewitt gained consensus First-Team All-Pro recognition by ranking among the league leaders with 14 receptions and 273 receiving yards. Repeating as a First-Team All-Pro in 1934, Hewitt led the NFL with five touchdown receptions. After a subpar 1935 campaign,

Hewitt rebounded in 1936 to earn All-Pro honors once again by catching 15 passes for a career-high 358 yards and six touchdowns.

As well as Hewitt played on offense, he proved to be even more of a force on defense, where his speed, strength, superior tackling ability, and uncanny sense of timing often prompted spectators to focus their attention on him, rather than on the football. Known for his explosiveness off the line of scrimmage, Hewitt acquired the nickname "The Offside Kid" due to his amazingly quick reaction to the center snap, which often enabled him to hit the ball-carrier almost as soon as the ball arrived. Responding to claims that he frequently crossed the line of scrimmage before the opposing center snapped the football, Hewitt stated on one occasion, "I just anticipate when the ball is going to be snapped and charge at the same time. Anyway, what is the head linesman for? It's up to him to call offside if he thinks I am."

Hewitt's aggressive style of play made him a personal favorite of Bears head coach George Halas, who called him "absolutely fearless," adding that "He was a happy-go-lucky guy—until he stepped onto the field—and then he was a terror on offense or defense. He asked no quarter nor gave any."

During his time in Chicago, Hewitt also became known for his unorthodox habit of playing without a helmet, which he explained by suggesting that donning headgear likely would have inhibited his play. Hewitt remained helmetless until 1939, when the NFL instituted a new rule requiring players to wear one.

Despite being only 27 years of age, Hewitt surprisingly elected to announce his retirement following the conclusion of the 1936 campaign, stating at the time, "Now's the time to quit. I want them to remember me as a good end. I've heard those boos from the grandstand before, and believe me, it's a lot more fun to quit with cheers instead ringing in your ears."

However, Hewitt decided to return to the playing field shortly after George Halas worked out a trade with the Eagles that sent him to Philadelphia in exchange for fullback Sam Francis, who the Eagles had earlier made the first overall pick of the 1937 NFL Draft. Talked out of retirement by Eagles owner Bert Bell, who offered to double his salary from $100 to $200 per game, Hewitt spent the next three seasons in Philadelphia, earning two more All-Pro selections. Choosing to retire again at the end of 1939, Hewitt remained away from the game for three years, before spending part of the 1943 season playing for a combined Steelers/Eagles squad known as the "Steagles." Retiring for good following the conclusion of the campaign, Hewitt ended his career with 103 receptions, 1,638 receiving yards, 26 touchdowns, and three TD passes. While playing for the Bears, Hewitt

Bill Hewitt (left), seen here with George Halas (middle) and Red Grange, proved to be one of the finest two-way ends of his era.
Courtesy of Boston Public Library, Leslie Jones Collection

made 52 receptions, amassed 939 receiving yards, scored 16 touchdowns, and threw all three of his TD passes.

Following his retirement, Hewitt worked for Supplee-Wills-Jones, a milk company in Pennsylvania, until September 1946. Unfortunately, he died just four months later, losing his life in an automobile accident in Sellersville, Pennsylvania, on January 14, 1947. Only 37 years old at the time of his passing, Hewitt later had his #56 retired by the Bears and received induction into the Pro Football Hall of Fame, being so honored in 1971.

## BEARS CAREER HIGHLIGHTS

### Best Season

Hewitt posted the best offensive numbers of his career in 1936, when, playing almost 60 minutes of every game due to injuries sustained by several of his teammates, he ranked among the NFL leaders with 15 receptions, 358 receiving yards, six TD catches, seven touchdowns, and 42 points scored. However, he had his finest all-around season in 1933, when, in addition to finishing third in the league with 14 receptions and 273 receiving yards, he threw three touchdown passes and performed remarkably well on defense. Although the NFL did not keep an official record of defensive statistics until years later, Hewitt is unofficially credited with throwing enemy ball-carriers for more than 300 yards in total losses over the course of the campaign, with his fabulous play on that side of the ball earning him consensus First-Team All-Pro honors for the first of three times.

### Memorable Moments/Greatest Performances

Hewitt contributed to a 34–0 win over the Chicago Cardinals on November 24, 1932, by scoring his first career TD on a 28-yard run.

Hewitt had a hand in both touchdowns the Bears scored during a 14–7 win over the Packers in the 1933 regular-season opener, throwing a 46-yard TD pass to Luke Johnsos and recovering a ball in the Green Bay end zone following a blocked field goal attempt by the Bears.

Although Hewitt made just one reception for 3 yards during the Bears' 23–21 win over the Giants in the 1933 NFL championship game, he played a key role in what was later described as "the greatest play of the game." With the Bears trailing the Giants by a score of 21–16 and in possession of the ball at the New York 22 yard line with five minutes remaining in the fourth quarter, Hewitt caught a jump pass from Bronko Nagurski and then lateraled the ball to right end Bill Karr, who ran the remaining 19 yards to give the Bears a 23–21 lead that they protected the rest of the way.

Hewitt helped lead the Bears to a 21–0 victory over the Boston Redskins on November 11, 1934, by making a pair of 20-yard touchdown receptions.

Hewitt led the Bears to a 17–0 win over the Eagles on September 27, 1936, by scoring both Chicago TDs on a 25-yard pass from Carl Brumbaugh and a 16-yard toss from Ray Nolting.

Hewitt scored the only touchdown the Bears recorded during a 21–10 loss to the Packers on November 1, 1936, when he returned his fumble recovery on defense 53 yards for a TD.

Hewitt turned in arguably his most memorable performance on October 22, 1933, when his spirited play helped lead the Bears to a 10–7 win over the Packers in a game that they trailed by seven points heading into the final four minutes. Praising Hewitt for his brilliant all-around play, the *Green Bay Press-Gazette* later reported:

> And this man Bill Hewitt, the Bears' left end—how he played football! It probably was his most inspired performance that kept up the Bear morale in the face of the Packer onslaught. It gave them courage to keep fighting until the end, and that determination not to be beaten was all that was needed. . . . Hewitt was a team by himself on the left side of the Bears line. The Packers would send two men and often three at him trying to clear the way for a ball carrier. But he would smash through all of them to break up the play. The Packers would plow and pass down the field, plowing over the weak side when they could not get through or around Hewitt. But when they got into the scoring territory, the demon end would turn on even more steam and stop plays on the opposite side of the line besides in his own territory. It was the most brilliant individual performance ever turned in by a player in a Packer-Bear game.

## Notable Achievements

- Averaged more than 20 yards per reception once (23.9 in 1936).
- Led NFL with five touchdown receptions in 1934.
- Finished second in NFL with six touchdown receptions and seven touchdowns in 1936.
- Finished third in NFL in receptions once and receiving yards twice.

- Led Bears in receptions three times and receiving yards twice.
- Three-time division champion (1932, 1933, and 1934).
- Two-time NFL champion (1932 and 1933).
- Three-time First-Team All-Pro selection (1933, 1934, and 1936).
- 1932 Second-Team All-Pro selection.
- NFL 1930s All-Decade Team.
- #56 retired by Bears.
- Named to NFL's 75th Anniversary All-Time Two-Way Team in 1994.
- Named to NFL 100 All-Time Team in 2019.
- Elected to Pro Football Hall of Fame in 1971.

# 27

## RICK CASARES

A powerful runner who longtime Bears linebacker Doug Buffone called "probably the toughest player pound-for-pound that ever played for the Chicago Bears," Rick Casares spent 10 seasons in the Windy City, rushing for the fourth most yards in franchise history. A major contributor to the Bears' successful run to the 1956 Western Division championship, Casares gained a league-leading 1,126 yards on the ground, establishing in the process a single-season franchise record that stood for another 10 years. The Bears' all-time leader in rushing yards, rushing attempts, and rushing touchdowns at the time of his retirement, Casares earned five Pro Bowl selections and two All-Pro nominations, leaving behind him a legacy that only a few other running backs in team annals have been able to surpass.

Born in Tampa, Florida, on July 4, 1931, Ricardo Jose Casares lost his father in a gangland slaying at the age of seven. Moving with his mother to Paterson, New Jersey, shortly thereafter, Casares grew up in a tough neighborhood, where he took up boxing. Developing a passion for the sport, Casares became a Golden Gloves boxing champion at the age of 15, after which he received a contract to turn pro. But, while young Rick had dreams of one day becoming a world champion, his mother felt differently, angering her son by refusing to sign the contract. Expressing his dissatisfaction with his mother's decision years later, Casares said, "I was frustrated by her decision. I wanted to box and turn pro, and she basically ended that dream."

Sent back to Tampa to live with his father's relatives, Casares subsequently established himself as an exceptional all-around athlete while attending Thomas Jefferson High School, excelling in basketball, football, and track, where he set the state record in the javelin throw. Performing brilliantly on the football field, Casares helped lead Jefferson High to two city championships, with his outstanding play earning him a scholarship to the University of Florida.

Continuing to star in multiple sports while in college, Casares gained All–SEC recognition in both football and basketball, excelling on the gridiron at halfback, fullback, quarterback, punter, and placekicker. However, Casares had to put his education and athletic career on hold after he was drafted into the Army following his junior year in 1953. Yet, even though Casares missed the next two seasons while serving in the military, he previously made such an impression on George Halas that the Bears selected him in the second round of the 1954 NFL Draft, with the 18th overall pick, knowing that he still had one year of military service remaining. Recalling how he learned of his selection by the Bears, Casares revealed, "I was stationed at Fort Jackson, South Carolina, when I got the call from the Bears telling me I was drafted. Honestly, I never dreamt of playing professional football, so, when I got the call, I was shocked."

Before joining the Bears, though, Casares briefly considered traveling north of the border to play for the Canadian Football League's Toronto Argonauts, who offered him the then-exorbitant sum of $20,000 to tote the football for them. But, with George Halas assuring him that the $10,000 contract he presented to him made him the team's highest paid player, Casares eventually decided to sign with the Bears, later telling *Cigar City* magazine, "Of course, I later learned he told everyone their contract was the highest on the team. He was a master negotiator."

Finally arriving in Chicago prior to the start of the 1955 campaign, Casares ended up having a solid rookie season, earning Pro Bowl honors for the first of five straight times by rushing for 672 yards, amassing 808 yards from scrimmage, scoring five touchdowns, and leading the league with a rushing average of 5.4 yards per carry. Casares followed that up with a sensational performance in 1956, gaining First-Team All-Pro recognition by leading the NFL with 1,126 yards rushing, 12 rushing touchdowns, and 14 TDs, while also placing near the top of the league rankings with 1,329 yards from scrimmage, 1,424 all-purpose yards, and a rushing average of 4.8 yards per carry. Although Casares subsequently posted far less impressive numbers in 1957, rushing for 700 yards, amassing 925 yards from scrimmage, scoring six touchdowns, and averaging just 3.4 yards per carry, he still managed to rank among the league leaders in each of the first three categories, earning in the process Second-Team All-Pro honors.

The NFL's most imposing runner, excluding Jim Brown, the 6'2", 226-pound Casares employed a bruising running style in which he attacked anyone who stood in his path. Preferring to run over his opponent, rather than run around him, Casares used his size and strength to his advantage, with Mike Ditka later calling him "the toughest guy I ever played with," and adding, "I idolized him because he was a tough guy that didn't wear it outside. He did everything by example. I saw the guy try to play a game on a broken ankle."

Although Casares assumed less of the team's offensive burden following the arrival of speedy halfback Willie Galimore, he continued his string of five straight Pro Bowl appearances in 1958 and 1959, concluding the first of those campaigns with 651 yards rushing, 941 yards from scrimmage, and three touchdowns, before gaining 699 yards on the ground, amassing 972 yards from scrimmage, and

Rick Casares led the NFL in rushing in 1956.
Courtesy of AlbersheimsStore.com

finishing third in the league with 12 touchdowns in the second. An excellent blocker, Casares further contributed to the Bears' offense by helping to create holes through which Galimore could run.

Although Casares led the Bears in carries (160) and yards rushing (566) for the sixth consecutive time in 1960, he complained publicly about his diminished role in the offense at season's end, prompting an angry George Halas to further reduce his number of carries the following year. Still, Casares made the most of his opportunities, gaining 588 yards on the ground and finishing third in the league with eight rushing touchdowns.

Unfortunately, the 1961 campaign proved to be Casares's last truly productive season. Hampered by injuries to his shoulders and ankle, he assumed a part-time role the following year, spending three more seasons in Chicago, before being dealt to the Washington Redskins following the conclusion of the 1964 campaign. Casares left the Bears with career totals of 5,657 yards rushing, 182 receptions, 1,538 receiving yards, 7,195 yards from scrimmage, 7,308 all-purpose yards, and 59 touchdowns, with 49 of those coming on the ground and the other 10 through the air.

Casares ended up spending just one season in Washington, appearing in only three games with the Redskins, before playing for the AFL's expansion Miami Dolphins in 1966. Announcing his retirement at season's end, Casares returned to his hometown of Tampa, Florida, where he opened a restaurant and spent his remaining years with his wife Polly, whom he met while in college. Looking back on his playing career years later, Casares told *Cigar City* magazine in 2011: "I never cared about individual numbers, but I did care about the NFL Hall of Fame. I think there are players in the Hall who I feel I was better than, but I guess the voters don't see it that way. . . . It would be a great honor. . . . But, if I do not get voted in, oh well. I got paid to play football. How can I complain about that?"

After undergoing numerous surgeries following the conclusion of his playing career, including two knee replacements, an ankle replacement, a shoulder replacement, and surgeries on his wrist and ribs, Casares suffered a heart attack that claimed his life on September 13, 2013. Upon his death at the age of 82, Casares's wife said, "Our mailbox was full every day. He answered everyone. He was just so flattered to be remembered."

## BEARS CAREER HIGHLIGHTS

### Best Season

Casares had easily the greatest season of his career in 1956, when he earned his lone First-Team All-Pro nomination by leading the NFL with 234 carries, 1,126 yards rushing, 12 rushing TDs, and 14 touchdowns, with his 1,126 yards gained on the ground representing the second-highest single-season total in league history at the time.

### Memorable Moments/Greatest Performances

Casares led the Bears to a 38–10 win over the Baltimore Colts on October 16, 1955, by carrying the ball nine times for 94 yards and two touchdowns, one of which came on a career-long 81-yard run.

Casares rushed for more than 100 yards for the first time in his career during a 52–31 victory over the Packers on November 6, 1955, gaining 115 yards on 16 carries.

Casares turned in an outstanding all-around effort against the Packers on October 7, 1956, leading the Bears to a 37–21 win by rushing for 139 yards, making three receptions for 50 yards, and scoring a pair of touchdowns.

Casares followed that up with another strong outing one week later, rushing for 112 yards and two touchdowns during a convincing 31–7 victory over the San Francisco 49ers.

Continuing his exceptional play against Baltimore on October 21, 1956, Casares rushed for 124 yards and two touchdowns during a 58–27 Bears win.

Although Casares gained only 57 yards on the ground during a 38–21 win over the 49ers the following week, he scored four times on short runs.

Casares led the Bears to a 35–24 victory over the Rams on November 4, 1956, by carrying the ball 25 times for 132 yards.

Casares rushed for a career-high 190 yards and one touchdown during a 38–21 win over the Detroit Lions in the final game of the 1956 regular season, with his TD coming on a 68-yard run.

Casares had another big game against the Lions on November 24, 1957, rushing for 116 yards and two touchdowns during a 27–7 Bears win.

Casares starred during a 24–10 victory over the Packers on November 9, 1958, carrying the ball 15 times for 113 yards and one touchdown, which came on a 64-yard run.

Casares proved to be the difference in a 27–21 win over the Steelers on December 6, 1959, rushing for 90 yards and four touchdowns, all of which came on runs of less than 5 yards.

Casares again lit the scoreboard multiple times during a 28–24 win over the Rams on November 26, 1961, gaining 78 yards on the ground and recording three short TD runs.

### Notable Achievements

- Rushed for more than 1,000 yards once (1,126 in 1956).
- Surpassed 1,000 yards from scrimmage once (1,329 in 1956), topping 900 yards three other times.
- Scored more than 10 touchdowns twice.
- Averaged more than 5 yards per carry once (5.4 in 1955).
- Led NFL in rushing attempts twice, yards rushing once, rushing touchdowns once, touchdowns once, and average yards per carry once.
- Finished second in NFL in rushing attempts once, yards rushing once, yards from scrimmage once, rushing touchdowns once, and points scored once.
- Finished third in NFL in rushing touchdowns twice and touchdowns scored once.
- Led Bears in rushing six times.

- Ranks among Bears career leaders with 1,386 rushing attempts (4th), 5,657 yards rushing (4th), 7,195 yards from scrimmage (4th), 49 rushing touchdowns (3rd), and 59 touchdowns (4th).
- Two-time division champion (1956 and 1963).
- 1963 NFL champion.
- Five-time Pro Bowl selection (1955, 1956, 1957, 1958, and 1959).
- 1956 First-Team All-Pro selection.
- 1957 Second-Team All-Pro selection.
- Two-time First-Team All–Western Conference selection (1956 and 1957).

# 28

# — STEVE MCMICHAEL —

**A** force on the interior of the Bears defense for more than a decade, Steve McMichael spent 13 seasons in Chicago anchoring one of the NFL's most formidable units from his left tackle position. Starting at that post from 1983 to 1993, McMichael helped the Bears win six division titles, one NFC championship, and one Super Bowl with his superior play against both the run and the pass, which earned him two Pro Bowl selections and four All-Pro nominations. One of the franchise's all-time leaders in sacks, tackles, and fumble recoveries, McMichael also proved to be one of the most durable players in team annals, appearing in 191 consecutive non-strike games during his time in the Windy City.

Born in Houston, Texas, on October 17, 1957, Stephen Douglas McMichael attended Freer High School, where he displayed an incredible amount of versatility on the gridiron. In addition to excelling at tackle, tight end, and fullback on offense, McMichael played end, tackle, and linebacker on defense, while also handling kickoff, extra-point, and field goal duties. Commenting on the youngster's performance on the defensive side of the ball, McMichael's college coach, Fred Akers, said, "He backed the line as well as anybody we've seen in high school. But he did it at Freer, so you don't know how that'll work out."

Everything worked out just fine after McMichael enrolled at the University of Texas, with the big defensive lineman forcing 11 fumbles and recording 30 sacks for the Longhorns from 1976 to 1979, with his dominant play at the point of attack earning him consensus First-Team All-America honors as a senior. Subsequently selected by the New England Patriots in the third round of the 1980 NFL Draft, with the 73rd overall pick, McMichael appeared in only six games as a rookie, before being released by the Patriots at the end of the year. Signed by the Bears shortly thereafter, McMichael spent the next two seasons assuming a backup role in Chicago, before finally breaking into the starting lineup in 1983.

Establishing himself as one of the Bears' better defensive players before long, McMichael made 37 tackles and finished second on the team with 8½ sacks in 1983, even though he started just 10 games. Improving upon those numbers the following year, the man who came to be known as "Mongo" recorded 42 tackles and 10 sacks for a Bears team that ended up losing to the San Francisco 49ers in the NFC championship game. McMichael then gained First-Team All-Pro recognition in 1985 by registering eight sacks and 44 tackles for the league's number 1 ranked defense, in helping the Bears capture the NFL championship. Continuing to perform at an extremely high level from 1986 to 1989, McMichael averaged 8½ sacks and 86 tackles during that four-year period, earning in the process Pro Bowl and All-Pro honors twice each.

Steve McMichael acquired the nickname "Mongo" during his time in Chicago.
Courtesy of George A. Kitrinos

Excelling against the run, McMichael did an outstanding job of using his burly 6'2", 270-pound frame to clog up the middle against opposing ball-carriers, enabling him to record more than 85 tackles in five different seasons. McMichael also possessed the strength and agility to emerge victorious whenever he faced single blocking in passing situations, allowing him to register at least 10 sacks three times.

One of the Bears' most popular players, McMichael became a favorite of the fans and local media because of his colorful personality, controversial comments, and insane antics that included howling like a hungry wolf on the practice field from time to time and stomping around the locker room wearing nothing but his game shoes in an effort to break in his cleats by game day. He also made it a practice to crash-test his helmet in the bathroom by banging his head against the wall several times, while screaming, "I feel nine or 10 sacks in this thing!"

McMichael's teammates had no problem with his outlandish behavior because they greatly appreciated everything he brought to the team. Speaking on his line-mate's behalf on one occasion, Dan Hampton said, "Nowadays, a lot of guys aren't willing to sacrifice themselves for the team because they're thinking about the big money down the road if they stay healthy. He's a guy you want in a foxhole with you, a tough guy in the old-fashioned sense of the term. Steve's attitude is, 'Damn the future, let's see who's better today.'"

Mike Ditka, who once called McMichael the toughest player he ever coached, stated, "Nobody loved Steve McMichael more than I did because he was my kind of player. He gave you everything he had."

And, as for his famous nickname, McMichael said, "Mongo was a character I played to intimidate the other team. And, when the other team underestimates you, it's their ass."

Although McMichael continued his string of 191 consecutive games played in 1990, he started only seven contests, limiting him to just four sacks and 71 tackles. However, after regaining his starting job the following year, McMichael went on to start every game in each of the next three seasons, gaining Second-Team All-Pro recognition in 1991 by recording nine sacks and 94 tackles, before registering 10½ sacks and 89 tackles in the ensuing campaign. Despite turning 36 years of age during the early stages of the 1993 season, McMichael continued to perform well, recording six sacks and 78 tackles, while also serving as a mentor to the team's younger defensive players brought in by new head coach Dave Wannstedt. But, with the Bears seeking to reduce his salary from $1 million to $300,000 at season's end to accommodate the league's new salary cap, McMichael signed a $450,000 one-year free-agent deal with the arch-rival Green Bay Packers, leaving Chicago with career totals of 92½ sacks, 814 tackles, 12 forced fumbles, 16 fumble recoveries, three safeties, and two interceptions, with his 92½ sacks representing the second-highest total in team annals and his three safeties representing a franchise record.

Expressing his satisfaction with the situation in Green Bay shortly after he joined the Packers, McMichael told *Sports Illustrated*, "I feel like I've been reborn in Green Bay. The people in this town revere the game. They're like rabid dogs. I feel young again. It doesn't matter which side of the Packer-Bear rivalry I'm playing on, as long as I'm playing in it."

McMichael ended up spending one year in Green Bay, recording just 2½ sacks and 28 tackles while starting at right tackle for the Packers in 1994, before announcing his retirement at season's end. Following his playing days, McMichael began a four-year career in wrestling, working for World Championship Wrestling (WCW) from 1996 to 1999, first as an announcer, and then as a wrestler. He later spent seven seasons serving as head coach of the Chicago Slaughter of the Indoor Football League. McMichael currently co-hosts a Bears pregame show with Jeff Dickerson on ESPN 1000 in Chicago.

## BEARS CAREER HIGHLIGHTS

### Best Season

Although McMichael earned First-Team All-Pro honors for the only two times in his career in 1985 and 1987, he performed slightly better in a few other seasons. En route to earning a Second-Team All-Pro nomination from the Newspaper Enterprise Association in 1988, McMichael recorded 88 tackles and a career-high 11½ sacks. He followed that up by registering 7½ sacks and a career-best 108 tackles in 1989. McMichael also recorded 10½ sacks, 89 tackles, and four forced fumbles in 1992. However, he had his finest all-around season for the Bears in 1986, earning Second-Team All-Pro honors for one of two times by registering eight sacks and 87 tackles (61 solo), intercepting a pass, forcing one fumble, and recovering two others, with his outstanding play on the interior of Chicago's d-line helping the Bears finish first in the league in points and yards allowed on defense.

### Memorable Moments/Greatest Performances

McMichael recorded the first two sacks of his career during a 20–17 win over the Lions on November 21, 1982.

McMichael sacked Joe Montana twice during a 13–3 win over the 49ers on November 27, 1983.

McMichael earned NFC Defensive Player of the Week honors by recording 2½ sacks during the Bears' 30–13 win over the Lions in the final game of the 1984 regular season.

McMichael registered the first of his franchise-record three career safeties when he brought down Green Bay quarterback Jim Zorn in the end zone during a 16–10 Bears win on November 3, 1985.

McMichael contributed to a 25–12 victory over the Packers on September 22, 1986, by recording two sacks, one of which resulted in a safety.

McMichael registered 2½ sacks during a 30–24 win over the Vikings on December 6, 1987.

McMichael helped lead the Bears to a 17–7 win over the Cowboys on October 16, 1988, by sacking Danny White three times.

McMichael made a huge play against the New York Jets on September 23, 1991, when, with the Bears trailing by a score of 13–6 and just 1:54 remaining in the fourth quarter, he forced a fumble by running back Blair Thomas, which he recovered at the New York 36 yard line. Quarterback Jim Harbaugh subsequently threw a game-tying touchdown pass to Neal

Anderson with only 18 seconds left on the clock. The Bears then went on to win the game in overtime when Harbaugh scored a touchdown on a 1-yard run.

### Notable Achievements

- Recorded second-longest consecutive games played streak in franchise history, appearing in 191 straight contests from 1981 to 1993.
- Recorded at least 10 sacks three times.
- Recorded more than 100 tackles once (108 in 1989), topping 80 tackles four other times.
- Led Bears in sacks twice.
- Holds Bears career record for most safeties (3).
- Ranks among Bears career leaders with 92½ sacks (2nd), 814 solo tackles (7th), 16 fumble recoveries (5th), and 191 games played (tied-2nd).
- Six-time division champion (1984, 1985, 1986, 1987, 1988, and 1990).
- 1985 NFC champion.
- Super Bowl XX champion.
- 1984 Week 16 NFC Defensive Player of the Week.
- Two-time Pro Bowl selection (1986 and 1987).
- Two-time First-Team All-Pro selection (1985 and 1987).
- Two-time Second-Team All-Pro selection (1986 and 1991).
- Two-time First-Team All-NFC selection (1986 and 1987).
- 1985 Second-Team All-NFC selection.
- Pro Football Reference All-1980s Second Team.

# 29

# RICHIE PETITBON

A n outstanding all-around athlete with an extremely high football IQ, Richie Petitbon spent 10 of his 14 NFL seasons in Chicago and established himself as one of the finest safeties in franchise history. Blessed with good size, exceptional speed, and the ability to see the entire field of play, Petitbon recorded the second-most interceptions in team annals, earning in the process four Pro Bowl selections and three All-Pro nominations. Extremely durable, Petitbon never missed a game in his 10 seasons with the Bears, appearing in 136 consecutive contests. Continuing to perform at an elite level after leaving Chicago following the conclusion of the 1968 campaign, Petitbon picked off 11 more passes while playing for the Los Angeles Rams and Washington Redskins, before beginning an extremely successful career in coaching.

Born to a French immigrant father and an American mother in New Orleans, Louisiana, on April 18, 1938, Richard Alvin Petitbon attended local Jesuit High School, where, in addition to serving as a member of a state championship football team in 1953, he starred in track and field. After turning down scholarship offers to play football at Louisiana State University and Tulane, Petitbon accepted a track and field scholarship to Loyola University, where he planned to study dentistry. However, after Loyola track coach "Boo" Jones attempted to convert him from a sprinter into a quarter-miler, Petitbon transferred to Tulane University at the end of his freshman year.

Developing into a two-way star on the gridiron while at Tulane, Petitbon excelled at quarterback and defensive back for the Green Wave, earning All–SEC honors as a junior by completing 52.8 percent of his passes, throwing for 728 yards and three touchdowns, and running for 188 yards and five TDs, while also averaging 27.6 yards per kickoff return. Subsequently selected by the Bears in the second round of the 1959 NFL Draft, with the 21st overall pick, even though he still had one year of college eligibility remaining, Petitbon chose to forgo his senior year and enter the NFL immediately.

Earning a starting job as a rookie, Petitbon performed well at cornerback, recording three interceptions, one of which he returned for a touchdown. Moved to safety by George Halas the following year, Petitbon quickly developed into one of the league's better players at that position, recording a total of 19 interceptions from 1961 to 1963. Playing his best ball for the Bears in 1962 and 1963, Petitbon gained Pro Bowl and All-Pro recognition both years, picking off six passes and leading the NFL with 212 interception-return yards in the first of those campaigns, before ranking among the league leaders with eight interceptions and 161 interception-return yards in the second.

In addition to using his speed, instincts, and intelligence to establish himself as one of the league's top ball-hawks, the 6'3", 206-pound Petitbon became known as a brutal tackler who instilled fear in opposing ball-carriers. A thinking man's football player, the well-read Petitbon also developed a reputation for being more worldly and thoughtful than most of his peers, contributing greatly to the success he later experienced as a defensive coordinator.

After failing to garner postseason honors in either of the previous two campaigns, Petitbon made the Pro Bowl in both 1966 and 1967, picking off a total of nine passes over the course of those two seasons. Petitbon then spent one more year in Chicago, before being dealt to the Los Angeles Rams prior to the start of the 1969 campaign. In his 10 seasons with the Bears, Petitbon recorded 37 interceptions, amassed 643 interception-return yards, recovered seven fumbles, and scored three touchdowns, with his 37 picks remaining a franchise record until Gary Fencik set a new mark nearly two decades later. Meanwhile, Petitbon's 643 interception-return yards also represent the second-highest total in franchise history.

After leaving the Bears, Petitbon split the next four years between the Los Angeles Rams

Richie Petitbon ranks second in franchise history in interceptions and interception-return yards.
Courtesy of MEARSonlineauctions.com

and the Washington Redskins, helping the former win a division title in 1969 and the latter capture the NFC championship in 1972, before announcing his retirement following the conclusion of the 1972 campaign. Ending his career with 48 interceptions, 801 interception-return yards, 13 fumble recoveries, and three touchdowns, Petitbon later received the honor of being named to the Pro Football Reference All-1960s Second Team.

Following his playing days, Petitbon began his coaching career in Houston, spending four years serving as an assistant under Oilers head coach Bum Phillips, before returning to Washington in 1978 to coach the Redskins' defensive secondary. Promoted to defensive coordinator when Joe Gibbs assumed head-coaching duties in Washington in 1981, Petitbon spent the next 12 years fulfilling that role, helping to lead the Redskins to three NFL championships. Named head coach when Gibbs retired in 1993, Petitbon remained in that position for just one season, before being relieved of his duties after the Redskins finished just 4-12 in 1993. Following his dismissal by Redskins owner Jack Kent Cooke, Petitbon never took another job in the NFL. Choosing to retire from football, Petitbon remained in the DC area until eventually moving to Virginia, where he became an avid golfer.

## BEARS CAREER HIGHLIGHTS

### Best Season

Petitbon had an outstanding season for the Bears in 1962, earning Second-Team All-Pro honors by intercepting six passes and setting a single-season franchise record by leading the NFL with 212 interception-return yards. Nevertheless, he performed slightly better the following year, gaining First-Team All-Pro recognition and helping the Bears capture the NFL championship in 1963 by recording a career-high eight interceptions, which he returned for a total of 161 yards.

### Memorable Moments/Greatest Performances

In an October 3, 1959, contest the Bears went on to win by a score of 26–21, Petitbon gave them an early 6–0 lead over the Baltimore Colts by returning his interception of a Johnny Unitas pass 33 yards for a touchdown.

Petitbon recorded a key interception during a 17–14 win over the Browns on December 10, 1961, subsequently returning the ball 43 yards into Cleveland territory.

Almost exactly one year later, during a 30–14 win over the Los Angeles Rams on December 9, 1962, Petitbon made the most memorable play of his career when he returned his interception of a Zeke Bratkowski pass 101 yards for a touchdown. Recalling the play years later, Petitbon said, "The Rams were driving toward what was home at Wrigley Field. We doubled the wide receiver, and I don't know if Bratkowski just didn't see it or what." After picking off Bratkowski's pass, Petitbon raced up the sideline, untouched, for a 101-yard return, remembering, "The first 50 yards, I was worried that someone was going to catch me, and the last 50 yards, I was afraid they weren't going to catch me."

Petitbon recorded another pick-six during a 37–21 win over the Detroit Lions on September 29, 1963, this time returning the ball 66 yards for a touchdown.

Petitbon intercepted two passes in one game for the first time in his career during a 27–7 victory over the San Francisco 49ers on December 8, 1963.

Petitbon played a huge role in the Bears' 14–10 win over the Giants in the 1963 NFL championship game, recovering a fumble early in the fourth quarter, before securing the victory with an end zone interception of a desperation pass thrown by Y. A. Tittle in the game's closing moments.

Although the Bears lost to the Packers by a score of 13–10 on September 24, 1967, Petitbon intercepted Bart Starr three times, returning his picks a total of 41 yards.

## Notable Achievements

- Never missed a game in his 10 seasons with the Bears, appearing in 136 consecutive contests.
- Recorded at least five interceptions four times.
- Amassed more than 100 interception-return yards twice.
- Led NFL with 212 interception-return yards in 1962.
- Finished third in NFL with eight interceptions in 1963.
- Led Bears in interceptions three times.
- Holds Bears single-game record for most interceptions (3 vs. Green Bay on September 24, 1967).
- Holds Bears single-season record for most interception-return yards (212 in 1962).
- Ranks among Bears career leaders with 37 interceptions (2nd), 643 interception-return yards (2nd), and three touchdown interceptions (tied-5th).

- 1963 division champion.
- 1963 NFL champion.
- Four-time Pro Bowl selection (1962, 1963, 1966, and 1967).
- 1963 First-Team All-Pro selection.
- Two-time Second-Team All-Pro selection (1962 and 1967).
- 1966 First-Team All–Western Conference selection.
- Pro Football Reference All-1960s Second Team.

# 30

## — JOE STYDAHAR —

The first lineman ever taken in the NFL Draft, and the first player ever selected by the Bears, "Jumbo" Joe Stydahar proved to be a pillar of strength on both sides of the ball during his nine seasons in Chicago. Excelling at tackle on both offense and defense, Stydahar helped lead the Bears to five division titles and three NFL championships between 1936 and 1946, with his dominant line play earning him four Pro Bowl selections, five All-Pro nominations, spots on the NFL 1930s All-Decade Team and the league's 75th Anniversary All-Time Two-Way Team, and a place in the Pro Football Hall of Fame.

Born in Kaylor, Pennsylvania, on March 17, 1912, Joseph Lee Stydahar moved with his family to Shinnston, West Virginia, at the age of eight, after which he spent part of his youth working with his Yugoslavian immigrant father in the coal mines. Starring in multiple sports while attending Shinnston High School, Stydahar, according to an article in the September 20, 1931, edition of the *Pittsburgh Press*, established himself as "the greatest schoolboy football and basketball player ever turned out by West Virginia."

Having earned All-Eastern honors on the gridiron while at Shinnston, Stydahar subsequently found himself being recruited by both the University of Pittsburgh and West Virginia University, with the latter ultimately procuring his services by hiding him in a fraternity house until Pittsburgh gave up looking for him.

Continuing to compete in multiple sports while at West Virginia, Stydahar served as captain of the school's basketball and football teams, manning the center position on the hardwood, while also excelling as a two-way tackle on the gridiron from 1933 to 1935. Gaining widespread acclaim for his outstanding play on both sides of the ball, Stydahar developed a reputation as a vicious tackler and bruising blocker, earning mention as an "unsung All-American" despite the lack of overall success experienced by WVU on the playing field. In discussing Stydahar, who blocked five punts and scored one touchdown on special teams as a junior in 1934, Heisman

Trophy winner Jay Berwanger said, "I played in two all-star games with him and thought he was the best tackle by far of that collegiate group. He proved to me in those two games that he was a tremendous player."

Subsequently selected by the Bears with the sixth overall pick of the first-ever NFL Draft held in 1936, Stydahar made an immediate impact as a rookie after laying claim to the starting left tackle job, gaining Second-Team All-Pro recognition by helping the Bears compile a record of 9-3. Establishing himself as the league's premier player at his position the following year, Stydahar earned First-Team All-Pro honors for the first of four straight times, tallying more points than any other player at any position in voting for the Associated Press All-Pro team, with the AP reporting:

> The standout player of the 1937 national pro football league season wasn't Slingin' Sammy Baugh, but Joe Stydahar, veteran tackle of the Chicago Bears. That was the way the coaches of the 10 league clubs figured, at least, when it came to casting their ballots for the All-League team. . . . Stydahar received 43 points out of a possible 50.

Stydahar also fared extremely well in the 1939 balloting, amassing the third-highest point total of any player in the league, with only Green Bay receiver Don Hutson and Bears teammate Dan Fortmann receiving more support.

Much of the success Stydahar experienced could be attributed to his tremendous power and outstanding speed. Despite being one of the league's biggest players throughout his career, Stydahar, who stood 6'4" and weighed almost 260 pounds, exhibited surprising quickness for a man of his proportions. He also possessed extremely large hands, which he used to ward off his opponent on both sides of the line of scrimmage.

One of the league's most intense players, Stydahar found himself unable to take the field on game day until he relieved the nervous tension in his stomach, with George Halas revealing years later:

> He could never eat breakfast on the morning of a game. In fact, Joe couldn't even stay in the locker room with the players because he always suffered a series of stomach eruptions starting about one hour before kickoff. The players called Joe's stomach "Old Faithful." You could set your watch by it. If some last-minute detail came up, one of the assistant coaches would have to run down to the

lavatory to tell Joe about it. . . . What Joe needed to quiet his stomach was a couple of good hard tackles—and he always got plenty once the game started.

Stydahar continued to dominate the opposition on both sides of the ball until he entered the Navy in 1943 to serve his country during World War II. During his two-year stint in the military, Stydahar served as a lieutenant and gunnery officer aboard the USS *Monterey* light aircraft carrier.

Displaying a considerable amount of rust upon his return to the Bears in 1945, Stydahar lost his starting job to veteran Al Babartsky. Appearing in only three games over the course of the campaign, the 33-year-old Stydahar made very little impact on a Bears team that finished just 3-7. When asked by George Halas at season's end how much he wished to be paid the following year, Stydahar answered, "I'm all washed up. Write in whatever you consider the right amount, and I'll sign it."

Exhibiting his appreciation for the many contributions Stydahar had made to the Bears through the years, Halas ended up paying the aging veteran twice what he had made before entering the service. Although Stydahar once again assumed a backup role in 1946, he provided veteran leadership to a Bears squad that went on to win the NFL championship—his third as a member of the team.

Choosing to announce his retirement following the conclusion of the campaign, Stydahar ended his playing career having appeared in a total of 84 games, recording during those contests one pass reception, one interception, two fumble recoveries, and 28 points, which came on 28 of 31 successful extra-point attempts as a part-time kicker.

Following his playing days, Stydahar began a career in coaching, serving as head

Joe Stydahar earned a spot on the NFL 1930s All-Decade Team with his outstanding play on both sides of the ball. Courtesy of RMYAuctions.com coach of the Los Angeles Rams from 1950 to 1952 and the Chicago Cardinals from 1953 to 1954. After being released by the Cardinals, Stydahar remained in the Chicago area, where he had formed a cardboard box business with a partner. Hired by George Halas as the Bears defensive line coach in 1963, Stydahar fulfilled that role for two years, before resigning from his position at the end of 1964, so that he might return to his cardboard box business. In his later years, Stydahar lived in Highland Park, Illinois, where he served as eastern regional manager for a container company until he suffered a fatal heart attack while on a business trip in Beckley, West Virginia, on March 23, 1977, just one week after celebrating his 65th birthday.

Upon learning of his passing, George Halas said, "Joe was something special for me. Football fans know him as the finest lineman drafted in the first round in 1936, as a true All-Pro, as a great football player, as one of the Bears' all-time greats, and as a Hall of Famer. But more important than any of the football accomplishments, Joe Stydahar was a man of outstanding character and loyalty . . . all things that made Joe a great football player were reflected in his successful business career."

## CAREER HIGHLIGHTS

### Best Season

Stydahar played his best ball for the Bears from 1937 to 1940, earning All-Pro honors in each of those four seasons. However, he gained consensus First-Team All-Pro recognition for the only time in his career in 1939, when, in addition to finishing third among all NFL players in points received in the AP All-Pro voting, he was rated as "the league's best tackle" and "one of the toughest linemen in the league to take out" by the United Press.

### Memorable Moments/Greatest Performances

Stydahar's superb blocking at the point of attack helped the Bears amass 406 yards of total offense during a 24–6 victory over the Brooklyn Dodgers on November 20, 1938, with 234 of those yards coming on the ground.

Stydahar once again dominated his opponent at the line of scrimmage in the 1939 regular-season opener, helping the Bears rush for 282 yards and amass 411 yards of total offense during a 30–21 win over the Cleveland Rams.

Stydahar recorded the only interception of his career in 1941, when he picked off a pass and returned the ball 55 yards into the opponent's territory.

## Notable Achievements

- Five-time division champion (1937, 1940, 1941, 1942, and 1946).
- Three-time NFL champion (1940, 1941, and 1946).
- Four-time Pro Bowl selection (1938, 1939, 1940, and 1941).
- Four-time First-Team All-Pro selection (1937, 1938, 1939, and 1940).
- 1936 Second-Team All-Pro selection.
- NFL 1930s All-Decade Team.
- Named to NFL's 75th Anniversary All-Time Two-Way Team in 1994.
- Elected to Pro Football Hall of Fame in 1967.

# 31

# GEORGE MUSSO

he first player in NFL history to earn All-Pro honors at two different positions on offense, George Musso spent his entire 12-year NFL career in Chicago, gaining All-Pro recognition a total of five times as a guard and tackle. Excelling at both posts for the Bears, Musso helped anchor the right side of Chicago's offensive line, while also serving as team captain for nine seasons. A durable 60-minute man, Musso starred as a middle guard (nose tackle) on defense as well, with his exceptional all-around play helping the Bears capture seven division titles and four league championships. Honored for his outstanding play on both sides of the ball long after he retired from the game, Musso received the distinctions of being named to the NFL's 75th Anniversary All-Time Two-Way Team and being elected to the Pro Football Hall of Fame.

Born in Collinsville, Illinois, on April 8, 1910, George Francis Musso starred in multiple sports while attending Collinsville High School, prompting James Millikin University to offer him an athletic scholarship. Continuing to compete in several sports while in college, Musso excelled in football, baseball, basketball, and track and field, with his exceptional play on the gridiron convincing George Halas to invite him to the Bears' training camp for a tryout in 1933.

Although the 6'2" Musso, who spent most of his pro career playing at close to 270 pounds, possessed great size for a player of his day, his awkwardness and overall physical appearance instilled serious doubts in Halas as to whether the massive lineman had any real chance of making the team when he first arrived at training camp. After seeing a picture of Musso sporting a mustache and wearing a Millikin College basketball uniform, Red Grange told Halas, "This guy will never make it. He looks like a walrus." And, after watching Musso at his first practice session, Halas agreed with Grange, telling him, "That kid is fat, slow, and ugly. You were right."

Nevertheless, star running back Bronko Nagurski, who befriended Musso during training camp, saw something in the youngster, looking past his heavy face and oddly proportioned body. Interceding on Musso's behalf when Halas informed the rookie that he planned to send him to a minor-league team in Cincinnati, Nagurski convinced the head coach to allow him to remain with the team for a few weeks. Nagurski then spent a considerable amount of time working with Musso, helping him to greatly improve his footwork and technique on both sides of the ball, with his protégé soon becoming a significant contributor on both offense and defense.

After laying claim to the starting right tackle job on offense midway through his rookie campaign, Musso remained the starter at that position in each of the next three seasons, earning Second-Team All-Pro honors in both 1933 and 1935. Shifted to right guard prior to the start of the 1937 campaign, Musso manned that post for the remainder of his career, gaining Pro Bowl and All-Pro recognition three times each over the course of his final eight seasons.

Although Musso performed extremely well at tackle, he proved to be even more effective at guard, with George Halas stating on one occasion, "George Musso is the greatest guard in the professional football ranks." Excelling as a downfield blocker,

George Musso earned All-Pro honors as both a guard and tackle on offense.
Courtesy of RMYAuctions.com

Musso explained the speed he exhibited when leading the way for Bronko Nagurski by saying, "If you didn't open the hole, he'd hit you in the back, and the next time you'd either open it or get out of the way quick."

An exceptional defender as well, Musso used his considerable bulk to clog up the middle against the run, often forcing opposing teams to alter their game plans on offense. Meanwhile, in discussing Musso's deceptive speed, teammate Aldo Forte said that he had "the mobility and quickness of a giant cat," adding, "He personified the Bears. Halas was 'Poppa Bear,' but teammates and opponents called George 'Big Bear.'"

Known affectionately to his teammates as "Moose," Musso spent his last nine years in Chicago serving as team captain, with Red Grange claiming that everyone on the squad had so much respect for him that "they wouldn't have anyone else."

After leading the Bears to the NFL championship in three of the previous four seasons, Musso assumed a somewhat diminished role in 1944, surrendering his starting job to 26-year-old rookie George Zorich. Choosing to announce his retirement following the conclusion of the campaign, Musso ended his playing career having appeared in 128 regular-season games and eight postseason contests, winning four of the seven championship games in which he competed. In addition to his many other accomplishments, Musso can lay claim to being the only player in NFL history to face two future presidents of the United States on the playing field. During his days at Millikin, Musso lined up against the much-lighter Ronald Reagan in a game against Eureka College. And, while playing for the Bears, he squared off against Gerald Ford, an All-American center from Michigan, during the 1935 College All-Star Game.

Following his playing days, Musso retired to Edwardsville, Illinois, where he opened a restaurant. He also later served as sheriff of Madison County, Illinois, and as county treasurer from the 1950s to the 1970s. After being involved in a near-fatal automobile accident in 1962 that left him with multiple fractures in his legs and pelvis, Musso lived another 38 years, passing away at his home in Edwardsville at the age of 90 on September 5, 2000, 18 years after the Pro Football Hall of Fame opened its doors to him.

## CAREER HIGHLIGHTS

### Best Season

Musso gained First-Team All-Pro recognition for the only time in his career in 1937, when he helped the Bears outscore their opponents by a combined margin of 201–100, en route to compiling a record of 9-1-1 during the regular season.

### Memorable Moments/Greatest Performances

Musso contributed to a 12–9 win over the Chicago Cardinals on October 15, 1933, when he blocked a punt out of the end zone, resulting in a safety for the Bears.

Musso's outstanding blocking at the point of attack helped running back Beattie Feathers rush for a game-high 114 yards and two touchdowns during a 41–7 rout of the Cincinnati Reds on October 21, 1934.

Musso once again dominated his opponent at the line of scrimmage on November 4, 1934, helping the Bears rush for 185 yards and amass nearly 300 yards of total offense during a 27–7 win over the Giants.

In addition to excelling on the offensive side of the ball, Musso recorded a sack during the Bears' 73–0 victory over the Washington Redskins in the 1940 NFL championship game.

### Notable Achievements

- Seven-time division champion (1933, 1934, 1937, 1940, 1941, 1942, and 1943).
- Four-time NFL champion (1933, 1940, 1941, and 1943).
- Three-time Pro Bowl selection (1939, 1940, and 1941).
- 1937 First-Team All-Pro selection.
- Four-time Second-Team All-Pro selection (1933, 1935, 1938, and 1939).
- Named to NFL's 75th Anniversary All-Time Two-Way Team in 1994.
- Elected to Pro Football Hall of Fame in 1982.

# 32

# JIMBO COVERT

Called "the best offensive tackle in the NFL" by teammate Walter Payton, Jimbo Covert ranked among the league's finest players at his position for most of his eight-year career, with only Cincinnati's Hall of Fame left tackle Anthony Munoz surpassing him in the eyes of many. An outstanding run-blocker who also excelled at providing blindside protection for the many quarterbacks that lined up behind center for the Bears from 1983 to 1990, Covert proved to be an invaluable member of Chicago teams that won six division titles, one NFC championship, and one Super Bowl. A two-time Pro Bowler, two-time All-Pro, and four-time All-NFC selection, Covert received the additional distinctions of being named NFC Offensive Lineman of the Year one season, before garnering NFL Offensive Lineman of the Year honors in the next. And, had Covert not been forced to retire early due to a badly injured back, he likely would have gained induction to the Pro Football Hall of Fame much earlier than he did.

Born in the steel-making town of Conway, Pennsylvania, on March 22, 1960, James Paul Covert attended Freedom Area High School in Beaver County, where he made a name for himself as an All-America wrestler and standout defensive lineman, helping lead the Bulldogs to a perfect 11-0 record and the Midwestern Athletic Conference (MAC) Championship as a senior in 1977. Recruited by several colleges after being named First-Team All-State by UPI, Covert ultimately chose to accept a scholarship from the University of Pittsburgh, where he spent his freshman year sitting on the bench, before redshirting the following season after injuring his shoulder. Upon returning to the team for spring practice, Covert asked to be moved to the offensive side of the ball, where he ended up starring at tackle for the next three seasons. Helping the Panthers compile an overall record of 31-5 during that time, Covert received First-Team All-America recognition from *Football News* and the Newspaper Enterprise Association (NEA) as a junior, before earning consensus All-America honors in his senior year, when he did not allow a single sack.

Flourishing under the tutelage of line coach Joe Moore while at Pitt, Covert received high praise from his mentor, who once said, "Jimbo is so good, it's like watching a clinic film. . . . After a play, I'm never surprised to see Jimbo and his man 10 or 15 yards downfield."

Extremely impressed with Covert's exceptional play at the collegiate level, the Bears made him the sixth overall pick of the 1983 NFL Draft, with head coach Mike Ditka later stating, "Jimbo's the guy we wanted. From Day 1, we put him at left tackle and moved on. You don't get too many people who come along who can make that impact. He had the respect of all his teammates and all his coaches."

Performing brilliantly his first year in the league, Covert earned a spot on the 1983 NFL All-Rookie Team by helping the Bears top the circuit in yards rushing for the first of four straight times. Covert also made a huge impact by raising the confidence level of the team's previously beleaguered offense, which had been abused by the club's more assertive defense for years. Recalling an incident that took place one day in practice after a whistle, fullback Matt Suhey revealed that 6'2", 270-pound defensive tackle Steve McMichael bumped the 6'4", 277-pound Covert, who subsequently turned and glared at his assailant. The two men then exchanged words, which led to shoves, with Suhey saying, "McMi-

Although injuries shortened his career, Jimbo Covert established himself as one of the finest offensive tackles in football during his time in Chicago.
Courtesy of MEARSonlineauctions.com

chael was a tough guy and a great player in his own right, but he picked on the wrong guy. Next thing I know, I saw McMichael's feet over his head and bam, right to the ground. He body slammed him and pancaked him. There weren't too many guys in the league who could have done that."

Mike Ditka, who observed the fracas from the sidelines, commented, "That set the tone for our offense, and our offense got better after that."

Named offensive co-captain the following year, Covert continued his exceptional play in each of the next three seasons, gaining Pro Bowl and

First-Team All-Pro recognition in both 1985 and 1986, while also being named NFC Offensive Lineman of the Year by the NFL Players Association in the first of those campaigns and being accorded NFL Offensive Lineman of the Year honors in the second. Meanwhile, as the individual accolades continued to mount, Covert established himself as one of the most respected tackles in the league, with Washington Redskins All-Pro defensive end Dexter Manley stating, "I think he's the best tackle in the game. It's between him and the kid from Minnesota, Gary Zimmerman."

Matt Suhey expressed his admiration for his former teammate by saying, "Everyone had tremendous respect for Jimbo. He had great leadership in his play, and he had a voice."

Suhey then added, "Everybody knew how good he was. He could pass protect, run block, everything. He had such great feet and such tremendous upper body strength. He and [Hall of Fame guard] Mike Munchak were the best linemen I played with, by far."

Perhaps the greatest praise for Covert, though, came from Hall of Fame head coach Bill Parcells, whose New York Giants squared off against the Bears three times between 1985 and 1990. With Covert holding legendary Giants pass-rusher Lawrence Taylor to no sacks in each of those three meetings, Parcells later told Dan Pompei of *The Athletic Chicago*, "Covert was better than all of those guys in the NFC at the time—way better. It's not close. He was one of the best in my 30 years in football. Other guys had to have help against Taylor."

Despite missing a few games with an ankle injury in 1987, Covert earned First-Team All-NFC honors for the third straight time. However, he suffered a far more serious injury the following year, rupturing a disc in his back during training camp. After undergoing surgery, Covert foolishly tried to return to the lineup six weeks later, forcing him to sit out the next few contests. Although Covert came back to start the Bears' final six games of the regular season and two playoff games, he never fully recovered, noting years later, "If I didn't come back so soon, I felt I could have played seven or eight more years."

Even though Covert spent the next two seasons playing at somewhat less than 100 percent, he missed a total of just two games in 1989 and 1990, with his strong play in the second of those campaigns gaining him Second-Team All-NFC recognition. But, after rupturing the same disc in his back during the 1991 preseason, Covert had to undergo spinal fusion, which forced him to retire prematurely at only 31 years of age. Covert subsequently began an extremely successful entrepreneurial career focused on health care sales, marketing, and acquisition initiatives. After being named president and CEO of The Institute for Transfusion Medicine in May 2007, Covert spent the next 10 years holding that prestigious position at a nonprofit organization that specialized in transfusion medicine and related services. Since ITXM merged with Blood Systems, Inc. in early 2017 to create the largest independent blood products and services company in the United States, Covert has been working in the private equity sector focused on health care–related investments. He is also a member of the University of Pittsburgh's Board of Trustees.

Although the relative brevity of Covert's playing career kept him out of the Pro Football Hall of Fame for many years, those who competed with and against him continued to express the belief that they considered him worthy of enshrinement, with Anthony Munoz saying, "I watched him quite a bit, and Jimbo Covert was one of the best I watched play. He's up there with Gary Zimmerman and the other guys who are in the Hall during that period. I liked his toughness, aggressiveness, and intensity. Whenever I watched him, he was getting after it."

When asked about the best offensive tackles he ever faced, Tampa Bay Buccaneers Hall of Fame defensive end Lee Roy Selmon once said, "From Chicago, there was a tackle by the name of Jim Covert who came in there from the University of Pittsburgh, and I found him to be a very talented and intelligent player. He used great techniques and was very physical. Also, Anthony Munoz, who played with the Cincinnati Bengals, who is in the Pro Football Hall of Fame."

In discussing his former teammate, Steve McMichael stated, "Covert was the best offensive lineman in the league before his back got hurt. If he'd had a long career, he'd be in the Hall of Fame, no question."

Covert finally received his just due when he gained induction to the Pro Football Hall of Fame as part of its centennial class of 2020.

## CAREER HIGHLIGHTS

### Best Season

Covert earned consensus First-Team All-Pro honors in both 1985 and 1986, with the first of those campaigns proving to be the finest of his career. Excelling at his left tackle post throughout the year, Covert helped the Bears amass more rushing yards than any other team in the NFL (2,761). They also finished second in the league in points scored (456) and boasted the league's fifth-highest rushing average, with Chicago running backs averaging a robust 4.5 yards per carry.

### Memorable Moments/Greatest Performances

Covert helped pave the way for Bears running backs to rush for a season-high 273 yards during a 27–0 win over the Tampa Bay Buccaneers on November 20, 1983.

Covert helped the Bears amass 480 yards of total offense during a 33–24 victory over the Minnesota Vikings on September 19, 1985.

Squaring off at different times against New York's top two pass-rushers in the divisional round of the 1985 NFC playoffs, Covert held Leonard Marshall and Lawrence Taylor to no sacks during the Bears' 21–0 win over the Giants.

Covert helped the Bears dominate the line of scrimmage during a 44–7 rout of the Cincinnati Bengals on September 28, 1986, with Chicago gaining 222 yards on the ground and amassing 476 yards of total offense during the contest.

Covert and his line-mates once again dominated the opposition at the point of attack on September 24, 1989, with the Bears rushing for 219 yards and amassing 542 yards of total offense during a 47–27 victory over the Detroit Lions.

### Notable Achievements

- Six-time division champion (1984, 1985, 1986, 1987, 1988, and 1990).
- 1985 NFC champion.
- Super Bowl XX champion.
- Member of 1983 NFL All-Rookie Team.
- Two-time Pro Bowl selection (1985 and 1986).
- Two-time First-Team All-Pro selection (1985 and 1986).
- Three-time First-Team All-NFC selection (1985, 1986, and 1987).
- 1990 Second-Team All-NFC selection.
- 1985 NFL Players Association NFC Offensive Lineman of the Year.
- 1986 Miller Lite NFL Offensive Lineman of the Year.
- NFL 1980s All-Decade Team.

# 33

## GEORGE MCAFEE

One of the NFL's most versatile players for much of the 1940s, George McAfee spent his entire eight-year career in Chicago, contributing to the Bears as a running back, receiver, defensive back, and return man. Nicknamed "One-Play McAfee" for his ability to quickly change the course of a game, McAfee ranked among the best athletes and most explosive players of his generation, with his speed, quickness, and tremendous balance giving him the ability to score from anywhere on the field. McAfee, who surpassed 1,000 all-purpose yards three times and recorded six interceptions twice, helped the Bears capture four division titles and three NFL championships, with his outstanding all-around play earning him one Pro Bowl selection and two All-Pro nominations. And, following the conclusion of his playing career, McAfee earned the additional distinctions of being named to the NFL 1940s All-Decade Team, the NFL's 75th Anniversary All-Time Two-Way Team, and the Pro Football Hall of Fame.

Born in Corbin, Kentucky, on March 13, 1918, George Anderson McAfee grew up in Ironton, Ohio, where he moved with his family as a youngster. After starring in football while attending Ironton High School, McAfee enrolled at Duke University in Durham, North Carolina. Continuing to excel on the gridiron in college, McAfee led Duke in rushing, receiving, scoring, kickoff returns, punt returns, interceptions, and punting as a senior in 1939, earning in the process First-Team All-America honors. An exceptional all-around athlete, McAfee also starred in baseball and track, batting .353 while patrolling center field for the Blue Devils, and capturing the 100-meter title at the Southern Conference track and field championships.

After being selected by the Eagles with the second overall pick of the 1940 NFL Draft, McAfee found himself heading to Chicago when the Bears acquired him for three players. Although George Halas initially had his doubts about McAfee's ability to compete in the NFL after he took a closer look at his slender 6-foot, 178-pound frame, "Papa Bear" soon changed his mind after watching him carry the ball for the first time in practice. Halas became even more convinced when McAfee gave the Bears a win over the Brooklyn Dodgers in their first preseason contest by returning a punt 75 yards for a touchdown in the closing moments.

McAfee ended up having a solid rookie season for the Bears, gaining Second-Team All-Pro recognition from the *New York Daily News* by carrying the ball 47 times for 253 yards and two touchdowns, gaining

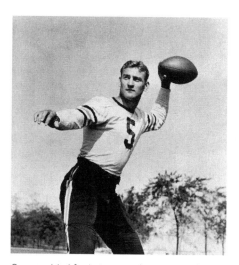

another 117 yards on seven pass receptions, returning one kickoff for a touchdown, intercepting four passes on defense, and averaging 38.7 yards per kick as the team's primary punter. Developing into a star his second year in the league, McAfee earned Pro Bowl and consensus First-Team All-Pro honors in 1941 by finishing second in the NFL with 474 yards rushing, 1,077 all-purpose yards, five rushing touchdowns, 12 TDs, and 72 points scored, while also ranking among the league leaders with 618 yards from scrimmage, 381 kickoff- and punt-return yards, three touchdown receptions, and six

George McAfee's tremendous versatility made him an invaluable member of the Bears for eight seasons.
Public domain

interceptions. Impressed with McAfee's brilliant play, Red Grange called him "the most dangerous man with the football in the game."

Legendary Packers head coach Curly Lambeau also had high praise for McAfee, calling him "the most talented back the Packers ever faced."

Meanwhile, John F. Kieran wrote in the *New York Times*, "The debate around Chicago has been as to whether McAfee is just as good as Jim Thorpe ever was, or better."

And, years later, when asked to compare rookie Gale Sayers to McAfee, George Halas answered, "The highest compliment you can pay any ballcarrier is just to compare him with McAfee."

McAfee's speed, balance, and cutting ability all contributed greatly to the success he experienced during the early stages of his career, with Chicago Cardinals head coach Jimmy Conzelman crediting his ability to elude opposing tacklers to his quickness and slippery running style. In addressing the last quality, Conzelman said, "That's something few really fast players ever developed. He puts the defense off balance and fakes with his head, as well as his arms and body." McAfee also pioneered the use of low-cut shoes in the NFL, believing that they helped increase his speed on the football field.

However, McAfee's greatest attribute may well have been his tremendous versatility, which enabled him to excel as a running back, receiver out of the backfield, cornerback, and kickoff and punt returner. In fact, the 12.8 yards per punt return average that McAfee compiled over the course of his career remained an NFL record for many years after he left the game.

Following his exceptional 1941 campaign, McAfee enlisted in the US Navy, where he spent the next three years serving his country during World War II. Explaining his decision years later, McAfee said, "I didn't want to be drafted. I enlisted, as did so many other young men at the time. I felt like it was my duty and the thing to do."

After returning to the Bears in 1945, McAfee appeared in a total of just six games the next two seasons, with his time on the playing field being limited by injuries and rust from his Navy tour. Sustaining a knee injury in 1946 that limited him to just three games, McAfee later said, "After I hurt my knee, I couldn't run like I had before, so I was happy to play mostly on defense."

Excelling at cornerback for the remainder of his career, McAfee recorded a total of 11 interceptions over the course of the next four seasons, with his six picks in 1949 placing him among the league leaders. Meanwhile, even though he lacked the same explosiveness he possessed earlier in his career, McAfee continued to contribute to the Bears on offense and special teams, amassing 701 yards from scrimmage and 1,034 all-purpose yards in 1947, before scoring eight touchdowns and accumulating 619 yards from scrimmage and 1,096 all-purpose yards the following year.

Choosing to announce his retirement following the conclusion of the 1950 campaign, McAfee ended his playing career with 1,685 rushing yards, 1,359 receiving yards, 1,431 punt-return yards, 488 kickoff-return yards, 5,313 all-purpose yards, 39 touchdowns, 25 interceptions, and 350 interception-return yards. In explaining his decision to retire when he did, McAfee said, "I just felt like I had enough. It was a long season, and I had a couple of small children and a business to run. I had just had enough. I got into the oil business the year before I left the Bears, so I blended into the business world. I didn't miss playing pro football."

McAfee spent the next three decades operating a Shell Oil distributorship in Durham, before finally retiring in 1981. Plagued by dementia in his later years, McAfee eventually moved into an assisted-living facility in Atlanta, where he died at the age of 90 on March 4, 2009, after wandering into a utility room and drinking a bottle of industrial-strength detergent. Following the announcement of his passing, the Bears issued a statement that read: "George McAfee helped establish the proud tradition of the Chicago Bears. His versatility led to his induction into the Pro Football Hall of Fame as he played offense, defense and special teams on three championship teams. George also served his country in the Navy during WWII. We are proud to have him as an integral part of our history and are saddened by his passing. Our thoughts and prayers are with his family."

## CAREER HIGHLIGHTS

### Best Season

McAfee had easily the finest all-around season of his career in 1941, when he earned his lone First-Team All-Pro selection by ranking among the league leaders with 474 yards rushing, 618 yards from scrimmage, 381 kickoff- and punt-return yards, 1,077 all-purpose yards, five rushing touchdowns, 11 touchdowns, 72 points scored, and six interceptions. McAfee, who returned only five punts all year, returned one of those for a touchdown, with his average of 31.6 yards per punt return setting a single-season franchise record that still stands.

### Memorable Moments/Greatest Performances

McAfee made his pro debut a memorable one, leading the Bears to a 41–10 rout of the Packers in the opening game of the 1940 regular season by returning a kickoff 93 yards for a touchdown, running 9 yards for another score, and throwing an 8-yard TD pass to Ken Kavanaugh.

McAfee contributed to the Bears' 73–0 manhandling of the Washington Redskins in the 1940 NFL championship game by intercepting a pass, which he returned 34 yards for a touchdown.

McAfee displayed his tremendous versatility during a 25–17 win over the Packers in the 1941 regular-season opener, throwing a 63-yard touchdown pass to Ken Kavanaugh, scoring himself on a 13-yard run, and returning a kickoff 51 yards.

McAfee exhibited his explosiveness against the Cleveland Rams the following week, returning a kickoff 97 yards for a touchdown during a 48–21 Chicago win.

McAfee led the Bears to a 53–7 mauling of the Chicago Cardinals on October 12, 1941, by scoring on a 59-yard run and a 74-yard punt return, while also intercepting a pass on defense.

McAfee scored in an unusual manner during a 31–13 win over the Rams on November 9, 1941, when, after teammate Bill Osmanski lateraled the ball to him following an interception, he took off down the sideline and avoided several would-be tacklers to complete a 41-yard TD interception return.

McAfee contributed to a 35–21 victory over the Redskins the following week by hauling in touchdown passes of 12 and 33 yards from Bob Snyder and recording an interception on defense.

McAfee ran for one score and picked off a pair of passes during a 24–7 win over the Detroit Lions on November 23, 1941.

McAfee proved to be the difference in a 34–24 win over the Cardinals in the 1941 regular-season finale, scoring two fourth-quarter TDs on a 39-yard pass from Sid Luckman and a 70-yard run.

McAfee then led the Bears to a 33–14 win over the Packers in their 1941 divisional round playoff game matchup by carrying the ball 14 times for 119 yards and returning two punts for 33 yards.

McAfee turned in another outstanding all-around performance against the Giants in the 1941 NFL championship game, leading the Bears to a 37–9 victory by gaining 81 yards and scoring one touchdown on the ground, while also making two receptions for 42 yards.

Making a triumphant return to the Bears after missing almost four full seasons due to time spent in the military during World War II, McAfee rushed for 105 yards and scored three touchdowns during a 28–7 win over the Pittsburgh Steelers on November 25, 1945, with the longest of his TDs coming on a 65-yard hookup with Sid Luckman.

McAfee helped lead the Bears to a 24–14 victory over the Giants in the 1946 NFL championship game by intercepting two passes and making four receptions for 57 yards.

Although the Bears lost to the Los Angeles Rams by a score of 17–14 on December 7, 1947, McAfee established career-high marks with nine receptions and 157 receiving yards.

McAfee excelled against the Rams once again on October 10, 1948, returning a punt 60 yards for a touchdown during a 42–21 Bears win.

McAfee proved to be too much for the Giants to handle on October 31, 1948, running for two TDs and scoring a third time on a 25-yard pass from Sid Luckman during a 35–14 Bears win.

McAfee all but clinched a 38–21 victory over the Philadelphia Eagles on October 16, 1949, when he gave the Bears a 14-point fourth-quarter lead by returning an interception 54 yards for a TD.

## Notable Achievements

- Amassed more than 1,000 all-purpose yards three times.
- Averaged more than 5 yards per carry three times.
- Recorded six interceptions twice.
- Led NFL in punt-return yardage once.
- Finished second in NFL in rushing yards once, all-purpose yards once, rushing touchdowns once, touchdowns once, points scored once, and punt-return average twice.
- Ranks among Bears career leaders with 1,431 punt-return yards (2nd), 39 touchdowns (8th), 25 interceptions (7th), and 350 interception-return yards (9th).
- Four-time division champion (1940, 1941, 1946, and 1950).
- Three-time NFL champion (1940, 1941, and 1946).
- 1941 Pro Bowl selection.
- 1941 First-Team All-Pro selection.
- 1948 Second-Team All-Pro selection.
- NFL 1940s All-Decade Team.
- #5 retired by Bears.
- Named to NFL's 75th Anniversary All-Time Two-Way Team in 1994.
- Elected to Pro Football Hall of Fame in 1966.

# 34

## — NEAL ANDERSON —

Drafted by the Bears in 1986 as the heir apparent to Walter Payton, Neal Anderson spent the next eight years trying to measure up to the enormously high standards set by arguably the greatest all-around running back in NFL history. Although Anderson found it impossible to reach the same level of excellence as his immediate predecessor, he nevertheless carved out quite a successful career for himself during his time in Chicago, ending his eight-year stay in the Windy City with the third most rushing yards in team annals. An outstanding runner, Anderson led the Bears in rushing seven times, gaining more than 1,000 yards on the ground on three separate occasions. An excellent receiver coming out of the backfield as well, Anderson led the team in receptions twice, with his pass-catching skills enabling him to also amass the third most yards from scrimmage in franchise history. Anderson's overall contributions on offense helped the Bears capture four division titles, earning him in the process four trips to the Pro Bowl, one All-Pro selection, and three All-NFC nominations.

Born in Graceville, Florida, on August 14, 1964, Charles Neal Anderson attended Graceville High School, where he starred for the Graceville Tigers football team at running back. After accepting a scholarship from the University of Florida in Gainesville, Anderson spent the next four years starting at halfback for the Gators, playing alongside fullback John L. Williams, who went on to play 10 seasons in the NFL. Displaying his explosiveness during his time at Gainesville, Anderson rushed for 197 yards against Kentucky as a freshman, recorded a 76-yard touchdown run against LSU as a sophomore, and rushed for 178 yards against Tennessee as a junior, with his longest run of the day being an 80-yard TD scamper. Ending his college career with 3,234 yards rushing, 30 touchdowns, and 14 games with at least 100 yards rushing, Anderson gained AP honorable mention All-America recognition twice and First-Team All–Southeastern Conference (SEC) honors as a senior in 1985.

Elated that Anderson lasted until the end of the first round of the 1986 NFL Draft, the Bears selected him with the 27th overall pick, knowing that Walter Payton planned to play only one or two more seasons. Anderson subsequently spent his first year in the league backing up Payton, gaining only 146 yards on the ground, but performing so well on the kickoff- and punt-coverage units that he earned All-Rookie honors for his outstanding play on special teams.

Accorded far more playing time on offense during the strike-shortened 1987 campaign, Anderson spent most of the year starting at fullback alongside Payton, rushing for 586 yards, gaining another 467 yards on 47 pass receptions, and scoring six touchdowns, with his 1,053 yards from scrimmage leading the team. Meanwhile, Anderson did an exceptional job of blocking for his running mate and picking up the blitz, thereby providing protection for Bear quarterbacks Jim McMahon and Mike Tomczak.

With Payton retiring at the end of the 1987 season, Anderson returned to his normal position of halfback, where he became the focal point of Chicago's offense. Excelling in that role for the next three years, Anderson played the best ball of his career, posting the following numbers during that time:

| YEAR | RUSH YD | REC YD | YD FROM SCRIMMAGE | TD |
| --- | --- | --- | --- | --- |
| 1988 | 1,106 | 371 | 1,477 | 12 |
| 1989 | 1,275 | 434 | 1,709 | 15 |
| 1990 | 1,078 | 484 | 1,562 | 13 |

Placing near the top of the league rankings in yards rushing, yards from scrimmage, and touchdowns all three years, Anderson earned three consecutive Pro Bowl and All-NFC selections, with his outstanding play in 1990 also gaining him Second-Team All-Pro recognition. Considered by many to be the best all-purpose back in the NFL throughout the period, the 5'11", 210-pound Anderson performed equally well as a runner, pass receiver, and blocker. Blessed with soft hands, Anderson caught more than 40 passes in a season five times, with his 50 receptions in 1989 proving to be his career-high mark. Also known for his ability to turn the corner with great speed, Anderson scored many of his touchdowns by diving for the end zone with a graceful leap, before grazing the pylon.

Yet, despite performing at an elite level, Anderson incurred the wrath of Bear fans when he held out for more money prior to the start of the 1990 season. Fans of the team grew increasingly disenchanted with him

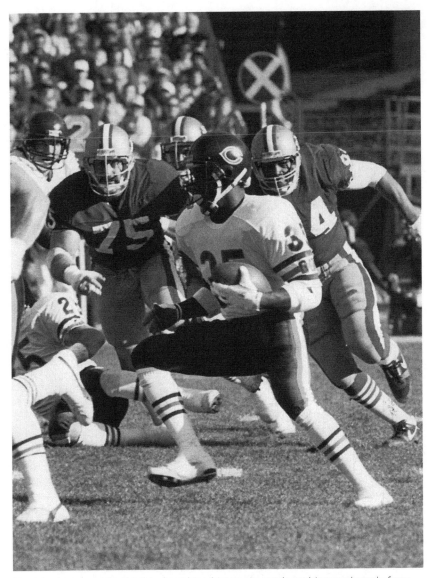

Neal Anderson ranks third in franchise history in yards rushing and yards from scrimmage.
Courtesy of George A. Kitrinos

the following year when his production began to wane after he suffered a pulled hamstring that forced him to miss three games. Further troubled by the arrest of his 63-year-old father, who was charged with the murder of his 37-year-old fiancée, Anderson failed to gain more than 1,000 yards on the ground for the first time in four years. Nevertheless, he still managed to earn his fourth straight trip to the Pro Bowl by rushing for 747 yards, amassing 1,115 yards from scrimmage, and scoring nine touchdowns.

Anderson's production continued to decline in 1992, as he began to share playing time with second-year halfback Darren Lewis. Still, he posted decent numbers, finishing the year with 582 yards rushing, 981 yards from scrimmage, and 11 touchdowns. After rushing for 646 yards, amassing 806 yards from scrimmage, and scoring only four touchdowns in a part-time role in 1993, Anderson elected to announce his retirement following the conclusion of the campaign, ending his career with 6,166 yards rushing, 302 receptions for 2,763 yards, 8,929 yards from scrimmage, and 71 touchdowns, with 51 of those coming on the ground and the other 20 through the air. In addition to amassing the third most yards rushing and yards from scrimmage in franchise history, Anderson continues to rank among the Bears' all-time leaders in all-purpose yards, receptions, rushing touchdowns, touchdowns, and points scored.

After retiring as an active player, Anderson returned to Gainesville, Florida, where he helped found a bank. He currently keeps himself busy by working on his 2,000-acre peanut farm, remaining active in the community, and playing golf.

## CAREER HIGHLIGHTS

### Best Season

Anderson had an outstanding year for the Bears in 1990, earning All-Pro honors for the only time in his career by rushing for 1,078 yards, amassing 1,562 yards from scrimmage, scoring 13 touchdowns, and averaging 4.1 yards per carry. However, he posted slightly better overall numbers in 1989, establishing career-high marks with 1,275 yards rushing, 1,709 yards from scrimmage, 15 touchdowns, and a rushing average of 4.7 yards per carry. Particularly effective in September, Anderson earned NFC Offensive Player of the Month honors by rushing for 359 yards and scoring four touchdowns during the Bears' three wins.

### Memorable Moments/Greatest Performances

Anderson scored the first touchdown of his career on a 58-yard pass from Doug Flutie during a 24–10 win over the Dallas Cowboys in the final game of the 1986 regular season.

Anderson had his breakout game against Tampa Bay on September 20, 1987, carrying the ball 16 times for 117 yards and one touchdown during a 20–3 Bears win.

Anderson led the Bears to a 34–7 victory over the Miami Dolphins in the 1988 regular-season opener by rushing for 123 yards and two touchdowns, with his outstanding performance earning him NFC Offensive Player of the Week honors for the only time in his career.

Anderson rushed for 139 yards and two touchdowns during a 16–0 win over the Packers on November 27, 1988, with one of his TDs coming on a career-long 80-yard run.

Anderson helped the Bears record a 17–14 victory over the Cincinnati Bengals in the opening game of the 1989 regular season by carrying the ball 21 times for 146 yards.

Anderson followed that up with an exceptional outing against Minnesota in Week 2, rushing for 97 yards and scoring three touchdowns during a 38–7 win, with two of his TDs coming on the ground and the other on a 24-yard pass from Mike Tomczak.

Turning in another outstanding performance against Detroit on September 24, 1989, Anderson clinched NFC Offensive Player of the Month honors by carrying the ball 16 times for 116 yards and one touchdown during a 47–27 win, scoring his TD on a 53-yard run.

Anderson provided most of the offense the Bears mounted when they defeated the Seattle Seahawks by a score of 17–0 in the 1990 regular-season opener, rushing for 101 yards, gaining another 42 yards on five pass receptions, and scoring both Chicago touchdowns on runs that covered 17 and 4 yards.

Anderson contributed to a 27–13 victory over the Packers on October 7, 1990, by rushing for 141 yards and one touchdown.

Anderson gave the Bears a 23–17 overtime win over the Detroit Lions on December 2, 1990, by hauling in a 50-yard touchdown pass from quarterback Jim Harbaugh.

Although Anderson carried the ball just eight times for 57 yards during a 20–17 win over the Giants on September 15, 1991, 42 of those yards came on a fourth-quarter touchdown run that gave the Bears the victory.

Anderson went over 100 yards rushing for the last time in his career when he carried the ball 23 times for 104 yards and one touchdown during a 47–17 win over the Tampa Bay Buccaneers on September 26, 1993.

**Notable Achievements**

- Rushed for more than 1,000 yards three times.
- Surpassed 50 receptions once and 400 receiving yards three times.
- Surpassed 1,000 yards from scrimmage five times, topping 1,500 yards twice.
- Scored more than 10 touchdowns four times.
- Finished third in NFL in yards from scrimmage once, touchdowns once, and rushing average once.
- Led Bears in rushing seven times and receptions twice.
- Ranks among Bears career leaders with 6,166 yards rushing (3rd), 8,929 yards from scrimmage (3rd), 8,955 all-purpose yards (5th), 302 receptions (8th), 51 rushing touchdowns (2nd), 71 touchdowns (2nd), and 426 points scored (8th).
- Four-time division champion (1986, 1987, 1988, and 1990).
- 1988 Week 1 NFC Offensive Player of the Week.
- September 1989 NFC Offensive Player of the Month.
- Four-time Pro Bowl selection (1988, 1989, 1990, and 1991).
- 1990 Second-Team All-Pro selection.
- Two-time First-Team All-NFC selection (1989 and 1990).
- 1988 Second-Team All-NFC selection.

# 35

## ⸺ JOHNNY MORRIS ⸺

**A**lthough Johnny Morris is perhaps remembered more for his lengthy stint as a sportscaster/sports director in the Chicago area, he previously spent 10 seasons playing for the Bears, amassing more receiving yards than anyone else in franchise history. After spending his first few seasons in the Windy City serving the Bears primarily as a backup running back/ return-man, Morris moved to wide receiver, where he compiled some of the most prolific receiving totals in team annals. In addition to gaining more yards through the air than any other player to don a Bears uniform, Morris ranks among the franchise's all-time leaders in receptions, touchdown receptions, yards from scrimmage, and all-purpose yards, accumulating more than 1,000 all-purpose yards on three separate occasions. The only player in Bears history to lead the league in all three major pass-receiving categories in the same season, Morris accomplished the feat in 1964, one year after he helped lead the team to the NFL championship.

Born in Long Beach, California, on September 26, 1935, Johnny Edward Morris attended Long Beach Polytechnic High School, where he starred at running back. After accepting an athletic scholarship to the University of California in Santa Barbara, Morris continued to perform well on the football field, while also excelling in track, where he tied the world record for the 50-yard dash.

Selected by the Bears in the 12th round of the 1958 NFL Draft, with the 137th overall pick, Morris spent his rookie season returning kickoffs and backing up Rick Casares and Willie Galimore in the offensive backfield. Doing a solid job in his dual role, Morris rushed for 239 yards, gained another 170 yards on 11 pass receptions, amassed a total of 904 all-purpose yards, scored two touchdowns, and finished second in the league with an average of 24.9 yards per kickoff return. Assuming a similar role the following year, Morris concluded the 1959 campaign with 312 yards rushing, 13 receptions for 197 yards, 1,118 all-purpose yards, and three touchdowns, one of which came on a 78-yard punt return.

Although Morris continued to see limited action on offense in 1960, his six touchdowns, rushing average of 5.7 yards per carry, 641 yards from scrimmage, and 1,100 all-purpose yards earned him Pro Bowl honors for the only time in his career. Finding a permanent home after the Bears moved him to flanker (wide receiver) prior to the start of the 1961 campaign in order to make better use of his soft hands and excellent speed, Morris made 36 receptions for 548 yards and four touchdowns. Emerging as one of the league's most dynamic offensive players the following year, Morris concluded the 1962 campaign with 58 receptions, 889 receiving yards, five touchdowns, and 1,104 all-purpose yards. After putting up solid numbers once again in 1963, Morris had the most productive season of his career in 1964, earning consensus First-Team All-Pro honors by leading the NFL with 93 receptions, 1,200 receiving yards, and 10 TD catches.

Johnny Morris amassed more receiving yards than any other player in franchise history.
Courtesy of MEARSonlineauctions.com

In addition to his exceptional quickness, Morris possessed outstanding moves and precise route-running ability, with Bears quarterback Bill Wade stating, "I thought Johnny Morris was a great football player. Without any question, I felt there were times when he could get clear against anybody in the business."

Focusing more on the 5'10", 180-pound Morris's toughness, Bears center Mike Pyle is quoted in the book *Papa Bear: The Life and Legacy of George Halas*, as saying, "Johnny had a special intensity. He was a player. He didn't play small. The great smaller players use their quickness and ability. Johnny held the world record for the 50-yard dash, and that's what you need on a football field. You don't run a 100, you run 30, 40, or 50. Johnny Morris was our punt returner, and I can't tell you how many times I'd come onto the football field and there'd be four or five guys on top of him. I just knew he'd pop up as soon as they were off. That's tough. He was tempered steel."

The 1964 season proved to be the high point of Morris's career. Assuming a somewhat diminished role in George Halas's new offense after the Bears drafted Gale Sayers the following year, Morris caught 53 passes for 846 yards and four touchdowns, before appearing in just two games due to injury in 1966. After making just 20 receptions for 231 yards and one touchdown in 1967, Morris announced his retirement following the conclusion of the campaign, ending his career with 356 receptions, 5,059 receiving yards, 1,040 yards rushing, 8,262 all-purpose yards, and 37 touchdowns.

Following his playing days, Morris, who joined WBBM-TV in Chicago as a sportscaster while still a member of the Bears, continued his career in broadcasting that lasted more than 30 years. Except for a six-year stint at rival WMAQ-TV, Morris remained at WBBM until 1992, during which time he popularized the use of the telestrator. Morris, who spent most of his time at WBBM serving as sports director, also worked as a network color commentator for Bears games from 1975 to 1986. After retiring to private life in 1996, Morris remained in the Chicago suburbs, where he currently lives. The survivor of a brain aneurysm he suffered more than a decade ago, Morris is 84 years old as of this writing.

## CAREER HIGHLIGHTS

### Best Season

Was there ever any doubt? Morris had easily the greatest season of his career in 1964, when he earned consensus First-Team All-Pro honors by leading the NFL with 93 receptions, 1,200 receiving yards, and 10 TD catches. Morris's 93 receptions remained a single-season franchise record until 2001, when Marty Booker caught 100 passes for the Bears. Meanwhile, his 1,200 receiving yards placed him first in team annals until Jeff Graham amassed 1,301 yards in 1995.

### Memorable Moments/Greatest Performances

Morris scored the first touchdown of his career on a 5-yard run during a 51–38 loss to the Baltimore Colts on October 4, 1958.

Although the Bears lost to the Los Angeles Rams by a score of 28–21 on October 11, 1959, Morris returned a punt 78 yards for a touchdown during the contest.

Morris went over 100 receiving yards for the first time as a pro during a 34–27 win over the Rams on October 9, 1960, finishing the game with three catches for 124 yards and two touchdowns, which came on hookups of 45 and 66 yards with quarterback Ed Brown.

Morris followed that up with another strong outing, carrying the ball seven times for 114 yards and two touchdowns during a 27–10 win over the 49ers on October 16, 1960, with his TD runs covering 61 and 37 yards.

Although the Bears suffered a 41–31 defeat at the hands of the 49ers on November 19, 1961, Morris had a big game, making five receptions for 123 yards and one touchdown, which came on a career-long 80-yard connection with quarterback Bill Wade.

Morris once again starred in defeat on October 14, 1962, when, during a 34–27 loss to the 49ers, he caught four passes for 122 yards and one touchdown, which came on a 73-yard hookup with Wade on the game's opening possession.

Morris had a huge day against Dallas on November 18, 1962, making 10 catches for 201 yards and one touchdown during a 34–33 victory over the Cowboys that the Bears won on a late field goal by Roger LeClerc. Morris's touchdown, which came on a 45-yard connection with Bill Wade late in the fourth quarter, set the stage for LeClerc's heroics, bringing the Bears to within two points of Dallas with just minutes remaining in the final period.

Morris contributed to a 24–14 win over the Lions in the final game of the 1963 regular season by making eight receptions for 171 yards and one touchdown, which he scored from 51 yards out.

Morris helped lead the Bears to a 34–28 victory over the Minnesota Vikings on September 20, 1964, by making 10 receptions for 135 yards and two touchdowns.

Morris continued his banner year by making 11 receptions for 147 yards and two touchdowns during a 38–17 win over the Rams on October 11, 1964, with the longest of his TDs coming on a 52-yard hookup with Bill Wade.

Although the Bears lost to the Baltimore Colts by a score of 40–24 on November 8, 1964, Morris caught 10 passes for 183 yards and one touchdown, collaborating with Rudy Bukich on a 63-yard scoring play.

## Notable Achievements

- Surpassed 50 receptions three times, topping 90 catches once (93 in 1964).

- Surpassed 800 receiving yards three times, topping 1,000 yards once (1,200 in 1964).
- Amassed more than 1,000 all-purpose yards three times.
- Led NFL with 93 receptions, 1,200 receiving yards, and 10 touchdown receptions in 1964.
- Finished second in NFL in kickoff-return average twice and kickoff- and punt-return yards once.
- Finished third in NFL in punt-return average once and punt-return yards once.
- Led Bears in receptions three times and receiving yards twice.
- Holds Bears career record for most receiving yards (5,059).
- Ranks among Bears career leaders with 356 receptions (3rd), 31 touchdown receptions (tied-5th), 37 touchdowns (tied-9th), 6,099 yards from scrimmage (6th), and 8,262 all-purpose yards (6th).
- 1963 division champion.
- 1963 NFL champion.
- 1960 Pro Bowl selection.
- 1964 First-Team All-Pro selection.
- 1964 First-Team All–Western Conference selection.

# 36

## ROOSEVELT TAYLOR

One of the best defensive backs to ever don a Bears jersey, Roosevelt Taylor spent 8½ seasons in Chicago, combining with Richie Petitbon to give the team arguably the league's finest pair of safeties. A playmaker who provided extra physicality on the back end of Chicago's defense, Taylor ranks among the franchise's all-time leaders in interceptions, interception-return yards, and touchdown interceptions, with his nine picks in 1963 leading the NFL. Extremely durable, Taylor never missed a game while with the Bears, appearing in 118 consecutive contests. Earning Pro Bowl and All-Pro honors twice each during his time in Chicago, Taylor accomplished all he did even though the Bears never intended to keep him after signing him as an undrafted free agent.

Born in New Orleans, Louisiana, on July 4, 1937, Roosevelt Taylor grew up in the city's Lower Ninth Ward, where he and his friends played football on the streets until they saw an opportunity to sneak onto the field at Holy Cross High School. Recalling his childhood days, Taylor said, "Holy Cross grass was cut and green, and we played ball until we saw the priests coming. Then we knew we were on our way out."

Establishing himself as a multi-sport star while attending local Joseph S. Clark High School, Taylor excelled in football, basketball, and track, with his exceptional play on the gridiron earning him All-City honors. Nevertheless, Taylor always maintained that he possessed more ability on the hardwood than anywhere else, claiming, "Basketball was my best sport. When I was in the 11th grade, I could dunk the basketball with two hands even though I was only 5'11". . . . That's one of the big reasons I made the pros [in football]. When they saw me jump up and grab the crossbar on the goalpost, it was over with."

After graduating from Clark, Taylor walked onto the Grambling State University football team, paying his own tuition his first semester, before earning an athletic scholarship. Developing into a two-way star during his time at Grambling, Taylor recorded touchdown runs of 87 and 75 yards in back-to-back games against Tennessee State and Texas Southern as a sophomore, before helping the school earn its first Southwestern Athletic Conference championship two years later.

Although all 14 NFL teams subsequently bypassed Taylor in the 1961 NFL Draft, he ended up signing with the Bears as a free agent, revealing the details of how he became a member of the team in Beth Gorr's 2005 book, *Bear Memories: The Chicago-Green Bay Rivalry*:

> I went to Grambling back in the late 1950s and early 1960s. This was in the days when, quite frankly, there weren't many African American players anywhere in the National Football League. . . . One of my friends on the Grambling team was a huge guy who went by the name of Ernie Ladd. Now, Ernie was a force to be reckoned with. He weighed over 300 pounds and stood at least 6'10½". Every professional team in the country knew of him.
>
> Coach Halas came up with an idea to recruit me since I was one of Ernie's closest friends. His idea was that Ladd would be much more likely to sign with a team that had his friend on the team. There were so few players from colleges down South in the NFL then that it could get sort of lonely for the players, particularly during their rookie year. If Ernie had me, the theory was, then he'd be much more comfortable.
>
> Halas went ahead and drafted Ernie, who, unfortunately for George, had much more interest in joining the AFL. . . . I came along as a free agent, signing with the Bears. . . . Well, Ernie never did get to Chicago. Instead, he signed with the San Diego Chargers. Now Halas was faced with a problem. What were the Bears going to do with a DB they weren't really all that interested in? I was already in Chicago, so they had to come up with a scheme to get rid of me quickly. The plan was to give me no guarantees for the long term at all. If I played well, I could stay, but it was made very clear that my services were required strictly on a week-to-week basis.
>
> What was I supposed to do? Give up and go home? That just wasn't an option. Instead, I had something to prove. But how was I going to do that when my coaches

had no confidence in me? I decided to excel at everything they put before me. That way, I couldn't be cut.

First up, the infamous "Halas Mile," a particularly brutal part of training camp. I worked my tail off, running that thing twice a day, every single day of the week. And, soon enough, I had the record at that distance. It made headlines in the local sports pages. Guess they couldn't cut me then.

Then it came time to prove myself on the field. In a game soon thereafter, I hit a #1 draft choice who went by the name of Tony Mason so hard that they had to bring an ambulance out on the field to get him to the locker room. He was out cold. The Bears couldn't cut me after that, either.

Soon came the annual College All-Star-Bears scrimmage. That time, I made a mark with kick-off returns. Ran them right back to the other end of the field, over and over. That bought me another five days on the team until they finally decided to keep me.

And look what happened. The one week I was to have been with the Bears lasted from 1961 to 1969. I was usually near the top of their interception list, and in 1963, I led the team with nine. I guess bringing me up from Grambling wasn't such a bad idea after all.

Proving to be a huge asset to the Bears over the course of those 8½ seasons, the 5'11", 186-pound Taylor used his speed, agility, soft hands, and excellent technique to pick off 23 passes, which he returned for a total of 414 yards and three touchdowns. Taylor also recovered 12 fumbles, amassed 598 kickoff-return yards, and scored three other TDs, with one of those coming on a fumble return and the other two on special teams. In addition to appearing in two Pro Bowls and being named All-Pro twice, Taylor gained First-Team All–Western Conference recognition in both 1963 and 1964, with his stellar play in the first of those campaigns helping the Bears capture the NFL title.

Crediting much of his success to his physical conditioning and pregame preparation, Taylor said, "I used to go out at 11:30 or 12 o'clock. I'd sneak out of the dormitory to go and work out. I'm a nut about training. I believe in training. Anybody who has ever trained with me will tell you 'That son of a gun never gets tired—he just runs and runs and keeps on bouncing.'"

Roosevelt Taylor led the NFL with nine interceptions in 1963.
Courtesy of MEARSonlineauctions.com

After Taylor earned Pro Bowl honors for the second time in his career in 1968, the Bears dealt him to the San Francisco 49ers for veteran offensive lineman Howard Mudd midway through the ensuing campaign, ending his 8½-year association with the club. Looking back at his lengthy stay in Chicago, Taylor said, "I think they got a pretty good deal with me. I was out there every second when I was with the Bears." He then added, "They gave me the break to play professional football, and all of the knowledge I grabbed in those years, I got it while with the Bears. When I left the Bears, I was considered an old-timer with the 49ers. It was my ninth year."

Taylor ended up spending 2½ seasons in San Francisco, intercepting a total of eight passes for the 49ers, in helping them capture two NFC Western Division titles. After playing for the Washington Redskins in 1972, Taylor announced his retirement following the conclusion of the campaign, ending his career with 32 interceptions, 486 interception-return yards, 13 fumble recoveries, and six touchdowns.

Following his playing days, Taylor became involved in 17 different businesses, including five lounges, two motels, ice cream shops, and a household cleaning company. Now retired at 82 years of age, Taylor currently lives in New Orleans, where he continues to hold the Bears close to his heart. Yet, he still questions their decision to trade him to the 49ers, saying, "I still hear about that when I go to Chicago and hang out with the boys. All of us got along great. I don't think I've ever had a squabble or anything with anybody. They talk about the worst trade the Bears ever made, trading me in mid-season for Howard Mudd."

## BEARS CAREER HIGHLIGHTS

### Best Season

Taylor had the finest season of his career in 1963, when he earned his lone First-Team All-Pro selection by leading the NFL with nine interceptions, finishing third in the league with 172 interception-return yards, and recovering three fumbles.

### Memorable Moments/Greatest Performances

Taylor scored the Bears' first points of the 1962 campaign when he returned his first career interception 43 yards for a touchdown during a 30–14 win over the San Francisco 49ers in the regular-season opener.

Taylor lit the scoreboard again when he returned a blocked punt 11 yards for a touchdown during a 30–14 win over the Los Angeles Rams on December 9, 1962.

Taylor picked off two passes in one game for the first time in his career during a 26–7 win over the Packers on November 17, 1963.

Taylor put the finishing touches on a 27–7 victory over the 49ers on December 8, 1963, by returning an interception 30 yards for a touchdown in the fourth quarter.

Although the Bears ultimately suffered a 30–28 defeat at the hands of the Los Angeles Rams on September 25, 1965, Taylor gave them a 7–6 lead midway through the second quarter when he returned a blocked field goal attempt by the Rams 60 yards for a touchdown.

Taylor crossed the opponent's goal line again during a 41–13 loss to the Pittsburgh Steelers in the 1967 regular-season opener when he returned a fumble 37 yards for a touchdown.

Taylor all but clinched a 29–16 victory over the Philadelphia Eagles on October 20, 1968, when he returned his fourth-quarter interception of a Norm Snead pass 96 yards for a touchdown.

## Notable Achievements

- Never missed a game in 8½ seasons with Bears, appearing in 118 straight contests.
- Recorded at least five interceptions twice.
- Amassed more than 100 interception-return yards once.
- Led NFL with nine interceptions in 1963.
- Finished second in NFL with 37 fumble-return yards in 1967.
- Finished third in NFL with 172 interception-return yards in 1963.
- Led Bears in interceptions twice.
- Ranks among Bears career leaders with 23 interceptions (10th), 414 interception-return yards (5th), and three touchdown interceptions (tied-5th).
- 1963 division champion.
- 1963 NFL champion.
- Two-time Pro Bowl selection (1963 and 1968).
- 1963 First-Team All-Pro selection.
- 1965 Second-Team All-Pro selection.
- Two-time First-Team All–Western Conference selection (1963 and 1964).

# 37

## — OLIN KREUTZ —

A key member of Bear teams that won four division titles and one NFC championship during the first decade of the 21st century, Olin Kreutz anchored Chicago's offensive line from his center position for 12 seasons, proving to be one of the NFL's most durable players. After missing nine games in 2000, Kreutz went on to start 159 of the Bears' next 160 contests, ending his 13-year stint in the Windy City tied for second in franchise history in games played. Along the way, Kreutz earned six trips to the Pro Bowl, two All-Pro selections, and three All-NFC nominations, with his strong play and outstanding leadership also earning him a spot on the NFL 2000s All-Decade Team.

Born in Honolulu, Hawaii, on June 9, 1977, Olin George Kreutz attended Saint Louis High School, where, in addition to starring on the gridiron, he excelled in wrestling and track and field, winning the Hawaii state heavyweight wrestling championship in his senior year. After also gaining All-State and High School All-America recognition in football as a senior, Kreutz accepted an athletic scholarship from the University of Washington. He then spent the next three seasons starting at center for the Huskies, making such a favorable impression on head coach Jim Lambright that the latter said, "If I were to choose one of a half-dozen of my players to have my back forever, it would be him. Once he decides he's on your side, he will be there. He takes great pride in his decisions."

Kreutz, who later became known for his fierce temper, first exhibited that side of his personality during spring practice prior to the start of his sophomore season at Washington, when he broke the jaw of teammate Sekou Wiggs following an argument that began on the playing field and carried over into the locker room. Delivering a blow so forceful that Wiggs had to have his jaw wired shut for more than a month, Kreutz subsequently found himself suspended from the team until he attended anger-management classes.

After returning to the playing field, Kreutz went on to earn consensus First-Team All-America and Pac-10 honors as a junior, prompting him to forgo his senior year and declare himself eligible for the 1998 NFL Draft, where the Bears selected him in the third round, with the 64th overall pick. Seeing very little action as a rookie, Kreutz started just one game, although he appeared in eight others. Assuming a far more prominent role the following year, Kreutz started every game at center, before missing more than half of the 2000 campaign due to injury. Reclaiming his starting job in 2001, Kreutz missed just one game over the course of the next 10 seasons, establishing himself as one of the league's top centers and true iron men.

Extremely consistent and reliable, Kreutz proved to be a pillar of strength in the middle of the offensive line for Bear teams that made four playoff appearances between 2001 and 2010, with his outstanding play earning him Pro Bowl honors six straight times, from 2001 to 2006. Big and strong, the 6'2", 292-pound Kreutz worked as hard as any other member of the team to remain at the top of his game, spending his off days lifting weights, and typically being the first player to arrive at the club's practice facility, and the last one to leave. Gradually emerging as one of the Bears' foremost leaders on the field and in the locker room, Kreutz drew high praise from head coach Lovie Smith, who said, "He's one of the best leaders I've been around at any level. . . . Just a real man."

Olin Kreutz is tied for second in franchise history with 191 games played.
Courtesy of Bearhanded via Wikipedia

A throwback of sorts, Kreutz became known for his mental and physical toughness—starting fights on the field or retaliating against opponents who took liberties with any of his teammates, with Bears linebacker Brian Urlacher stating, "Olin is one of my favorite people on the team. Number 1 thing, I'm glad he's on my team because I wouldn't want to play against him." Identified by *Sports Illustrated* as one of the 10 most feared players in the NFL, Kreutz even inspired fear in his own teammates, repeating his earlier college indiscretion by breaking the jaw of fellow Bears offensive lineman Fred Miller during a dispute at an FBI shooting range in 2005.

After spending the previous seven seasons serving as a team captain, Kreutz turned down a $4 million, one-year offer made by the Bears early in 2011 to pursue other options. Stating at the time that those options included retirement, Kreutz told Brad Biggs of the *Chicago Tribune*, "That is a decision I am still making. I am sure I will have an opportunity. I am just not sure if I want to play for anyone else. Retirement is definitely an option."

Kreutz also made it clear that he harbored no ill feelings toward the Bears or their general manager, Jerry Angelo, saying, "Jerry has been good to me too. He's given me a lot of money, and I've been there a long time. It felt like maybe it was time to move on. I just got that feeling. If I was right, if I was wrong, if the offer was fair, I have enough money. So, the offer wasn't a big hurdle for me. It was a feeling I had, just maybe they wanted to move on no matter what the offer was."

Kreutz then added, "At this point in my career, the offer of money is not a big deal to me. It's just a feeling I had. I don't want to taint anyone. Both sides have won since I've been here. I've won. They've treated me good. They've given me everything I've asked for, and I think I've played my ass off for them."

Kreutz ended up signing a one-year contract with the New Orleans Saints worth $2 million, with an additional $2 million in incentives. But, after experiencing philosophical differences with the team's offensive line coach, Kreutz left the Saints during the early stages of the campaign, claiming that he had lost his passion for the game. In announcing Kreutz's decision, his agent, Mark Bartelstein, said, "He decided, 'If I can't bring that same passion every day to work, I'm not gonna just sit here and collect a paycheck.' That's the way he is. Olin's a little different than most guys. People say all the time that it's not about the money. That's really how it is with him. It never has been."

After remaining away from the game for three years, Kreutz returned to Chicago in 2015 to join James Williams and Hub Arkush on the Bears' postgame radio show, replacing the recently deceased Doug Buffone.

## BEARS CAREER HIGHLIGHTS

### Best Season

Kreutz earned First-Team All-Pro honors for the only time in his career in 2006, when he helped the Super Bowl–bound Bears score a total of 427 points, which represents the third-highest figure in franchise history.

### Memorable Moments/Greatest Performances

Kreutz anchored an offensive line that enabled the Bears to rush for 203 yards and amass 435 yards of total offense during a 24–0 win over the Cincinnati Bengals on October 21, 2001.

Kreutz and his line-mates dominated the Tampa Bay Buccaneers at the point of attack on December 16, 2001, with the Bears rushing for 207 yards and accumulating a total of 379 yards on offense during a 27–3 win.

Kreutz helped pave the way for the Bears to gain 187 yards on the ground during a convincing 38–6 victory over the Lions on September 18, 2005, with Thomas Jones rushing for 139 yards and two touchdowns.

Kreutz and the rest of Chicago's offensive line once again dominated the opposition at the line of scrimmage on November 23, 2008, with the Bears rushing for a season-high 208 yards during a 27–3 win over the St. Louis Rams.

### Notable Achievements

- Missed just one game in final 10 seasons with Bears, starting 159 out of 160 contests.
- Tied for second in franchise history with 191 games played.
- Four-time division champion (2001, 2005, 2006, and 2010).
- 2006 NFC champion.
- Six-time Pro Bowl selection (2001, 2002, 2003, 2004, 2005, and 2006).
- 2006 First-Team All-Pro selection.
- 2005 Second-Team All-Pro selection.
- Three-time First-Team All-NFC selection (2001, 2004, and 2005).
- NFL 2000s All-Decade Team.

# 38

## ── DOUG BUFFONE ──

Spending much of his career playing in the shadow of the incomparable Dick Butkus, Doug Buffone often found himself being overlooked and underappreciated by most NFL observers. Nevertheless, Buffone established himself as one of the league's finest all-around linebackers during his 14 years in the Windy City, proving to be one of the few bright spots on teams that consistently posted losing records. An outstanding run-defender, Buffone recorded more than 100 tackles in seven different seasons, bringing down opposing ball-carriers a total of 1,257 times over the course of his career. Excellent in pass coverage as well, Buffone recorded 24 interceptions, which represents the highest total ever compiled by a Bears linebacker. An exceptional leader, Buffone served as defensive captain his last eight years in Chicago. And, following the conclusion of his playing career, Buffone continued his association with the Bears as a broadcaster, using his affable personality, honesty, and unbridled enthusiasm to become one of the most beloved figures in franchise history.

Born in Yatesboro, Pennsylvania, on June 27, 1944, Douglas John Buffone attended Shannock Valley High School in nearby Rural Valley, where his athletic prowess earned him a scholarship to the University of Louisville. Excelling on the gridiron at center and middle linebacker for the Cardinals, Buffone recorded a total of 479 tackles in his three seasons as a starter, becoming in the process one of only four players in school history to lead the team in stops three straight times. Commenting on Buffone's brilliant play, Louisville head coach Frank Camp, who also tutored future NFL stars Johnny Unitas, Ernie Green, and Lenny Lyles, called the linebacker "the most complete ball player I've ever coached."

Subsequently selected by the San Diego Chargers in the eighth round of the 1966 AFL Draft, with the 72nd overall pick, Buffone instead elected to sign with the Bears, who chose him in the fourth round of that year's NFL Draft, with the 60th overall pick. After spending his rookie season playing mostly on special teams, Buffone laid claim to the starting left-outside linebacker job in 1967—a position he held for the next 13 years.

Playing alongside Dick Butkus from 1967 to 1973, Buffone combined with the NFL's most intimidating defensive player to give the Bears an imposing pair of linebackers. While Butkus laid waste to enemy ball-carriers with his bone-jarring hits and vicious tackles, Buffone simply went about the business of recording more than 100 tackles virtually every year, making as many as 158 stops in 1972. Blessed with good speed and excellent instincts, the 6-foot, 230-pound Buffone also did an outstanding job in pass coverage, recording at least three

Doug Buffone's total of 24 career interceptions represents a franchise record for linebackers. Courtesy of MEARSonlineauctions.com

interceptions four times. One of the league's top blitzing linebackers, Buffone also excelled at applying pressure to opposing quarterbacks, with his unofficial total of 18 sacks in 1968 representing one of the highest single-season marks in franchise history.

Commenting on the manner with which Buffone performed his job in virtual anonymity, Bears defensive tackle Jim Osborne said, "There were some guys that had to do a lot of the dirty work, and it had to be done, and he was one of those guys that made certain that it was being done. You couldn't have had a better guy on the team, and in the locker room."

In discussing Buffone, who played in every game his first 10 years in Chicago, Dick Butkus stated, "It seemed to me he was lucky that he never had any serious injuries while he played with me. He had like bird legs but a developed upper body."

Acknowledging the fact that his own presence on the team may well have prevented Buffone from gaining the sort of recognition he deserved, Butkus added, "I never heard him gripe. He was a Pro Bowler in my eyes on my team."

Buffone's string of 142 consecutive games played ended when he suffered an injury in Week 2 of the 1976 campaign that sidelined him for the rest of the year. However, he returned to the Bears the following season, missing just two more games, before announcing his retirement following the conclusion of the 1979 campaign. In addition to recording 1,257 tackles and 24 interceptions, Buffone registered 37 sacks, recovered nine fumbles, forced nine others, amassed 211 interception-return yards, and scored one defensive touchdown during his career. Appearing in a total of 186 games with the Bears, Buffone retired as the franchise's all-time leader in that category (he has since slipped to fifth).

Following his playing days, Buffone remained in the Chicago area, where he became a restauranteur, founded a newspaper known as *Doug Buffone's Chicago Bear Report*, and began a career in broadcasting, co-hosting *Chicago NFL Live* and a popular Bears radio postgame show on WSCR with former teammate Ed O'Bradovich. Using his frankness, sense of humor, and passion for the team he loved to attract legions of younger listeners who never saw him perform on the football field, Buffone reached a level of celebrity he never attained during his playing career.

Unfortunately, Buffone's lengthy association with the Bears ended on April 20, 2015, when he died in his sleep in his Chicago home, at the age of 70. Upon learning of his passing, Bears chairman George McCaskey issued a statement that read:

> We are terribly saddened to hear of Doug's passing. He will always be celebrated as one of the Bears greats for his contributions to his team and the fans who loved him. There was no one tougher on Sundays than Doug Buffone. And he proved it each week over his 14-year career, a tenure record he shared with another great, Bill George, for 33 seasons. His retirement ended a link to our founder, as he was the last active player to play for George Halas.

Mike Ditka said of his former teammate, "He was a great guy, a great friend, and a hell of a football player. But forget the football—he was one of the good guys. For a sports guy who was pretty big in our town, he handled himself very, very well. He was very humble. He was a good guy—period. I don't know any other way to put it. I never heard anybody say anything about Doug that wasn't complimentary."

Ditka then added, "Doug had a lot of passion for the Bears. I don't think anybody that has played for the Bears ever had more."

Commenting on the loss of his longtime friend, Ed O'Bradovich stated, "Being with Doug the last 49 years, I know that no one person could love a family more than Doug. I know that no one person that played the game of football loved it more than Doug did. The bottom line is he was true and loyal to his family, to football, and to his friends. I cannot tell you how much I will miss him."

## CAREER HIGHLIGHTS

### Best Season

Buffone performed exceptionally well for the Bears in 1972, recording one interception and a career-high 158 tackles over the course of the campaign. He had another outstanding all-around year in 1975, finishing the season with five forced fumbles, one fumble recovery, one interception, and 99 tackles, seven of which resulted in a loss. However, Buffone turned in his most dominant performance in 1968, when, in addition to finishing second on the team in tackles, he recorded an unofficial total of 18 sacks.

### Memorable Moments/Greatest Performances

Buffone recorded his first interception as a pro when he picked off a Bart Starr pass during a 13–10 loss to the Packers on September 24, 1967.

Buffone scored his lone career touchdown when he returned a fumble 1 yard for a TD during a 27–13 win over the Lions on November 5, 1967.

Buffone helped lead the Bears to a 24–10 victory over the New Orleans Saints on October 6, 1974, by recording a game-high 11 solo tackles.

Buffone picked off two passes during a 16–13 win over the 49ers on September 10, 1978.

Buffone recorded the final two interceptions of his career during a 27–7 loss to the Patriots on October 14, 1979.

### Notable Achievements

- Played in every game first 10 years with Bears, appearing in 142 consecutive contests.
- Recorded more than 100 tackles seven times.
- Recorded unofficial total of 18 sacks in 1968.
- Ranks among Bears career leaders with 1,257 tackles (4th), 24 interceptions (tied-8th), and 186 games played (tied-5th).
- Served as Bears defensive captain from 1972 to 1979.

# 39

# OTIS WILSON

Perhaps the most athletically gifted member of one of the greatest defenses in NFL history, Otis Wilson used his speed, strength, and tenacity to track down opposing ball-carriers and apply pressure to opposing quarterbacks for the Bears during the 1980s. A solid run-defender and elite pass-rusher, Wilson served as Chicago's designated blitzer during the championship campaign of 1985, finishing second on the team with 10½ sacks, with his outstanding play earning him Pro Bowl and Second-Team All-Pro honors. Although Wilson never again earned either distinction, he proved to be a force at linebacker for most of his eight years in the Windy City, helping the Bears win four division titles, one NFC championship, and one Super Bowl.

Born in Brooklyn, New York, on September 15, 1957, Otis Ray Wilson grew up in the borough's rugged Brownsville section, where he avoided trouble by playing sports. After starring on the gridiron at Thomas Jefferson High School, Wilson accepted an athletic scholarship from Syracuse University, where he remained just one year before transferring to the University of Louisville. Excelling for the Cardinals at linebacker for three seasons, Wilson recorded a total of 484 tackles during his college career, gaining First-Team All-America recognition as a senior in 1979.

Selected by the Bears in the first round of the 1980 NFL Draft, with the 19th overall pick, Wilson spent most of his rookie season playing on special teams, although he managed to intercept two passes in limited action on defense. Replacing Jerry Muckensturm at starting left-outside linebacker the following year, Wilson performed well, recording 4½ sacks and recovering three fumbles for a Bears team that finished just 6-10. After two more solid seasons, Wilson began to emerge as a top defender in 1984, earning Second-Team All-NFC honors by registering 6½ sacks, with his strong play helping the Bears capture their first of five straight division titles. Wilson subsequently established himself as a full-fledged star in 1985, recording a career-high 10½ sacks and three interceptions, while also registering two fumble recoveries, one safety, and one touchdown for the NFL champions.

Proving to be the perfect complement to Wilber Marshall and Mike Singletary, Wilson combined with those two men to form one of the greatest linebacking trios in NFL history. While Marshall roamed the field in freelance fashion and Singletary anchored the Bears' defense from his middle linebacker position, calling the signals on that side of the ball while also focusing on stopping the run and covering backs coming out of the backfield, Wilson filled any holes left unattended and served as the team's primary blitzer, forcing many errant throws by opposing quarterbacks.

In comparing Wilson to Singletary, teammate Doug Plank said, "You know, Otis and Singletary were two different kinds of players. Mike was mechanical. He was the train on the track going downhill. Otis could go left and right like nobody's business. He could defend wide receivers, and he was just murder coming off the edge. Speed personified."

Plank then went on to compare Wilson to Marshall, stating, "I can never recall any player on any team consistently holding Otis on a block. Wilber was a fabulous player, but he was different than Otis. Again, it's a fast and loose concept. Wilber was stiffer than Otis. . . . Otis wasn't thick. His upper body was like a Greek god. He should have been a statue inside the remains of the Acropolis."

Steve McMichael provided additional insight when he said, "Otis and Wilber were both more complete than Mike Singletary—better players. They were both faster and more athletic than Singletary, and O and Wilber would intercept passes, while Singletary would just knock them down."

McMichael also stated that, although the 6'2", 227-pound Wilson made good use of his considerable physical gifts, he also excelled in the mental aspect of the game, suggesting, "When he joined the Bears, he picked up a bad rap as a slow learner. So, people underestimated his football IQ, and that's just wrong. Let me tell ya something, when that's the case, a guy's gonna get his ass handed to him. Otis had terrific football intelligence."

Otis Wilson finished second on the 1985 Bears with 10½ sacks.
Courtesy of MearsonlineAuctions.com

Wilson further contributed to the Bears' mystique with his "Junkyard Dog" persona, frequently barking like a dog after making a big play, which led to chants of "Woof, Woof, Woof" resonating in the stands at Soldier Field for the next decade.

Although the 1985 campaign proved to be the finest of Wilson's career, he performed very well once again the following year, finishing the 1986 season with eight sacks, two interceptions, and three fumble recoveries. However, after getting off to an excellent start in 1987, recording 6½ sacks in the first seven games, Wilson tore his ACL, forcing him to miss the rest of the year, and all of 1988 as well. Ready to return to the team in 1989, Wilson suffered the indignity of being released by the Bears, who subsequently replaced him in the lineup with Ron Rivera. Wilson left Chicago with career totals of 514 tackles, 40½ sacks, 10 interceptions, eight fumble recoveries, and two touchdowns.

Following Wilson's release, rumors surfaced that his close relationship with former Bears defensive coordinator Buddy Ryan, who had since assumed head-coaching duties in Philadelphia, may well have contributed to his dismissal. Although Wilson's inability to take the field for nearly two years and his role in the 1987 players' strike previously caused him to fall out of favor with Mike Ditka, many believe that his alleged meeting with Ryan at a hotel in Chicago two nights before the Bears met the Eagles in the 1988 playoffs ultimately sealed his fate.

After leaving the Bears, Wilson signed with the Los Angeles Raiders, with whom he spent one undistinguished season, appearing in just one game, before retiring at the end of the year after sustaining another injury. Since retiring as an active player, Wilson has spent much of his time focusing on his nonprofit organization, The Otis Wilson Charitable Association, which provides an all-inclusive health and fitness program for at-risk youth. The organization, which remains active in the Chicago area, sponsors many events to fund its programs. Wilson has also co-authored the book, *If These Walls Could Talk: Chicago Bears*, which Triumph Books released in September 2017.

In discussing his former teammate, Steve McMichael stated, "If you talk about left-side linebackers in the 1980s, Otis was better than Carl Banks, the guy who played on the other side of L.T. Otis was really Von Miller before Von Miller, and you know what kind of money Denver pays Miller."

McMichael added, "Some guys are born into this world to play football, just like gladiators were born to fight in ancient Rome. Otis was a gladiator. He made toast out of rival players."

## BEARS CAREER HIGHLIGHTS

### Best Season

Wilson had his best season for the Bears in 1985, when he earned his only trip to the Pro Bowl and lone All-Pro nomination by recording a career-high 10½ sacks, recovering two fumbles, and intercepting three passes, one of which he returned for a touchdown.

### Memorable Moments/Greatest Performances

Wilson recorded the first interception of his career during a 22–3 win over the New Orleans Saints on September 14, 1980.

Although the Bears suffered a 26–23 overtime loss to Tampa Bay in the final game of the 1982 regular season, Wilson scored his first career touchdown on a 39-yard pick-six.

Wilson recorded two sacks during a 30–13 win over the Lions in the 1984 regular-season finale.

Wilson contributed to a 23–7 victory over the Packers on October 21, 1985, by tackling Green Bay quarterback Jim Zorn in the end zone for a safety.

Wilson scored the last of his two career touchdowns when he returned his interception of a Tommy Kramer pass 23 yards for a TD during a 27–9 win over the Vikings on October 27, 1985.

Wilson earned NFC Defensive Player of the Week honors by recording a sack, recovering a fumble, and applying constant pressure to Dallas quarterbacks Danny White and Gary Hogeboom during a 44–0 rout of the Cowboys on November 17, 1985.

Wilson registered two sacks during the Bears' 46–10 mauling of the Patriots in Super Bowl XX.

Wilson helped lead the Bears to a 13–10 victory over the Atlanta Falcons on November 16, 1986, by recording two sacks.

Wilson earned NFC Defensive Player of the Week honors for the second and final time by recording two sacks during the Bears' 24–10 win over Dallas in the 1986 regular-season finale.

### Notable Achievements

- Recorded 10½ sacks in 1985.
- Tied for ninth in franchise history with 40½ career sacks.

- Four-time division champion (1984, 1985, 1986, and 1987).
- 1985 NFC champion.
- Super Bowl XX champion.
- Two-time NFC Defensive Player of the Week.
- 1985 Pro Bowl selection.
- 1985 Second-Team All-Pro selection.
- 1985 First-Team All-NFC selection.
- 1984 Second-Team All-NFC selection.

# 40

## — GEORGE TRAFTON —

Nicknamed "The Brute," George Trafton proved to be one of the NFL's most universally disliked players during the league's formative years, with legendary running back Red Grange once calling him "the toughest, meanest, most ornery critter alive." Extremely talented as well, Trafton anchored the Bears' offensive line from his center position for 12 seasons, helping them win two league championships. Also excelling on the defensive side of the ball, Trafton earned All-League honors five times with his outstanding all-around play. And, following the conclusion of his playing career, Trafton received the additional distinctions of being named to the NFL 1920s All-Decade Team and being elected to the Pro Football Hall of Fame.

Born in Chicago, Illinois, on December 6, 1896, George Edward Trafton attended Oak Park and River Forest High School, where he played football under legendary head coach Bob Zuppke. Following his graduation, Trafton spent two years working and playing semipro football, before enlisting in the Army in 1918. Enrolling at the University of Notre Dame following his discharge from the military one year later, Trafton served as a member of that institution's football, basketball, and track-and-field teams, with his exceptional play on the gridiron helping to lead the Fighting Irish to an undefeated record and the National Championship in 1919. However, after it surfaced that Trafton had played semipro ball under an assumed name, thereby making him ineligible to compete for Notre Dame in any future sporting events, head coach Knute Rockne kicked him off the team, prompting Trafton to leave school.

Subsequently recruited by George Halas to play for the Decatur Staleys of the newly formed American Professional Football Association, Trafton joined the team prior to the start of the 1920 campaign. Starting for the Staleys at center on offense and tackle on defense, Trafton earned First-Team All-APFA honors in the league's inaugural season, helping the Staleys compile a record of 10-1-2 in the process. Continuing to perform well when the team relocated to Chicago the following year, Trafton served as a key member of a Staleys squad that captured the first league championship in franchise history. Choosing to leave the Staleys at season's end to become the offensive line coach at Northwestern University, Trafton fulfilled that role for one season, before Big Ten rules prohibiting professional players from serving as coaches forced him to resign his post.

Returning to the newly named Bears in 1923, Trafton began a 10-year stint in the Windy City, establishing himself as arguably the league's top center. The first player at that position to snap the football with just one hand, Trafton, according to an old Bears' press book, "never made a bad snap in 201 games or 158 hours of actual competition." The 6'2", 230-pound Trafton also possessed outstanding size, strength, and mobility, making him an exceptional lead blocker.

George Trafton earned All-League honors five times with his outstanding two-way play.
Public domain, photographer unknown

Yet, even though Trafton's brilliant play at center earned him All-Pro honors four times between 1923 and 1927, he admitted that he derived much more pleasure from playing defense, stating on one occasion, "That I loved. You could really find the action on defense." Taking great pride in his ability to perform well on both sides of the ball, Trafton said, "Imagine . . . when I started with the Bears, we had 15 players. You were hired to play a football game, and you played it—all 60 minutes of it."

One of the first interior linemen to rove on defense, Trafton became known for his hard-hitting, aggressive style of play, which made him extremely unpopular with fans of opposing teams. Commenting on the anger that Trafton inspired in fans throughout the league, one reporter claimed that he "was strongly disliked in every NFL city, with the exception of Green Bay and Rock Island, where he was hated."

The physical nature of Trafton's game caused him to develop an affinity for boxing, which he briefly participated in himself. While still playing for the Bears in 1929, Trafton decided to test his pugilistic skills, engaging in a few bouts, before being suspended indefinitely in 1930 for allegedly "taking a dive" against future world heavyweight champion Primo Carnera.

Trafton remained with the Bears through the end of 1932, helping them win the NFL championship in his final season. During his 12 years in Chicago, the Bears posted a losing record just once, winning at least nine games on seven separate occasions.

Following his retirement, Trafton operated a boxing gymnasium in Chicago for nearly a decade, while also serving as a boxing manager. He later held assistant coaching jobs with the Bears, Rams, and Packers, before becoming head coach of the Winnipeg Blue Bombers of the Canadian Football League in 1951. After remaining in that post for three years, Trafton returned to Los Angeles, where he spent several years working in the real estate and property management business. Inducted into the Pro Football Hall of Fame in 1964, Trafton found himself suffering from poor health in his later years. After undergoing hip surgery in April 1971 to treat an injury that he traced back to his playing days, Trafton spent the next six months residing at the Villa Gardens Convalescent Home in Los Angeles. He passed away at the age of 74 on September 5, 1971, with a friend noting at the time, "George just plain wore out." Trafton's funeral service was subsequently held in Los Angeles, with his pallbearers including former teammates and fellow Hall of Famers George Halas, Ed Healey, and Link Lyman.

## CAREER HIGHLIGHTS

### Best Season

Although Trafton also performed exceptionally well for the Bears in 1926, helping them outscore the opposition by a combined margin of 216–63, he had his finest all-around season in 1924, when he earned his lone First-Team All-Pro selection.

### Memorable Moments/Greatest Performances

Trafton excelled on both sides of the ball during a 29–0 win over Rockford A.C. on October 31, 1920.

Trafton and the rest of Chicago's offensive line dominated the opposition at the point of attack during a 26–0 victory over the Oorang Indians on November 4, 1923, with the Bears scoring three touchdowns on the ground during the contest.

Trafton and his line-mates controlled the line of scrimmage during victories of 34–0 over the Louisville Colonels on November 7, 1926, and 35–0 over the Canton Bulldogs on November 28, 1926.

Although the Bears lost to the Packers by a score of 14–10 on September 27, 1925, Trafton accounted for their only touchdown when he blocked a punt, which teammate Don Murry subsequently recovered in the Green Bay end zone.

The most famous (or infamous) moment of Trafton's career took place during a scoreless tie with the Rock Island Independents on November 7, 1920, when he reportedly knocked unconscious four Rock Island players over a span of only 12 plays. Chased from the city following the conclusion of the contest by angry Rock Island fans, who pelted him with whatever objects they had at their disposal, Trafton finally escaped with the help of a passing motorist. With the two teams engaging in another extremely physical battle the next time they met in Rock Island, the hometown fans once again became quite irritable, prompting George Halas to hand over to Trafton for safekeeping the $7,000 that represented Chicago's share of the gate receipts. Explaining his actions, Halas later said, "I knew that if trouble came, I'd be running only for the $7,000. Trafton would be running for his life."

## Notable Achievements

- 1932 division champion.
- 1921 APFA (American Professional Football Association) champion.
- 1932 NFL champion.
- 1920 First-Team All-APFA selection.
- 1924 First-Team All-Pro selection.
- Three-time Second-Team All-Pro selection (1923, 1926, and 1927).
- NFL 1920s All-Decade Team.
- Elected to Pro Football Hall of Fame in 1964.

# 41

## — HARLON HILL —

H is period of dominance limited to three short seasons by a series of injuries he sustained during the early stages of his career, Harlon Hill never attained the level of greatness for which he appeared destined his first few years in Chicago. Nevertheless, the speedy Hill established himself as arguably the NFL's most potent offensive weapon from 1954 to 1956, leading the league in touchdown receptions, touchdowns, and average yards per reception twice each during that time. The first winner of the NFL Rookie of the Year award, Hill followed that up by becoming the inaugural winner of the Jim Thorpe Trophy as the most outstanding professional football player of the year. A three-time Pro Bowl selection and three-time All-Pro, Hill continues to rank second in Bears' history in receiving yards and touchdown receptions nearly 60 years after he played his last game as a member of the team.

Born in Killen, Alabama, on May 4, 1932, Harlon Junious Hill attended Lauderdale County High School in nearby Rogersville, where he starred as a receiver and defensive back. Continuing to excel on both sides of the ball at tiny Florence State Teacher's College (now known as the University of North Alabama), Hill earned NAIA All-America honors as a senior in 1953.

Despite being virtually unknown to the rest of the league, Hill became the 174th overall pick of the 1954 NFL Draft when the Bears selected him in the 15th round. Commenting years later on his unexpected selection, Hill said, "How many players ever make it to the pros from a college the size of Florence State? I'd never even considered that path."

Hill continued, "Being from a small college, it was sort of a coincidence that I was discovered. One of the scouts from the Bears was at the Blue-Gray Game in Montgomery. A coach from Jacksonville State, who I had played against for four years, mentioned my name to him [George Halas] and told him a little about me. George Halas called Coach Self and asked for a film. He must have liked something he saw. I was drafted in the 15th round."

Revealing that he didn't even realize at the time that he had been drafted by the Bears, Hill told Pro Football Researchers in 1983: "I was surprised when I found out I was drafted by the Bears. I had no idea I had been 'discovered.' I really did not know much about the National Football League. I was walking across campus and Mr. Van Pelt—who is still down

Harlon Hill earned NFL Rookie of the Year honors in 1954.
Courtesy of MEARSonlineauctions.com

there—he came up to me and told me about it. I did not know what to think, but, after I found out what it was all about, naturally I was elated."

Hill added, "I was overwhelmed. I had such limited experience at that time. The city of Chicago itself was dazzling to me. Just think of the impression a place like that would have made from a boy raised in a small town in Alabama. And to play on an NFL team? That was completely unbelievable."

Although Hill arrived at his first Bears training camp with little fanfare, he made an immediate impression on his new teammates, with linebacker George Connor later being quoted in the George Halas autobiography entitled *Papa Bear* as saying, "Harlon Hill was the best piece of raw-boned talent I ever saw walk into a training camp. I came home from camp one weekend and told my brother, 'You should see this kid we got from Alabama. He can run all day and all night and never break a sweat, never drop a football.'"

Taking the NFL by storm in 1954, Hill earned Rookie of the Year, Pro Bowl, and All-Pro honors by making 45 receptions, finishing second in the league with 1,124 receiving yards, and topping the circuit with 12 touchdowns and an average of 25.0 yards per reception. Although somewhat less productive in 1955, Hill still managed to lead the NFL with nine touchdowns and rank among the league leaders with 42 receptions and 789 receiving yards, earning in the process Pro Bowl and All-Pro honors for the second straight time, while also being named NFL Player of the Year by the Newspaper Enterprise Association (NEA). Hill followed that up with an exceptional 1956 campaign, earning Pro Bowl and All-Pro honors once again by placing near the top of the league rankings with 47 receptions, 1,128 receiving yards, 1,152 yards from scrimmage, and 11 touchdown catches, while also leading the league with an average of 24.0 yards per reception.

Blessed with 9.7 speed, sure hands, and good size, the 6'3", 200-pound Hill developed a reputation as the NFL's most feared deep threat his first three years in the league, with sportswriters often comparing him to Green Bay Packers Hall of Fame wideout Don Hutson. An extremely acrobatic receiver who possessed exceptional body control, Hill also became known for his ability to make improbable catches, with George Halas claiming that he "had an uncanny knack for pulling down impossible passes."

Unfortunately, Hill suffered a back injury during the Bears' 47–7 loss to the Giants in the 1956 NFL championship game that proved to be just the first in a serious of injuries that led to a precipitous fall in his offensive production. Missing the final four games of the 1957 season after separating his shoulder, Hill finished the year with just 21 receptions, 483 receiving yards, and two touchdowns. After rupturing his Achilles tendon in 1958, Hill appeared in only eight contests, making just 27 receptions for 365 yards and three touchdowns. Although Hill returned to action in 1959 after undergoing surgery during the offseason, he failed to regain much of his speed and agility, recording 36 receptions for 578 yards and three touchdowns, before assuming a backup role the following year.

Even though injuries proved to be a major factor in Hill's failure to perform at the same lofty level he attained his first three years in the league, his fall from grace could also be attributed, at least to some degree, to his growing dependence on alcohol. Admitting years later that he let his early success go to his head, Hill began drinking too much after 1956, causing his level of play to deteriorate somewhat.

Moved to safety in 1961, Hill recorded three interceptions, which he returned for a total of 52 yards. Dealt to the Pittsburgh Steelers following the conclusion of the campaign, Hill ended his time in Chicago with 226 receptions, 4,616 receiving yards, 40 touchdown catches, and an average of 20.4 yards per reception that ranks as the third highest in franchise history among players with at least 100 catches.

After leaving the Bears, Hill returned to wide receiver, where he made just seven receptions for 101 yards while splitting the 1962 season between the Steelers and Detroit Lions, before announcing his retirement. Following his playing days, Hill became sober, moved back to Alabama, and enjoyed a long career in secondary education, eventually serving as the principal at Brooks High School in Killen from 1980 to 1992. In 1986, Hill became the namesake for the Harlon Hill Trophy, which is presented annually to the NCAA Division II College Football Player of the Year. Hill lived until March 21, 2013, when he passed away at the age of 80 following a long battle with lung disease.

## BEARS CAREER HIGHLIGHTS

### Best Season

Hill posted nearly identical numbers in 1954 and 1956, concluding the first of those campaigns with 45 receptions, 1,124 receiving yards, and 12 touchdowns, and finishing the second with 47 catches, 1,128 receiving yards, and 11 TDs. Since Hill earned consensus First-Team All-Pro honors in 1956 and only made Second-Team All-Pro two years earlier, we'll identify the 1956 season as the finest of his career.

## Memorable Moments/Greatest Performances

Hill made a huge impact in his first game as a pro, catching four passes for 140 yards and one touchdown during a 48–23 loss to the Detroit Lions in the 1954 regular-season opener, with his first career TD coming on a 64-yard connection with Zeke Bratkowski.

Hill scored the first points of a 28–9 victory over the Baltimore Colts on October 10, 1954, when he collaborated with George Blanda on a 76-yard scoring play. He finished the game with three receptions for 144 yards and that one TD.

Hill led the Bears to a 31–27 win over the San Francisco 49ers on October 31, 1954, by making seven receptions for 214 yards and four touchdowns, which came on hookups of 47, 20, and 11 yards with George Blanda and a 66-yard connection with Ed Brown with just 30 seconds remaining in the fourth quarter that provided the margin of victory.

Hill continued his extraordinary rookie campaign by making six receptions for 117 yards and one touchdown during a 29–7 win over the Chicago Cardinals on December 5, 1954.

Hill helped lead the Bears to a 31–20 victory over the Los Angeles Rams on October 30, 1955, by making eight receptions for 151 yards and three touchdowns, one of which came on an 86-yard connection with Ed Brown.

Hill and Brown collaborated on another long scoring play against the Rams on November 13, 1955, with Hill hauling in an 84-yard TD pass from his quarterback during a 24–3 Bears win. He finished the game with three catches for 113 yards and that one TD.

Hill contributed to a 58–27 victory over the Baltimore Colts on October 21, 1956, by making nine receptions for 198 yards and two touchdowns, the longest of which covered 68 yards.

Hill followed that up with a strong outing against San Francisco, making seven receptions for 142 yards during a 38–21 Bears win on October 28, 1956.

Continuing his success against Green Bay two weeks later, Hill made four receptions for 121 yards and two touchdowns during a 38–14 victory, with his longest reception of the day being a 70-yard TD connection with Ed Brown.

Hill helped lead the Bears to a 30–21 win over the Rams on November 18, 1956, by making five catches for 121 yards and one touchdown, which came on a 68-yard pass from Brown.

Hill helped the Bears forge a 17–17 tie with the Giants on November 25, 1956, by making a pair of fourth-quarter touchdown receptions that covered 79 and 56 yards, with the 56-yarder being a sensational over-the-shoulder juggling catch that came in the game's closing moments.

Although the Bears lost to the Rams by a score of 28–21 on October 11, 1959, Hill turned in an outstanding effort, making five catches for 147 yards and one touchdown, which came on a career-long 88-yard hookup with Ed Brown.

## Notable Achievements

- Surpassed 1,000 receiving yards twice.
- Scored more than 10 touchdowns twice.
- Averaged more than 20 yards per reception three times.
- Led NFL in touchdown receptions twice, touchdowns twice, and average yards per reception twice.
- Finished second in NFL in receiving yards twice and touchdown receptions once.
- Finished third in NFL in receiving yards once, yards from scrimmage once, touchdowns once, and average yards per reception once.
- Led Bears in receptions three times and receiving yards three times.
- Ranks among Bears career leaders with 4,616 receiving yards (2nd), 40 touchdown receptions (2nd), and 40 touchdowns (7th).
- 1956 division champion.
- 1954 NFL Rookie of the Year.
- 1955 NEA NFL Player of the Year.
- Three-time Pro Bowl selection (1954, 1955, and 1956).
- Two-time First-Team All-Pro selection (1955 and 1956).
- 1954 Second-Team All-Pro selection.
- 1956 First-Team All–Western Conference selection.

# 42

## — WILBER MARSHALL —

One of the finest all-around linebackers of his time, Wilber Marshall performed so well in all phases of the game that he earned a spot on this list even though he spent just four seasons in Chicago. Blessed with speed, power, and intelligence, Marshall starred at right-outside linebacker for the Bears from 1984 to 1987, contributing greatly to teams that won four division titles, one NFC championship, and one Super Bowl. Garnering Pro Bowl recognition twice and All-Pro honors once during his time in the Windy City, Marshall continued to perform at an elite level after he left the Bears following the conclusion of the 1987 campaign, earning another Pro Bowl selection and two more All-Pro nominations as a member of the Washington Redskins.

Born in Titusville, Florida, on April 18, 1962, Wilber Buddyhia Marshall grew up with his 10 brothers and sisters in nearby Mims, where he helped his father pick oranges in the fields until nightfall after attending football practice at Astronaut High School. Starring for the Astronaut War Eagles at tight end on offense and linebacker on defense, Marshall earned *Parade* magazine high school All-America honors, prompting the University of Florida in Gainesville to offer him an athletic scholarship.

Playing linebacker exclusively for the Gators, Marshall performed brilliantly from 1980 to 1983, recording career totals of 23 sacks and 343 tackles, with his magnificent play gaining him First-Team All–SEC recognition in each of his final three seasons. Also accorded First-Team All-America honors in his junior and senior years, Marshall received the additional distinctions of twice being named a finalist for the Lombardi Award as the best player in college football and being named National Defensive Player of the Year by ABC Sports in 1983.

Subsequently selected by the Bears with the 11th overall pick of the 1984 NFL Draft, Marshall spent his rookie season playing mostly on special teams, often incurring the wrath of defensive coordinator Buddy Ryan, who mercilessly referred to him as "Stupid." Recalling how Ryan treated him during his first season in Chicago, Marshall said, "He drilled me. When I told him I wanted to play, he said, 'No way, you're a rookie.' I had to be intelligent enough to figure out how to get on the field. Then, when Al Harris sat out the 1985 season in a contract dispute, that was my chance, and I convinced him I could do it."

Finally getting his opportunity to start in 1985, Marshall recorded 78 tackles, six sacks, and four interceptions, with his addition to Mike Singletary and Otis Wilson giving the Bears arguably the finest trio of line-backers in the NFL. Marshall followed that up with an even stronger 1986 campaign, gaining Pro Bowl and First-Team All-Pro recognition by making 105 tackles, registering 5½ sacks, picking off five passes, scoring two touchdowns, and finishing second in the league with four forced fumbles.

Allowed to freelance quite a bit by Chicago's coaching staff, Marshall assumed a diverse role on defense, often playing near the line of scrimmage, while also frequently dropping into pass coverage. An excellent blitzer, the 6'1", 231-pound Marshall used his strength and quickness to apply pressure to opposing quarterbacks. Even more outstanding in pass coverage, Marshall possessed the ability to run with most of the league's wide receivers and running backs, with former teammate Steve McMichael stating, "You've got to understand how fast Wilber Marshall was. If the perception is that he was linebacker fast, that's wrong. He was defensive back fast."

In discussing Marshall's varied skill set, Buddy Ryan once said, "No question about it. Wilber was Hall of Fame-caliber. He was one of the only linebackers who could blitz, sack the quarterback, and make interceptions. He could bump and run with wideouts. He was gifted."

Described by fellow Bears linebacker Otis Wilson as "Determined, nasty, hard-hitting, smart, knowledgeable—a pit bull," Marshall also became known for his ability to deliver jarring hits to the opposition. However, Dan Hampton stressed that his teammate played well within the rules of the game, stating, "Understand what I'm going to tell you. Wilber wasn't a dirty player—he was a *vicious* player. He played the game with an inner rage. He'd knock the living [stuff] out of you every chance he got. That creates an intimidation and fear that players don't want to talk about or acknowledge."

Former Bears cornerback Leslie Frazier related the following incident that took place during the championship campaign of 1985: "We were playing the Colts that championship season and someone gave him a cheap shot, and he said, 'Les, I'm going to get him, you watch, I'm going to get that guy.' We were lining up for a field goal, and Wilber just absolutely cleaned his clock. They had to take him out on a stretcher. I wanted to be in a foxhole with him."

Marshall had another outstanding year in 1987, earning his second straight Pro Bowl nomination by recording 93 tackles and five sacks, before becoming the first free agent in 11 years to sign with another NFL team following the conclusion of the campaign. Electing to accept a five-year, $6 million contract offer from the Washington Redskins, Marshall drew heavy compensation in return, with the Redskins having to surrender their first-round pick in each of the next two drafts to the Bears, who chose not to match the offer.

In explaining his decision, Marshall said at the time, "I wouldn't have minded staying in Chicago. We'd been talking contract with the Bears, but they told my agent his demands were ridiculous. I preferred to play in Washington. When you're a linebacker, you look at who you're lining up behind, and I'll have Dexter Manley and Darryl Grant in front of me on the right side. The Redskins' whole defensive line is great . . . this unit could be more powerful than the one I played on in the last few years."

Wilber Marshall helped the Bears win the division title in each of his four seasons with the team.
Courtesy of SportsMemorabilia.com

Marshall continued, "The Bears tried to get me to drop the no-trade provision in the deal I'd signed with Washington. They got Walter Payton to talk to me about it. He called me from Phoenix. I thought there was someone listening in on the speaker phone. I said, 'Walter, if they want to ask me, they don't need you to do it for them.' Without the no-trade, they could have signed me and then traded me for higher draft choices. It wouldn't have been right. I made a deal with the Skins. I want to be better than I was for the last four years. I know I've got it in me. I think I can make NFL Player of the Year. That's my goal, and I won't stop until I get there."

Upon learning of the impending departure of Marshall, who recorded 295 tackles, 16½ sacks, nine interceptions, eight forced fumbles, five fumble recoveries, and two touchdowns during his time in Chicago, Dan

Hampton said, "He's the best player on our football team. If anybody deserves a lot of money, it's Wilber Marshall. I'm sad as heck Wilber is leaving, but you have to be pragmatic."

Meanwhile, Washington general manager Bobby Beathard gushed, "Wilber is a great addition to the Redskins. It isn't often a player of his caliber is available. . . . He's a great blitzer and cover guy. He can run stride for stride with wideouts."

Marshall ended up spending five very successful seasons in Washington, registering 621 tackles, 24½ sacks, 12 interceptions, and 13 forced fumbles, with his exceptional play earning him one trip to the Pro Bowl and two All-Pro nominations. He then split the next three seasons between the Houston Oilers, Arizona Cardinals, and New York Jets, before retiring at the end of 1995 with career totals of 1,043 tackles, 45 sacks, 23 interceptions, 304 interception-return yards, 24 forced fumbles, 16 fumble recoveries, and four touchdowns.

Although the Pro Football Hall of Fame has not yet opened its doors to him, Marshall feels that he is worthy of that honor, telling sportswriter Rick "Goose" Gosselin, "Hate to say it, but I do believe I should be there. I'm probably the only linebacker in history . . . that I know of . . . that played outside and inside linebacker [on the same Super Bowl unit]. They had Mike [Singletary] sitting on the sidelines when I'm playing middle linebacker on third down. So, I wasn't just a rush guy, like the guys on the end that you see going 90 percent of the time. Ten percent of the time they may drop. So, I had a lot to learn."

Former Bears safety Shaun Gayle expressed similar sentiments when he said, "Wilber Marshall should be on his way to the Hall of Fame. He was a defensive coordinator's dream. Usually, you can't find a guy who can rush the passer, cover a running back in the slot, drop back in coverage, and plug the hole. Now, they substitute three guys. If you look at the way linebackers are judged, they either do one or two things very well. But, when you find a player so versatile, sometimes they don't get all the accolades and recognition—except from the players they played against."

Mike Ditka also had high praise for Marshall, stating, "There was a time when I thought Wilber Marshall was the best outside linebacker in football when we had him. He would put some hurt on you."

Meanwhile, Leslie Frazier said of his former teammate, "He was a tremendous athlete, and we missed him and his talent. Who knows if he would have stayed and we had a healthy quarterback, what would have happened?"

Unfortunately, Marshall has experienced a considerable amount of adversity since his playing career ended, spending most of his retirement battling the NFL for disability benefits needed to pay for surgeries to repair his injured spine, shoulder, and knees. Forced to file for bankruptcy at one point, Marshall eventually returned to his hometown of Titusville, Florida, where he currently lives. Choosing to remain away from Chicago due to his ongoing dispute over retroactive payments, Marshall nevertheless continues to hold the Bears and their fans close to his heart, saying, "I hope Bears fans will forgive me for not being at the reunions. I want people to know I'm not bitter toward everybody in Chicago. I loved the team, and I loved the fans. They treated me like the king of England, and I played my heart out for them. But the reason I haven't been there is to fight for my life. I don't want to be run over."

## BEARS CAREER HIGHLIGHTS

### Best Season

Marshall played his best ball for the Bears in 1986, when he earned First-Team All-Pro honors by making 105 tackles, intercepting five passes, recording 5½ sacks, forcing four fumbles, recovering three others, and scoring two touchdowns.

### Memorable Moments/Greatest Performances

Marshall recorded the first sack of his career during a 20–7 win over the Patriots on September 15, 1985.

Just four days later, during a 33–24 Thursday night win over the Vikings, Marshall recorded his first career interception, which he subsequently returned 14 yards.

Marshall sacked Joe Montana twice during a 26–10 win over the 49ers on October 13, 1985.

Marshall delivered his most memorable hit as a member of the Bears during a 37–17 win over the Lions in the 1985 regular-season finale, when he leveled Joe Ferguson with a stunning blow that left the Detroit quarterback lying flat on his back, totally unconscious.

Marshall provided the highlight of the 1985 NFC championship game when, after teammate Richard Dent sacked Rams quarterback Dieter Brock early in the fourth quarter, causing him to fumble, Marshall picked up the loose football and ran 52 yards through the falling snow at Soldier Field for a touchdown. Later identified by Fox News Chicago as the most iconic moment of the season, Marshall's fumble recovery and subsequent TD run put the finishing touches on a 24–0 win over the overmatched Rams.

Marshall excelled for the Bears in Super Bowl XX, recording a sack and recovering a fumble during the Bears' 46–10 trouncing of the New England Patriots.

Marshall helped lead the Bears to a 41–31 victory over the Browns in the opening game of the 1986 regular season by returning his interception of a Bernie Kosar pass 58 yards for a TD.

Marshall lit the scoreboard again when he returned a fumble 12 yards for a touchdown during a 13–7 win over the Detroit Lions on October 26, 1986.

Marshall played a key role in another victory over the Lions on December 15, 1986, when he recorded two sacks during a 16–13 Bears win.

Marshall helped the Bears end the 1986 regular season in style by intercepting a pass and recording a sack during a 24–10 win over the Dallas Cowboys on December 21.

Marshall recorded a career-high three sacks during a 34–19 victory over the New York Giants in the opening game of the 1987 regular season.

## Notable Achievements

- Recorded 105 tackles in 1986.
- Intercepted five passes in 1986.
- Recorded at least five sacks three times.
- Finished second in NFL with four forced fumbles in 1986.
- Four-time division champion (1984, 1985, 1986, and 1987).
- 1985 NFC champion.
- Super Bowl XX champion.
- December 1986 NFC Defensive Player of the Month.
- Two-time Pro Bowl selection (1986 and 1987).
- 1986 First-Team All-Pro selection.
- 1986 First-Team All-NFC selection.
- 1987 Second-Team All-NFC selection.

# 43

# LINK LYMAN

A winner wherever he went, Roy "Link" Lyman won four league championships over the course of his 11-year NFL career, never playing for a team with a losing record. Spending his final seven seasons in Chicago, Lyman helped lead the Bears to two division titles and one NFL championship, with the team compiling an overall record of 68-20-8 with him serving as a member of the squad. Excelling at tackle on both sides of the ball, Lyman gained All-Pro recognition a total of seven times, being so honored four times while playing for the Bears. And, long after his playing career ended, Lyman received the additional distinction of being named to the Pro Football Hall of Fame.

Born in Table Rock, Nebraska, on November 30, 1898, William Roy Lyman grew up with his seven younger siblings in Rawlins County, Kansas, where his father raised cattle and sold real estate. Unable to play football at McDonald Rural High School since, as he recalled, there were only "six or seven boys in the whole school," Lyman had to wait until he enrolled at the University of Nebraska to begin his career on the gridiron. Quickly developing an affinity for the sport, Lyman remembered, "From the first day, I just loved the game, and we had some pretty good teams, too." Starring at offensive and defensive tackle for the Cornhuskers, Lyman earned Missouri Valley and All-Western honors in 1918, 1919, and 1921, choosing not to return to the university in 1920 after getting married the previous winter. Receiving high praise in the 1922 Nebraska yearbook, Lyman, it said, "was, without doubt, our fastest lineman. Roy is a big man, weighing 200 pounds, and he could get down under punts almost as quickly as the ends. Roy proved to be a ground-gainer on tackle-around plays before the season was over."

Following his graduation, Lyman signed with the NFL's Canton Bulldogs, whose head coach and star player, Guy Chamberlain, also graduated from Nebraska. Lyman spent the next 3½ seasons with the Bulldogs, helping them capture the league championship in 1922, 1923, and 1924,

Link Lyman gained All-Pro recognition in four of his seven seasons with the Bears.
Public domain, photographer unknown

before joining the Frankford Yellow Jackets for the final four games of the 1925 campaign. Establishing himself as one of the NFL's best two-way tackles during his time in Canton, Lyman gained All-Pro recognition from at least one major news publication each year, from 1923 to 1925.

After spending the 1925 offseason playing for the Bears during their winter barnstorming tour that featured Red Grange, Lyman decided to remain with the team in 1926. He subsequently helped them go a combined 28-9-6 over the course of the next three seasons, with his exceptional play on both sides of the ball prompting DeKalb, Illinois's *Daily Chronicle* to call him "the daddy of all tackles" and proclaim that "No man in the league can get down the field faster, and he's nearly impregnable on defense."

Meanwhile, Red Grange, who benefited greatly from Lyman's outstanding blocking, suggested, "Lyman is almost a football line by himself."

Possessing surprising speed and quickness for a man his size, the 6'2", 233-pound Lyman excelled as a downfield blocker and proved to be a demon on special teams. George Halas also maintained that Lyman improved with age, claiming years later that he was "stronger and tougher during his last two seasons than when he first joined the team eight years earlier."

Yet, Lyman's greatest claim to fame lay in the manner with which he influenced future generations of defensive players by constantly shifting positions, thereby disrupting the blocking assignments of opposing offensive linemen. Steve Owen, who played with Lyman in 1925 and later coached the Giants for many years, recalled, "Link was the first lineman I ever saw who moved from the assigned defensive position before the ball was snapped. It was difficult to play against him because he would vary his moves and, no matter how you reacted, you could be wrong."

Meanwhile, Lyman's Pro Football Hall of Fame biography reads: "The constant shifting by defensive players before each play in modern professional football can be traced back to Lyman, who regularly resorted to similar ploys. His sliding, shifting style of defensive line play confused his opponents and made him one of the most respected players of his time. Lyman explained that the idea of shifting was an instinctive move to fool a blocker. He had a unique ability to diagnose a play, and many times he would make his move just as the ball was snapped."

Lyman elected to retire from the NFL following the conclusion of the 1928 campaign, but, after spending one year playing semipro ball in Texas and working in the ranching business, he decided to return to the Bears in 1930. He remained in Chicago for the next two years, before retiring again at the end of 1931 to resume his semipro career and return to his ranch. After another one-year hiatus, Lyman rejoined the Bears in 1933, helping lead them to a regular-season record of 10-2-1 and a 23–21 victory over the New York Giants in the NFL championship game. He subsequently spent the 1934 season serving as a key member of a Bears team that finished a perfect 13-0 during the regular season, before losing to the Giants by a score of 30–13 in the NFL title game. Retiring for good at season's end, Lyman left Chicago having blocked for legendary running backs Red Grange and Bronko Nagurski, as well as the less-famous Beattie Feathers, who, with the help of Lyman, became the first player in league history to rush for 1,000 yards in a season. A true iron man, Lyman appeared in a total of 286 professional games over the course of his career (including unofficial games), logging a total of 211½ hours of playing time in the process, with both those figures representing NFL records at the time of his retirement.

Following his playing days, Lyman returned to the University of Nebraska, where he served as line coach from 1935 to 1941, before being relieved of his duties. Lyman subsequently accepted a position with the Equitable Life Assurance Society, eventually becoming an insurance executive with the firm. After being elected to the Pro Football Hall of Fame eight years earlier, Lyman died in an automobile accident on December 28, 1972, perishing when his car crashed into the back of a semi-trailer truck 12 miles south of Baker, California. Lyman was 74 years old at the time of his passing.

One of the greatest linemen of his era, Lyman receives the following words of praise in the *National Football League Encyclopedia*: "He did it all a little bit better than anyone else of his era, and there seems to be little doubt that he would have done it just as well in any era."

## BEARS CAREER HIGHLIGHTS

### Best Season

Lyman played arguably the best ball of his career in his final NFL season, earning First-Team All-Pro honors in 1934 by helping the Bears outscore their opponents by a combined margin of 286–86.

### Memorable Moments/Greatest Performances

Lyman starred on both sides of the ball in consecutive weeks in 1928, leading the Bears to 27–0 wins over the New York Yankees and the Dayton Triangles on November 4 and November 11 of that year.

Although the Bears lost to the Frankford Yellow Jackets by a score of 13–12 on October 25, 1931, Lyman scored the only touchdown of his career when he recovered a fumble in the Frankford end zone.

Lyman's late fumble recovery led to a last-minute field goal by Jack Manders that gave the Bears a 10–9 victory over the New York Giants on November 18, 1934. The win improved the Bears' record to 10-0, with Lyman's big play helping to preserve their undefeated regular season.

### Notable Achievements

- Two-time division champion (1933 and 1934).
- 1933 NFL champion.
- Two-time First-Team All-Pro selection (1930 and 1934).
- Two-time Second-Team All-Pro selection (1928 and 1931).
- Elected to Pro Football Hall of Fame in 1964.

# 44

## — WILLIE GALIMORE —

Often described as one of the most elusive runners in NFL history, Willie "The Wisp" Galimore blended 9.6 speed with extraordinary quickness and tremendous cutback ability to establish himself as the most explosive running back of his time. Playing for the Bears from 1957 to 1963, Galimore surpassed 1,000 yards from scrimmage once and 1,000 all-purpose yards twice, even though he spent most of his time in Chicago sharing running duties with Rick Casares. A member of the Bears squad that captured the NFL championship in 1963, Galimore earned Pro Bowl and All-Pro honors once each, before tragically losing his life in an automobile accident prior to the start of the 1964 campaign.

Born in St. Augustine, Florida, on March 30, 1935, Willie Lee Galimore attended local Excelsior High School, where he starred in football and basketball, prompting historically black Florida A&M University to offer him an athletic scholarship. Choosing to focus exclusively on football while in college, Galimore spent the next four years starring at halfback for the Rattlers, gaining a total of 3,596 yards on the ground, en route to earning Black College All-America honors three straight times from 1954 to 1956. Leading his school to an overall record of 33-4-1 and four consecutive trips to the Orange Blossom Classic game, which pitted the top two teams in black college football against one another each year, Galimore saved some of his finest performances for his trips to Miami, rushing for 295 yards against Maryland State in 1954, before scoring four touchdowns against Tennessee State in his final college game two years later.

Called "the finest player I ever coached" by legendary Florida A&M head coach Jake Gaither, Galimore also drew high praise from assistant coach Costa Kittles, who said, "He had something many running backs don't have—both the short stride and the long stride. You need the short stride to change directions. Once he broke clean, he had the long stride to break away from you. As a receiver, I saw him make a lot of one-hand catches like someone picking grapes from a vine. In terms of a total football player, he was the best Florida A&M ever had."

After scoring 16 touchdowns and averaging 9.5 yards per carry as a senior in 1956, Galimore entered that year's NFL Draft, where the Bears selected him in the fifth round, with the 58th overall pick. Performing well as a rookie in 1957, Galimore combined with fullback Rick Casares to give the Bears one of the league's top running back tandems. In addition to rushing for 538 yards, Galimore gained another 201 yards on 15 pass receptions, amassed 879 all-purpose yards, and scored seven touchdowns. Improving upon those numbers the following year, Galimore earned Pro Bowl and Second-Team All-Pro honors by ranking among the league leaders with 619 yards rushing, 1,108 all-purpose yards, eight rushing touchdowns, 12 TDs, and a rushing average of 4.8 yards per carry. Plagued by injuries in each of the next two seasons, Galimore amassed a total of just 567 yards on the ground and scored only four touchdowns. However, he rebounded in 1961 to score seven touchdowns and establish career-high marks with 707 yards rushing, 33 receptions, 502 receiving yards, 1,209 yards from scrimmage, and 1,291 all-purpose yards.

While the numbers Galimore compiled his first few years in the league might seem modest to some, it must be remembered that George Halas employed his running backs in a rather unusual fashion, preferring to split the workload between them, rather than relying heavily on one member of his offensive backfield to shoulder much of the burden. Yet, despite his somewhat limited usage, Galimore emerged as one of the NFL's top offensive threats, and easily its most electrifying runner. Standing 6'1" and weighing 187 pounds, Galimore had the build and speed of a wide receiver, possessing more quickness than any other player in the game at that time. Also blessed with outstanding instincts, exceptional peripheral vision, and the ability to move laterally extraordinarily well, Galimore, it was said, could run side-to-side just as fast as most men could run down the field in a straight line.

Commenting on his former teammate's running style, Bears quarterback Bill Wade said, "Willie was nicknamed 'Willie the Wisp,' and, in reality, that was the way he ran. All of a sudden, you'd see him break out into the open and you didn't know where he came from. . . . Willie was unbelievably quick going downfield. He wasn't sideways or this way. He just zoomed down the field and seemed to be so fast nobody could catch him."

Wade added, "He could get downfield so fast on the defensive halfback and the free safety that the free safety was not free anymore. This had the effect of two great halfbacks in professional football."

Willie Galimore proved to be the most explosive running back of his time.
Courtesy of AlbersheimsStore.com

In discussing Galimore, Philadelphia Eagles Hall of Fame center/line-backer Chuck Bednarik stated, "He had speed like you wouldn't believe. One motion, the same speed, to be able to cut back. The only difference between him and [Hugh] McElhenny, Willie was faster. To me, it seemed like he did the 100 in 9.2. Fantastic!"

San Francisco 49ers great Leo Nomellini claimed, "Willie Galimore could turn the corner faster than most fellows could run forward. I've seen him do that."

Galimore lost some of his blinding speed after he suffered a knee injury that limited him to just seven games and 289 yards from scrimmage in 1962. Returning to the Bears a bit slower the following year, Galimore accumulated just 452 yards from scrimmage, although he managed to score five touchdowns for the eventual NFL champions.

Sadly, Galimore never appeared in another game with the Bears, tragically losing his life while driving back with teammate John "Bo" Farrington to the dorms at the team's training camp on July 27, 1964. Their automobile overturned on a country road in Rensselaer, Indiana, and Galimore, 29, and Farrington, 28, both perished instantly. Haunted by the loss of their teammates, which they recalled every time they looked at each other and saw the commemorative black armbands they wore on their jerseys all year, the Bears stumbled to a 5-9 record in 1964.

Reflecting back years later on his former teammate, who ended his career with 2,985 yards rushing, 87 receptions for 1,201 yards, 4,186 yards from scrimmage, 5,286 all-purpose yards, and 37 touchdowns, Doug Atkins told NFL Films: "It seems like everybody forgot him. And he made some runs that I've never seen a back do yet. I have never seen anyone, and I don't believe you have in any of your film, catch him from behind, or from an angle. . . . He was amazing. I always thought he was one of the best runners, and I never could understand why he didn't get more recognition."

## CAREER HIGHLIGHTS

### Best Season

Although Galimore earned Pro Bowl and All-Pro honors for the only time in 1958 by rushing for 619 yards, finishing third in the league with 12 touchdowns, and amassing 770 yards from scrimmage and 1,108 all-purpose yards, he posted slightly better overall numbers in 1961, concluding the campaign with 707 yards rushing, seven touchdowns, 1,209 yards from scrimmage, and 1,291 all-purpose yards.

### Memorable Moments/Greatest Performances

Galimore scored the first touchdown of his career during a 21–10 loss to the Baltimore Colts on October 5, 1957, when he collaborated with quarterback Ed Brown on a 56-yard scoring play.

Galimore led the Bears to a 34–26 victory over the Los Angeles Rams on October 20, 1957, by carrying the ball 24 times for 153 yards, gaining another 60 yards on two pass receptions, and scoring four touchdowns, the longest of which came on an 18-yard run.

Galimore gained 84 yards on just eight carries during a 14–6 win over the Chicago Cardinals on December 8, 1957, with most of those yards coming on a 67-yard TD run.

Galimore proved to be the difference in a 34–20 win over the Packers in the 1958 regular-season opener, rushing for 45 yards, making three receptions for 88 yards, and scoring three TDs, the longest of which came on a 79-yard catch-and-run on a pass thrown by Ed Brown.

Although the Bears lost to the Colts by a score of 51–38 on October 4, 1958, Galimore turned in an outstanding all-around effort, rushing for 96 yards and scoring on a 99-yard kickoff return.

Despite rushing for only 19 yards during a 24–10 win over the Colts on October 15, 1961, Galimore played an important role in the victory, making seven receptions for 149 yards and one TD, with his 84-yard fourth-quarter connection with Ed Brown putting the Bears ahead to stay.

Galimore's 52-yard touchdown reception late in the fourth quarter gave the Bears a 28–24 victory over the Rams on November 26, 1961. He finished the game with 55 yards rushing, four receptions for 85 yards, and that one TD.

Galimore contributed to a 52–35 win over the Vikings in the final game of the 1961 regular season by carrying the ball 13 times for 97 yards, making three receptions for 41 yards, and scoring two touchdowns, one of which came on an electrifying 60-yard run.

Galimore displayed his explosiveness in the 1962 regular-season opener, leading the Bears to a 30–14 victory over the 49ers by rushing for 181 yards and two touchdowns, which came on runs that covered 37 and 77 yards.

## Notable Achievements

- Amassed more than 1,000 yards from scrimmage once (1,209 in 1961).
- Amassed more than 1,000 all-purpose yards twice.
- Scored 12 touchdowns in 1958.
- Averaged at least 5 yards per carry twice.
- Finished third in NFL with eight rushing touchdowns and 12 touchdowns in 1958.
- Led Bears with 707 yards rushing in 1961.

- Ranks among Bears career leaders with 2,985 yards rushing (10th), 26 rushing touchdowns (tied-7th), and 37 touchdowns (tied-9th).
- 1963 division champion.
- 1963 NFL champion.
- 1958 Pro Bowl selection.
- 1958 Second-Team All-Pro selection.
- #28 retired by Bears.

# 45

# DAVE DUERSON

A hard-hitting defensive back who combined with Gary Fencik to give the Bears one of the NFL's most formidable safety tandems, Dave Duerson spent seven of his 11 NFL seasons in Chicago, serving as a key member of Bear teams that won four division titles, one NFC championship, and one Super Bowl. An outstanding tackler and excellent blitzer with a nose for the football, Duerson recorded 16 sacks and 18 interceptions during his time in the Windy City, bringing down opposing quarterbacks behind the line of scrimmage seven times one season, while also picking off at least five passes twice. A tremendous leader and positive influence in the locker room as well, Duerson contributed to the success of the Bears in many ways, with his significant role on one of the most dominant defenses of all time earning him four trips to the Pro Bowl, two All-Pro nominations, and three All-NFC selections. Yet, unfortunately, Duerson is perhaps remembered most for taking his own life nearly two decades after his playing career ended, leaving us at only 50 years of age.

Born in Muncie, Indiana, on November 28, 1960, David Russell Duerson attended Muncie Northside High School, where he starred in baseball, football, and basketball. Particularly outstanding in the first two sports, Duerson gained recognition as 1979 Indiana Mr. Football, before being offered a contract to sign with the Los Angeles Dodgers, who felt he had the ability to either pitch or play the outfield in the major leagues one day. Choosing to pursue a career in football instead, Duerson declined the Dodgers' offer and accepted an athletic scholarship from the University of Notre Dame.

Duerson subsequently went on to star at Notre Dame for four seasons, setting the school record for most career interception-return yardage (256), en route to earning All-America honors twice, with his exceptional play prompting the Bears to select him in the third round of the 1983 NFL Draft, with the 64th overall pick. After seriously considering going to law school or beginning a career in politics, Duerson ultimately elected to sign with the Bears, thereby fulfilling his dream of playing in the NFL.

Failing to make much of an impression on defensive coordinator Buddy Ryan following his arrival in Chicago, Duerson saw very little action on defense over the course of his first two NFL seasons, spending most of his time playing on special teams and backing up starting strong safety Todd Bell. Commenting on the level of disdain that Ryan displayed toward Duerson during that time, former teammate Dan Hampton said, "Buddy wanted smashmouth, and Duerson wouldn't nail guys. In practice, Buddy would yell, 'That shit ain't cuttin' it! You dive on the ground again, I'm firing you!'"

Duerson finally received his opportunity to assume a more significant role on defense in 1985, when Bell remained away from the team for the entire year while holding out for more money. Yet, even though Ryan turned to him in his time of need, Duerson later revealed that he did so reluctantly, recalling, "I played through that whole season with Buddy telling me that he was rooting for me to screw up. So, I became an All-Pro myself."

Performing at an elite level his first year as a full-time starter, Duerson contributed significantly to the league's top-ranked defense, earning Pro Bowl honors for the first of four straight times by picking off five passes and recording two sacks. In discussing the impact that Duerson made after he joined the starting unit, Mike Ditka said, "He was a hell of a football player. He came in at the right time for us because that's when Todd Bell held out. He fit right in, became a starter. We liked everything about him at Notre Dame. He rounded out that defense. He fit in perfectly with Gary Fencik back there and was one of the leaders of our team."

Dave Duerson combined with Gary Fencik to give the Bears one of the NFL's most formidable safety tandems.
Courtesy of MEARSonlineauctions.com

Continuing his strong play in 1986, Duerson gained Second-Team All-Pro recognition for the first of two straight times by intercepting six passes and registering seven sacks, which remained a record for defensive backs until 2005. Excelling against the run as well, the 6'1", 207-pound Duerson developed into a ferocious hitter after submitting to Ryan's wishes, doing an outstanding job of jamming runners at the line of scrimmage, while also applying pressure to opposing quarterbacks via the blitz and covering runners coming out of the backfield. One of the Bears' leaders on defense, Duerson combined with linebacker Otis Wilson to develop the unit's calling card, standing over their victims and barking like junkyard dogs after delivering especially vicious hits to the opposition.

Duerson remained in Chicago for three more years, earning two more Pro Bowl selections and another All-Pro nomination, before being released by the Bears following the conclusion of the 1989 campaign. In addition to his 16 sacks and 18 interceptions, Duerson ended his time in the Windy City with 221 interception-return yards, 566 tackles, seven forced fumbles, and four fumble recoveries.

Following his release by the Bears, Duerson signed with the Giants, with whom he won the Super Bowl in his only year in New York. He subsequently spent the next three years with the Phoenix Cardinals, before retiring at the end of 1993 with career totals of 20 interceptions, 226 interception-return yards, 16 sacks, five fumble recoveries, and one defensive touchdown.

After retiring as an active player, Duerson began a successful career in business, purchasing three McDonald's franchises in Louisville, Kentucky, before establishing Duerson Foods, which supplied sausages to fast food chains. However, after remaining profitable for nearly a decade, Duerson's business began to suffer losses, with his errors in judgment contributing to its decline, as his former wife, Alicia, noted when she said, "He was making hasty decisions. A lot of things that would come natural to him wouldn't anymore. He started to lose his ability to function, to think things clearly through."

And, as Duerson's financial losses continued to mount, his physical and mental state grew increasingly precarious. Plagued by severe headaches, sharp mood swings, and frequent memory loss, Duerson began to lash out verbally at those around him. Finally reaching his nadir in February 2005, Duerson attacked his wife in a hotel room in Indiana, leading to his arrest and the couple's divorce two years later. With Duerson's business failing, he went bankrupt, forcing him to surrender his house and celebrity lifestyle. Looking back at that dark period in her former husband's life, Alicia said, "David was so disappointed in himself. He was a very proud person, and he couldn't handle the failure of it. We had built this beautiful life together, and he lost it all."

With Duerson having also lost his position as a University of Notre Dame trustee, he settled in Miami, where he eventually began working as a consultant and hosting an internet radio sports talk show called *Double Time with Double D* on Voice America. Sadly, while still fulfilling both roles, Duerson took his own life, with police finding him dead from a self-inflicted gunshot wound to his chest at his Sunny Isles Beach, Florida, home on February 17, 2011. Also discovered on the premises was a note that read: "Please, see that my brain is given to the NFL's brain bank."

Studies subsequently revealed that Duerson suffered from "moderately advanced" chronic traumatic encephalopathy (CTE) likely brought on by his career in football, with Dr. Ann McKee, a neuropathologist and co-director of the Boston University School of Medicine Center for the Study of Traumatic Encephalopathy stating, "Dave Duerson had classic pathology of CTE and no evidence of any other disease. He had severe involvement of areas that control judgment, inhibition, impulse control, mood and memory."

Upon learning of Duerson's death, Ray Ellis, the sports channel director at Voice America Sports, said, "If you looked at him visually, Dave Duerson looked like he could play strong safety today." Ellis, who also mentioned that Duerson recently told him that he had gotten engaged and planned to marry sometime later that year, then added, "There was so much more to Dave than being a former Chicago Bear. Dave took pride in his accomplishments off the field."

Former Bears teammate Richard Dent stated, "It's just so unfortunate. I'm just speechless right now. It's very hard to take."

In trying to express his emotions at the time, Walter Payton's older brother, Eddie, said, "When I lost Walter, he [Duerson] was the first there. When he lost his mother, I was the first there. Through all of it, his strength helped me through tough times, and we actually became like brothers."

## BEARS CAREER HIGHLIGHTS

### Best Season

Duerson had his finest season for the Bears in 1986, when he earned one of his two All-Pro nominations by recording 87 tackles and establishing career-high marks with six interceptions, 139 interception-return yards, and seven sacks.

## Memorable Moments/Greatest Performances

Duerson recorded the first two sacks of his career during a 20–7 loss to the San Diego Chargers on December 3, 1984.

Duerson recorded his first interception as a pro the following week when he picked off a Rich Campbell pass during a 20–14 loss to the Packers on December 9, 1984.

Duerson starred during a 13–10 overtime victory over the Philadelphia Eagles on September 14, 1986, recording a sack and an interception, which he returned 22 yards.

Duerson contributed to a 23–0 win over the Vikings on October 5, 1986, by intercepting a pass and sacking Minnesota quarterback Tommy Kramer twice.

Duerson helped lead the Bears to a 13–10 win over the Atlanta Falcons on November 16, 1986, by recording an interception and a sack.

## Notable Achievements

- Recorded at least five interceptions twice.
- Amassed 139 interception-return yards in 1986.
- Recorded seven sacks in 1986.
- Four-time division champion (1984, 1985, 1986, and 1987).
- 1985 NFC champion.
- Super Bowl XX champion.
- 1987 NFL Man of the Year.
- Four-time Pro Bowl selection (1985, 1986, 1987, and 1988).
- Two-time Second-Team All-Pro selection (1986 and 1987).
- 1986 First-Team All-NFC selection.
- Two-time Second-Team All-NFC selection (1987 and 1988).

# 46

## KEN KAVANAUGH

The Bears' first true deep threat at wide receiver, Ken Kavanaugh used his soft hands and exceptional running speed to score more touchdowns through the air than anyone else in franchise history. Despite playing for Bears teams that depended primarily on their running game to overpower the opposition, Kavanaugh managed to record 50 TD receptions over the course of his career—a figure that remains easily the highest total in team annals some 70 years after his retirement. Kavanaugh also holds the franchise record for highest receiving average, averaging 22.4 yards per catch his eight years in the league, with his outstanding play, which helped the Bears win three NFL championships, earning him two trips to the Pro Bowl, three All-Pro selections, and a spot on the NFL 1940s All-Decade Team. Kavanaugh accomplished all he did even though he missed three peak seasons due to time spent in the military during World War II.

Born in Little Rock, Arkansas, on November 23, 1916, Kenneth William Kavanaugh attended Little Rock Central High School, where he starred in football as a two-way end. Establishing himself as a star in multiple sports after enrolling at Louisiana State University in 1936, Kavanaugh excelled in both baseball and football, performing well enough on the diamond to be offered a minor-league contract by the St. Louis Cardinals following his graduation. Proving to be even more proficient on the gridiron, Kavanaugh earned All–SEC honors three straight times, also gaining consensus All-America recognition as a senior in 1939, when he led the nation with 30 receptions and 467 receiving yards.

Although Kavanaugh pitched briefly in the Cardinals organization in 1940, he elected to focus exclusively on football shortly after the Bears selected him in the third round of the 1940 NFL Draft, with the 22nd overall pick. Arriving in Chicago in time for the start of the 1940 season, Kavanaugh had a solid rookie year, earning Pro Bowl honors for the first of two straight times by leading the Bears with 12 receptions, 276 receiving yards, and three TD catches. He followed that up by ranking among the

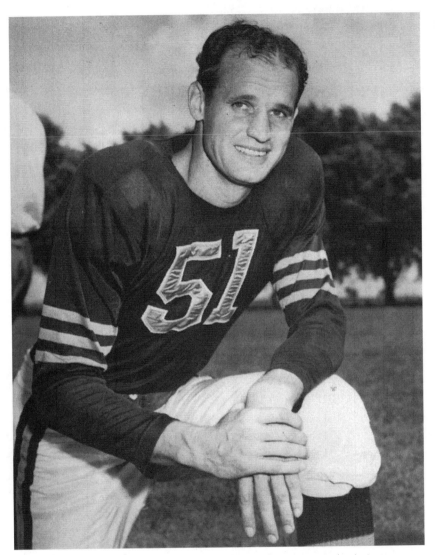

Ken Kavanaugh caught more touchdown passes than anyone else in team annals.
Public domain, photographer unknown

league leaders with 314 receiving yards and six TD catches in 1941, before entering the US Air Force, where he spent the next three and one-half years serving as a bomber pilot. Stationed in England much of that time, Kavanaugh, who eventually reached the rank of captain, flew more than 30 missions between 1942 and 1944.

Returning to the Bears prior to the start of the 1945 season, Kavanaugh caught 25 passes and led the team with 543 receiving yards and six touchdown receptions, establishing new career highs in each of the first two categories. After earning Second-Team All-Pro honors for the first of three straight times in 1946 by making 18 receptions for 337 yards and five touchdowns, Kavanaugh had the finest statistical season of his career the following year, catching 32 passes, finishing third in the NFL with 818 receiving yards, and leading the league with 13 touchdown receptions, with the last figure representing a single-season franchise record.

Used primarily by the Bears as a long-distance touchdown threat, Kavanaugh never made more than 32 receptions in any single season. However, he proved to be one of the most dangerous receivers in the game for much of his career, combining with Sid Luckman to form a deadly passing duo. Standing 6'3" and weighing 207 pounds, Kavanaugh possessed outstanding size for a receiver of his day, often using his height to his advantage, as LSU head coach Bernie Moore noted when he called him "a pass completer rather than a receiver, simply because he'd catch passes no one else could get to." Kavanaugh's speed also made him a threat to score from anywhere on the field, with the receiver averaging a touchdown for nearly every third catch. An outstanding postseason performer as well, Kavanaugh scored a touchdown in each of his three NFL championship game appearances.

After making 18 receptions for 352 yards and six touchdowns in 1948, Kavanaugh had his last big year for the Bears in 1949, concluding the campaign with 29 receptions, 655 receiving yards, and a league-leading nine TD catches. He spent one more year in Chicago, making 17 receptions for 331 yards and two touchdowns in 1950, before announcing his retirement at season's end. In addition to his franchise-record 50 touchdown catches, Kavanaugh ended his career with 162 receptions, 3,626 receiving yards, and two defensive touchdowns.

Following his playing days, Kavanaugh began a lengthy career in coaching, serving as an assistant coach with the Bears in 1951, before assuming a similar role at Boston College (1952–1953), Villanova University (1954), and with the New York Giants (1955–1970). He then served as a scout within the Giants organization from 1971 to 1999, before retiring to Sarasota, Florida, where he passed away at the age of 90, on January 25, 2007, following a bout with pneumonia.

## CAREER HIGHLIGHTS

### Best Season

Kavanaugh had his most productive season for the Bears in 1947, when he established career-high marks in receptions (32), receiving yards (818), and touchdown catches (13), leading the league in the last category. Along the way, Kavanaugh set a Bears record by making at least one touchdown reception in seven straight games.

### Memorable Moments/Greatest Performances

Kavanaugh excelled in his pro debut, catching touchdown passes of 8 yards from George McAfee and 39 yards from Bob Snyder during a 41–10 win over the Packers in the opening game of the 1940 regular season.

Kavanaugh contributed to a 47–25 victory over the Cleveland Rams on November 24, 1940, by making three receptions for 100 yards and one touchdown, which came on a 74-yard connection with Sid Luckman.

Kavanaugh scored Chicago's first points of the 1941 campaign when he gathered in a 63-yard TD pass from George McAfee during a 25–17 win over the Packers in the regular-season opener.

Kavanaugh punctuated the Bears' 37–9 win over the Giants in the 1941 NFL championship game by scoring a touchdown with just nine seconds remaining in the fourth quarter when he recovered a fumble, which he returned 42 yards for the game's final score.

Although the Bears lost to the Washington Redskins by a score of 28–21 on November 18, 1945, Kavanaugh had a big day, making six receptions for 138 yards and two touchdowns, which came on passes from Sid Luckman that covered 33 and 48 yards.

Kavanaugh proved to be the difference in a 27–21 win over the Los Angeles Rams on November 10, 1946, making six receptions for 146 yards and three touchdowns, with his TDs coming on hookups of 38, 34, and 28 yards with Luckman.

Kavanaugh scored the first points of the 1946 NFL title game when he gathered in a 21-yard touchdown pass from Sid Luckman. The Bears went on to defeat the Giants by a score of 24–14.

Despite making just two receptions during the Bears' 40–7 rout of the Philadelphia Eagles on October 12, 1947, Kavanaugh proved to be a huge factor in the game, scoring a pair of touchdowns on connections with Sid Luckman that covered 74 and 70 yards.

Kavanaugh helped the Bears record a 28–24 victory over the Boston Yanks on November 2, 1947, by making eight catches for 129 yards and three touchdowns, with his last two TDs erasing a 24–14 fourth-quarter deficit.

Kavanaugh followed that up by collaborating with Sid Luckman on a career-long 81-yard touchdown reception during a 20–17 win over the Packers on November 9, 1947. He finished the game with four catches for 103 yards and that one TD.

Kavanaugh recorded another 81-yard TD reception during a 31–21 win over the Redskins on November 20, 1949, this time hooking up with quarterback Johnny Lujack.

Kavanaugh contributed to a 52–21 win over the Chicago Cardinals in the final game of the 1949 regular season by making six receptions for 137 yards and two touchdowns, which came on connections of 17 and 37 yards with Lujack.

Although the Bears lost to the New York Yanks by a score of 38–27 on October 29, 1950, Kavanaugh had a huge game, making eight receptions for 177 yards and one touchdown, which came on a 67-yard hookup with Lujack.

## Notable Achievements

- Surpassed 800 receiving yards once (818 in 1947).
- Made 13 touchdown receptions in 1947.
- Averaged more than 20 yards per reception five times.
- Led NFL in touchdown receptions twice.
- Finished second in NFL in touchdown receptions once, touchdowns once, and average yards per reception twice.
- Finished third in NFL in receiving yards once, TD catches once, and touchdowns once.
- Led Bears in receptions twice and receiving yards three times.
- Holds Bears single-season record for most touchdown receptions (13 in 1947).
- Holds Bears career record for most touchdown receptions (50).
- Ranks among Bears career leaders with 3,626 receiving yards (10th) and 52 touchdowns (6th).
- Four-time division champion (1940, 1941, 1946, and 1950).
- Three-time NFL champion (1940, 1941, and 1946).
- Two-time Pro Bowl selection (1940 and 1941).
- Three-time Second-Team All-Pro selection (1946, 1947, and 1948).
- NFL 1940s All-Decade Team.

# 47

## — LARRY MORRIS —

The third and final member of the Bears' outstanding linebacking trio of the late 1950s and early 1960s to make our list, Larry Morris spent seven seasons in Chicago, establishing himself as a tremendous big-game player. The MVP of the 1963 NFL championship game, Morris led the Bears to a 14–10 victory over the New York Giants, with his extraordinary performance in that contest proving to be the highlight of his career. Yet, Morris, who acquired the nickname "The Brahma Bull" during his time in Chicago, contributed to the Bears in many other ways during his seven-year stay in the Windy City, with his exceptional all-around play earning him one All-Pro selection and a spot on the NFL 1960s All-Decade Team.

Born in Decatur, Georgia, on December 10, 1933, Lawrence Cleo Morris lost his father at the age of 10, after which his mother supported the family by working as a bookkeeper. Keeping himself busy after school by doing chin-ups, pushups, and running, Morris attended Georgia Military Academy and Boys High School, where he starred as a center fielder on the diamond and a fullback and linebacker on the gridiron, leading his school to back-to-back state football championships in his junior and senior years. Praising Morris for the brilliance he exhibited on the football field during his time at Boys High, head football coach Charlie Waller, who later coached for the San Diego Chargers, said, "Larry was not only one of the greatest players I ever coached, but one of the greatest I have ever seen—college or pro."

After turning down a contract offer from the Class AA Atlanta Crackers, Morris enrolled at Georgia Tech University, where he spent the next four years lettering in baseball and football. Earning All–SEC honors multiple times in both sports, Morris proved to be particularly proficient on the gridiron, leading the Yellow Jackets to an overall record of 40-5-2, with his exceptional play at center and linebacker also gaining him All-America recognition twice. Turning in what Tech head coach Bobby Dodd later called "the finest individual performance I have ever seen," Morris provided the highlight of his college career when he recorded 24 solo tackles during a 7–3 win over arch-rival Georgia in 1954.

Commenting on Morris's magnificent performance, *Atlanta Journal* sports editor Ed Danforth wrote, "Morris hit a peak of brilliance. He played 60 minutes in the highest tradition of his craft."

Also expressing his admiration for Morris's superb play, former University of Georgia head coach and *Atlanta Journal* football analyst Harry Mehre, who covered the game for that newspaper, wrote, "Morris was everywhere, rushing the passer, a human wrecking ball as a middle linebacker, and springing to the flanks, where he personally stopped eight Bulldog scoring threats."

Unaffected by his sudden celebrity, the quiet and unassuming Morris simply said, "My tackles were made possible because our linemen wiped out the interference to give me a clear shot at the ball carriers."

Dodd, though, continued to praise his squad's finest player by stating, "If my future depended on one game, I would rather have Larry Morris going for me than any other player I ever saw."

Subsequently selected by the Los Angeles Rams with the seventh overall pick of the 1955 NFL Draft, Morris spent most of his first two NFL seasons serving the Rams primarily as a blocking fullback, before being moved to linebacker in 1957. In discussing the 6'2", 225-pound Morris's blocking ability, legendary Army halfback and former Rams teammate Glenn Davis said, "Larry was not only a devastating linebacker, he was like a steamroller blocking at fullback. It was easy for us to gain yardage when he was knocking down two and sometimes three players on every play."

Meanwhile, Rams head coach Sid Gillman marveled at Morris's tremendous versatility, suggesting, "He could have played 10 positions, everywhere but quarterback. He was the kind of player a coach dreams about. He had size, speed, and desire. And he only knew one speed—full. He didn't 'talk the talk,' as they say today. He was all action."

After spending the previous season playing linebacker for the Rams, Morris missed the entire 1958 campaign with an injury. Dealt to the Bears at season's end, Morris began a seven-year stint in Chicago, during which time the team compiled an overall record of 55-36-3. Manning the right-outside linebacker position his entire time in Chicago, Morris combined with Bill George, Joe Fortunato, and, later, Dick Butkus, to give the Bears the league's most formidable linebacking corps.

Extremely consistent and reliable, Morris often found himself being overshadowed by some of the Bears' more flamboyant defenders—most notably George, Butkus, and Doug Atkins. Nevertheless, he proved to be a huge contributor on that side of the ball, with Johnny Morris (no relation) saying of his former teammate, "He had pretty good speed for a linebacker and was as effective against the pass as the run," and then adding, "Although he had an easygoing personality, he was a great player in a violent game."

Morris reached the apex of his career in 1963, when he helped lead the Bears to the NFL title, earning in the process his lone All-Pro selection. He remained in Chicago for two more years, before spending his final season serving as a backup with his hometown team, the Atlanta Falcons. Retiring following the conclusion of the 1966 campaign,

Larry Morris earned game MVP honors for his performance against the Giants in the 1963 NFL championship game. Public domain, photographer unknown

Morris ended his career with six interceptions, 53 interception-return yards, nine fumble recoveries, and one defensive touchdown, compiling virtually all those numbers as a member of the Bears.

Following his playing days, Morris briefly entered the political arena, serving one term in the Georgia State Legislature, before beginning a successful career in the real estate development business in Gainesville, Florida. After developing dementia during the late 1980s, Morris retired to private life, spending the next two decades suffering from declining health, before passing away at the age of 79, on December 19, 2012.

Attributing his condition to football, Morris's widow, Kay, said that her husband suffered several concussions during his career, prompting her to donate his brain to Boston University for research to determine the effects of football on former players. Mrs. Morris, who claimed that her husband began exhibiting symptoms of memory loss in his 40s, stated, "He loved the game, but he had no idea he was exchanging 20 years of quality life for the game." She added, "He and I used to tell each other 'I love you' every time we talked on the phone, every time we said good night. I missed that when that stopped. It was a big adjustment." Mrs. Morris also revealed that, in her husband's last days, "The children pulled my bed up next to him, and

I got to snuggle up with him, and that felt good. We let him know that it was all right, that he had struggled a long time."

## BEARS CAREER HIGHLIGHTS

### Best Season

Morris had his finest all-around season in 1963, when, in addition to earning All-Pro honors for the only time in his career, he led the Bears to a hard-fought 14–10 victory over the New York Giants in the NFL championship game with his stellar play on defense.

### Memorable Moments/Greatest Performances

Morris scored his only touchdown as a member of the Bears during a 26–21 win over the Los Angeles Rams on November 1, 1959, when he returned a fumble 19 yards for a TD.

Morris recorded a key interception during a 21–20 win over the Baltimore Colts on October 29, 1961, subsequently returning his pick of a Johnny Unitas pass 25 yards.

Morris intercepted two passes in one game for the only time in his career during a 13–0 win over the Minnesota Vikings on October 7, 1962.

Morris turned in the most memorable performance of his career in the 1963 NFL championship game, earning game MVP honors by making 16 tackles, recording a sack, and intercepting a Y. A. Tittle screen pass, which he subsequently returned 61 yards to the Giants' 6 yard line, to help set up one of the Bears' two touchdowns. Following the conclusion of the contest, George Halas grabbed Morris, hugged his neck, and said, "You are the greatest Bear of all."

### Notable Achievements

- 1963 division champion.
- 1963 NFL champion.
- 1963 NFL Championship Game MVP.
- 1963 Second-Team All-Pro selection.
- NFL 1960s All-Decade Team.

# 48

## KHALIL MACK

Although Khalil Mack has spent just two full seasons in Chicago, the tremendous overall impact he made on the Bears following his arrival in the Windy City prior to the start of the 2018 campaign earned him a spot on this list. One of the most dominant defensive players in the NFL, Mack helped lead the Bears to a 12-4 record and their first NFC North Division title in nearly a decade his first year in Chicago, with his stellar play gaining him Pro Bowl and consensus First-Team All-Pro recognition. Even though the Bears and Mack took a step backwards in 2019, the defensive end/linebacker remained the backbone of the Chicago defense and a force to be reckoned with, earning his fifth consecutive trip to the Pro Bowl.

Born in Fort Pierce, Florida, on February 22, 1991, Khalil Mack displayed an affinity for sports at an early age, spending his formative years competing in baseball, basketball, and football. Especially proficient on the hardwood, Mack viewed basketball as his ticket to a college scholarship, until a torn patella tendon he sustained prior to the start of his sophomore year at local Fort Pierce Westwood High School forced him to alter his plans. Quickly transitioning to football, Mack began his career on the gridiron at quarterback, before an inability to deliver the ball accurately from short range prompted him to move to linebacker. Proving to be extremely successful at his new post, Mack recorded 140 tackles and nine sacks as a senior, earning in the process Third-Team All-State and First-Team All-Area recognition.

Subsequently offered a scholarship by the State University of New York at Buffalo, Mack spent his freshman year redshirting at that Division I school, gradually transforming himself from a relatively lean 215-pounder into a man among boys. Recalling the work ethic that Mack displayed during his earliest days at Buffalo, Robert Wimberly, who recruited him for the school, said, "He was out on the field by himself when all the other young men that redshirted were leaving the facility—he was there for an

Khalil Mack led the Bears to their first playoff appearance in eight years in 2018.
Courtesy of Joe Glorioso of All-Pro Reels

extended period of time. For most freshmen, especially in Buffalo weather, that's dedication. He always pushed himself."

Jon Fuller, assistant AD/communications at Buffalo, added, "Very quiet, humble kid. Kind of shied away from the spotlight."

Mack ended up starting for four years at Buffalo, earning First-Team All–MAC honors three times, while also gaining recognition as the 2013 MAC Defensive Player of the Year and Second-Team All-America honors as a senior.

Extremely impressed with Mack's brilliant play at the collegiate level, the Oakland Raiders selected him with the fifth overall pick of the 2014

NFL Draft, after which he went on to have a fabulous rookie season. Starting all 16 games at right-outside linebacker for the Raiders in 2014, the 6'3", 269-pound Mack recorded four sacks and 75 tackles, 16 of which went for a loss, earning in the process a spot on the NFL All-Rookie Team and a third-place finish in the NFL Defensive Rookie of the Year balloting, with only Aaron Donald of the Rams and C. J. Mosley of the Ravens receiving more support among the voters. Splitting the ensuing campaign between linebacker and right defensive end, Mack registered 77 tackles and finished second in the league with 15 sacks, with his superb play at both positions gaining him Pro Bowl and First-Team All-Pro recognition. Mack followed that up with two more outstanding seasons, earning NFL Defensive Player of the Year honors in 2016 by recording 11 sacks, 73 tackles, five forced fumbles, three fumble recoveries, one interception, and one touchdown, before earning his third straight trip to the Pro Bowl by registering 10½ sacks and 78 tackles in 2017.

Nevertheless, with Mack and the Raiders reaching an impasse in contract negotiations at season's end, Oakland completed a blockbuster trade with the Bears on September 1, 2018, that sent the star defender and two future draft picks to Chicago for a pair of first-round draft picks, a sixth-round pick in the 2019 NFL Draft, and a third-round pick in the 2020 draft. Upon learning of the deal, Mack said, "Coming from where I came from, which is a great organization, coming to . . . a real, rich history-based organization, especially for the defensive side of the ball, it's going to be exciting. And it's new, but I'm looking forward to it."

After signing a six-year contract with the Bears worth $141 million that made him the highest-paid defensive player in NFL history, Mack led Chicago to the division title in 2018 by recording 12½ sacks, 47 tackles, six forced fumbles, two fumble recoveries, and one interception, which he returned for a touchdown. Accomplishing all he did despite missing two games with an ankle injury, Mack gained Pro Bowl and First-Team All-Pro recognition, before being further honored during the offseason by being named the winner of the Butkus Award as the league's top linebacker.

Certainly, Mack's ability to apply pressure to opposing quarterbacks off the edge contributed greatly to the success the Bears experienced his first year in Chicago. Mack's size, strength, quickness, agility, and tremendous determination all help make him an elite pass-rusher. He also is an outstanding defender against the run and is quite capable of covering backs coming out of the backfield, although the Bears rarely use him in that manner. But, as much as anything, Mack's strong work ethic, leadership ability, and intelligence helped resuscitate the Bears defense, with teammate Prince

Amukamara saying, "I feel like he does a lot of film study. He knows what to expect. In the middle of getting double- and triple-teamed, he knows what's coming and he's still successful."

In discussing Mack's selfless attitude and ability to lead by example, Bears head coach Matt Nagy stated, "He's selfless. He's all about 'we.' He's all about his teammates."

Philadelphia Eagles tight end Zach Ertz also praised Mack when he said, "He's a monster, first and foremost. He's one of the top three players in the league on defense."

Unfortunately, with opposing teams paying an inordinate amount of attention to Mack in 2019, both he and the Bears regressed somewhat, with the team failing to make the playoffs and Mack recording just 8½ sacks. However, more sagacious use of Mack in more varied defensive schemes will likely allow him to return to top form moving forward—something that will be necessary if the Bears are going to reestablish themselves as contenders in the NFC North over the course of the next few seasons. Since Mack is only 29 years old as of this writing, there is certainly every reason to believe that he will soon reclaim his spot among the NFL's elite defenders.

## BEARS CAREER HIGHLIGHTS

### Best Season

Mack had his most impactful season as a member of the Bears in 2018, leading them to the division title by recording a team-high 12½ sacks, while also finishing third in the league with six forced fumbles. Particularly effective during the early stages of the campaign, Mack earned NFC Defensive Player of the Month honors for September by registering at least one sack and one forced fumble in each of Chicago's first four games.

### Memorable Moments/Greatest Performances

Although the Bears suffered a 24–23 defeat at the hands of the Packers in the 2018 regular-season opener, Mack turned in a memorable performance in his first game as a member of the team. After earlier preventing a Green Bay score by recording a strip-sack of backup quarterback DeShone Kizer and recovering the ball at the Chicago 21 yard line, Mack intercepted a Kizer pass, which he returned 27 yards for a touchdown with only 39 seconds remaining in the first half.

Mack keyed a 16–14 victory over the Arizona Cardinals on September 23, 2018, by registering two sacks, five solo tackles, and one forced fumble.

Mack helped the Bears clinch the division title with a 24–17 win over the Packers on December 16, 2018, by recording 2½ sacks and six tackles, two of which resulted in losses.

Mack turned in his most dominant performance of the 2019 campaign on September 23, leading the Bears to a 31–15 victory over the Washington Redskins by recording two sacks, making four tackles, and forcing two fumbles.

Mack followed that up with another strong outing against Minnesota on September 29, registering 1½ sacks and one forced fumble during a 16–6 win over the Vikings.

### Notable Achievements

- Has scored one defensive touchdown.
- Recorded 12½ sacks in 2018.
- Finished third in NFL with six forced fumbles in 2018.
- Finished fourth in NFL with five forced fumbles in 2019.
- Has led Bears in sacks twice.
- 2018 division champion.
- September 2018 NFC Defensive Player of the Month.
- Two-time Pro Bowl selection (2018 and 2019).
- 2018 First-Team All-Pro selection.

# 49

## — JIM MCMAHON —

One of the most charismatic and controversial figures in NFL history, Jim McMahon spent seven turbulent seasons in Chicago, quarreling at various times with team ownership, head coach Mike Ditka, and even NFL commissioner Pete Rozelle. Marching to the beat of a different drum, McMahon endeared himself to some of his teammates with his unique behavior, while alienating himself from others. Yet, despite the many distractions that McMahon created during his seven-year stint in the Windy City, the Bears proved to be a significantly better team with him behind center, compiling an overall record of 46-15 with him starting at quarterback, while posting a mark of 27-16 with someone else calling the signals for them. And, with the enigmatic McMahon serving as their primary QB, the Bears won five division titles, one NFC championship, and one Super Bowl.

Born in Jersey City, New Jersey, on August 21, 1959, James Robert McMahon grew up in San Jose, California, after moving there with his family at the age of three. Losing most of the vision in his right eye as a youngster, McMahon later explained, "I was playing Cowboys and Indians with my brothers as a kid. Tried to untie a knot in my gun holster with a fork and it slipped. Had two prongs go through my eye." Although doctors managed to save the eye, McMahon's vision remained severely impaired and extremely sensitive to light, causing him to regularly wear sunglasses indoors as he grew older.

After starring on the gridiron for two years at San Jose's Andrew Hill High School, McMahon moved with his family once again, this time to Roy, Utah, where he spent his junior and senior years playing football and baseball at Roy High School. With his first choice, Notre Dame, subsequently showing no interest in him, McMahon accepted a scholarship from Brigham Young University, a Mormon school in Provo, Utah, where he spent his freshman year serving as punter, before sharing quarterback duties with future NFL signal-caller Marc Wilson his sophomore year. Laying claim to the starting job as a junior, McMahon went on to set 71 NCAA records, earning in the process All-America honors twice. Particularly impressive as a senior in 1981, McMahon led BYU to the Western Athletic Conference championship by passing for 3,555 yards and 30 touchdowns, with his exceptional play enabling him to finish third in the Heisman Trophy balloting. McMahon also won the Davey O'Brien Award, presented annually to the best quarterback in all of college football.

Making a strong impression on Steve Young, who served as his backup in his final year at BYU, McMahon later received the following words of praise from the Hall of Fame quarterback: "I always admired him. I learned to play by watching him. I watched him drop, I watched him throw. I'm grateful in so many ways for Jim that he probably doesn't even realize."

While McMahon performed exceptionally well on the football field during his time at BYU, he caused a considerable amount of consternation to school officials with his atypical conduct off the playing field. Not one to yield to authority, McMahon failed to follow the rules of the Mormon church, which shunned the use of alcohol and tobacco.

Continuing to behave unconventionally after the Bears selected him with the fifth overall pick of the 1982 NFL Draft, McMahon showed up at his first public function as a member of the team with beer in hand, leaving an unfavorable first impression on George Halas and new head coach Mike Ditka. Nevertheless, Ditka didn't wait long to turn over the starting quarterback job to McMahon, who had a solid first season, earning a spot on the NFL All-Rookie Team by completing 57.1 percent of his passes, while also throwing for 1,501 yards and nine touchdowns in just seven starts during the strike-shortened 1982 campaign. Although McMahon posted unspectacular numbers the following year, finishing the 1983 season with 2,184 yards passing, 12 touchdown passes, and 13 interceptions, he helped the Bears improve their record from 3-6 to 8-8. Despite missing the final six games of the 1984 season with a lacerated kidney, McMahon helped the Bears take another step forward, leading them to a record of 7-2 in games that he started, with the team posting an overall mark of 10-6 that earned them their first division title in more than two decades. McMahon and the Bears then reached the pinnacle of their sport in 1985, with the team losing just one game during the regular season, before laying waste to anyone they faced in the playoffs, which culminated with a 46–10 mauling of the Patriots in Super Bowl XX.

Clearly a better team with McMahon behind center, the Bears benefited greatly from their quarterback's knowledge of the game and ability to read defenses. Blessed with an intuitive grasp of in-game situations,

McMahon frequently changed plays at the line of scrimmage, a practice that infuriated Mike Ditka, even though it most often led to success. The 6'1", 200-pound McMahon also possessed good mobility and excellent awareness, with Ditka saying, "He has a great feel for the rush. He knows how to move away, to slide away. If you do that with enough success, it can become frustrating for the defensive people who are rushing. When they think they have the quarterback trapped two or three times in a game and he gets away, that gets a little frustrating."

One of the finest rollout passers of his time, McMahon explained that coaching in his youth had taught him to square his shoulders to the direction he wanted to throw the football. Doing so enabled him to execute passes with tight spirals and a high degree of accuracy when running to either side.

Adding to McMahon's effectiveness was the relationship he shared with his offensive linemen, with Ditka stating, "Those guys would have done anything to protect Jim McMahon. He didn't play the game like a quarterback. He didn't have any respect for his body. He played the game with reckless abandon."

Ditka added, "He makes you think about stereotypes. You take your so-called general: He's out there, but he's not really in the battle with his troops. It's the opposite with Jim. He thinks he's the best passer, the best runner, the best blocker there is on the team. A lot of players wouldn't do what he does. A lot shouldn't . . . I just wish he would be more discreet about some of the things he does."

Right tackle Keith Van Horne said of his quarterback, "He always wants to be one of the guys. He likes to get down in the trenches with us, get dirty or get turf burns. He wants marks on his helmet."

Meanwhile, former NFL head coach Ron Meyer claimed, "I don't think he ever took a safe slide like you see quarterbacks today. Is that smart? Probably not, but does that win? You bet, and that's Jim McMahon."

Also known for his eccentric behavior off the playing field, McMahon constantly challenged authority, with his dispute with then NFL commissioner Pete Rozelle providing the most notable example of his rebellious nature. After being fined by Rozelle for wearing a headband that featured an unauthorized corporate logo, McMahon showed up on the field one week later donning a headband that read "Rozelle," with the commissioner himself admitting afterwards that he found humor in McMahon's response.

In defense of his teammate, though, Gary Fencik said, "He's not abusive. He doesn't break any laws of society. But he's not one to turn down a drink with the boys, either. That's one of the things that has allowed him to become so close to the other guys on the team. He scoffs at the holier-than-thou adulation most quarterbacks receive."

Fencik then added, "When you see the things Jim is doing, it's almost unimaginable that he's in a Bears uniform. But you have got to have that magic, and that's essentially what Jim brings to this team. Now, we're psychologically hooked on him. He can do no wrong."

Unfortunately, the magic that McMahon brought to the Bears began to dissipate during the latter stages of the 1986 campaign, when, after being body-slammed to the ground by Green Bay nose tackle Charles Martin on what could only be described as an intentionally late and dirty hit,

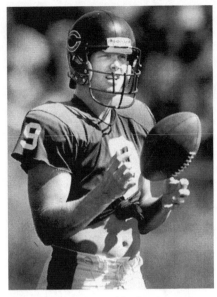

Jim McMahon proved to be an extremely controversial figure during his seven seasons in Chicago.
Courtesy of MearsonlineAuctions.com

the quarterback missed the remainder of the season with a badly injured shoulder. Although the Bears finished the regular season with a record of 14-2, they subsequently found themselves unable to defend their Super Bowl championship without the services of their starting quarterback, suffering a 27–13 defeat at the hands of the Washington Redskins in the divisional round of the postseason tournament. Missing a considerable amount of time in each of the next two seasons as well, the oft-injured McMahon started a total of only 15 games, with the Bears failing to make it back to the Super Bowl both years.

McMahon subsequently wore out his welcome in Chicago by quarreling with Bears president Mike McCaskey and head coach Mike Ditka during the 1988 offseason, prompting the team to trade him to the San Diego Chargers for a conditional pick in the 1990 NFL Draft. Appearing in just 66 out of a possible 104 games during his seven seasons in Chicago, McMahon threw for 11,203 yards, tossed 67 touchdown passes and 56 interceptions, completed 57.8 percent of his passes, and posted a QBR of 80.4. He also ran for 1,284 yards and scored 17 touchdowns, with 15 of those coming on runs and the other two on pass receptions.

Expressing the sentiments of several members of the Bears' defense years later, Dan Hampton criticized McMahon for his reckless style of play, stating during a January 2015 interview, "Unfortunately, McMahon was only healthy a handful of games throughout his career after '86 and '87. It was intolerable. . . . When he left, I was glad. . . . It's a team. And everybody has to pull on the rope. Nobody can ride in the wagon. . . . Mike Ditka, as open-minded as he is—and he was kind of a party guy when he played—but you cannot run an NFL franchise with a quarterback that you cannot depend on. It's just impossible."

After leaving the Bears, McMahon lived a somewhat nomadic existence for the next eight years, spending one season in San Diego, three in Philadelphia, one in Minnesota, one in Arizona, and two in Green Bay, serving as a backup much of the time, before announcing his retirement following the conclusion of the 1996 campaign. Over the course of 15 NFL seasons, McMahon amassed 18,148 passing yards, threw 100 touchdown passes and 90 interceptions, completed 58 percent of his passes, and posted a QBR of 78.2.

Since retiring as an active player, McMahon has experienced numerous physical problems resulting from the concussions, broken neck, and lacerated kidney he sustained during his playing career. Diagnosed with early onset dementia in September 2012, McMahon admits, "There are a lot of times when I walk into a room and forget why I walked in there."

Plagued by headaches, dizziness, depression, and memory loss, McMahon says, "All my joints hurt but the headaches are the worst. My head used to hurt so bad I would mostly stay in my room for months at a time with the shades down. Any kind of light hurt. Often, I couldn't remember where I was or what I was supposed to do. The pain was like somebody sticking ice picks in my head."

McMahon, who has fluid drained from his brain by New York chiropractor Scott Rosa four times per year, states:

> The first time he did it, my head was so full of stuff it literally felt like a toilet being flushed. I could actually feel the stuff draining out of my head. There's no cure for this condition, so I go back to New York every three months because the fluid keeps building up in my brain. . . . During the three months before my next check-up, I get increasingly bad headaches. It's hell getting on a plane with your head all swelled up. I literally squeeze my head for four or five hours on a flight. But, as soon as he adjusts me, I'm good again. . . . In between my visits to New

York, the only way I can ease the pain is to smoke a joint. Here in Arizona, it's legal medically to relieve inflammation. I use Cannabidiol—a marijuana derivative known as CBD—which would work for a large percentage of the population with chronic injuries and doesn't make you feel stoned. . . . When I was playing, the team doctors would hand out painkillers—Vicodin, Percocet, or Oxycontin— like candy, and keep shooting you up to deaden joint pain. But, according to the NFL, you can't smoke a joint because that's bad and addictive. That's ridiculous. Marijuana is a medicinal herb, not a drug, it's not addictive, and it's not a chemical. It's been demonized because it's got natural healing properties. I was in pain my whole career, and some weeks I'd be forced to take more than 100 pills.

McMahon, who has lived in Scottsdale, Arizona, since 2010 and spends most of his time with his family and playing golf in charity events and fundraisers for veterans, now says, "Growing up, I wanted to be a professional athlete. I accomplished that. I didn't want to have a job. I accomplished that. Now, I just want to have a good time—just play golf, enjoy life, and watch my kids grow up. Hopefully, they'll do better than I did."

## BEARS CAREER HIGHLIGHTS

### Best Season

Although McMahon posted comparable numbers in one or two other seasons, he played his best ball for the Bears in 1985, leading them to a perfect 11-0 record in his 11 starts behind center by passing for 2,392 yards, throwing a career-high 15 touchdown passes, running for 252 yards and three touchdowns, making one TD reception, completing 56.9 percent of his passes, and compiling a passer rating of 82.6, with his solid play earning him Pro Bowl honors for the only time in his career.

### Memorable Moments/Greatest Performances

McMahon completed his first touchdown pass as a pro when he hit Ken Margerum with an 11-yard scoring strike during a 20–17 win over the Detroit Lions on November 21, 1982.

McMahon led the Bears to a 26–13 victory over the New England Patriots on December 5, 1982, by running for one touchdown and completing 15 of 21 pass attempts for 192 yards and two TDs, the longest of which went 17 yards to Ken Margerum.

Although the Bears lost to the Packers by a score of 31–28 on December 4, 1983, McMahon performed well in defeat, passing for 298 yards and one touchdown, which came on a career-long 87-yard connection with Willie Gault.

McMahon led the Bears to a 44–9 rout of the Tampa Bay Buccaneers on October 21, 1984, by completing 12 of 18 pass attempts for 219 yards and three touchdowns, the longest of which went 49 yards to Brad Anderson.

McMahon earned NFC Offensive Player of the Week honors by scoring twice from the 1 yard line on quarterback sneaks and completing 23 of 34 pass attempts for 274 yards and two touchdowns during a 38–28 win over Tampa Bay in the 1985 regular-season opener.

McMahon led the Bears to a lopsided 45–10 victory over the Washington Redskins on September 29, 1985, by completing 13 of 19 pass attempts for 160 yards and three touchdowns, the longest of which went 33 yards to Walter Payton. McMahon also caught a 13-yard TD pass from Payton during the contest.

McMahon turned in a solid performance against the Patriots in Super Bowl XX, completing 12 of 20 pass attempts for 256 yards, throwing no interceptions, and scoring on a pair of short TD runs.

McMahon led the Bears to a 44–7 rout of the Cincinnati Bengals on September 28, 1986, by running for one touchdown and throwing for 211 yards and three TDs, with the longest of those coming on a 53-yard connection with Willie Gault.

Although the Bears lost to the Denver Broncos by a score of 31–29 on November 16, 1987, McMahon passed for a career-high 311 yards and three touchdowns during the contest, scoring the Bears' final TD himself on a 1-yard run.

McMahon guided the Bears to a 24–3 victory over the Buffalo Bills on October 2, 1988, finishing the game 20-of-27 for 260 yards and two touchdowns, the longest of which went 63 yards to Ron Morris.

McMahon performed well once again two weeks later, throwing for a season-high 284 yards and one touchdown during a 17–7 win over the Dallas Cowboys on October 16, 1988.

McMahon turned in the most memorable performance of his career before a national television audience on Thursday night, September 19,

1985, when he brought the Bears back from a second-half deficit to the Minnesota Vikings after spending the first 2½ quarters sitting on the bench. Slated to serve as Steve Fuller's backup after spending most of the previous week recovering from a neck injury, McMahon sat and watched as the Vikings built a 17–9 lead midway through the third quarter. After finally convincing head coach Mike Ditka to allow him to enter the fray, McMahon proceeded to throw a 70-yard touchdown pass to Willie Gault on his first play from scrimmage. McMahon subsequently completed two more TD passes in the third quarter, with both of those going to Dennis McKinnon. The Bears went on to win the game by a score of 33–24, with McMahon throwing for 236 yards and those three touchdowns. Expressing his and his teammates' astonishment with McMahon's extraordinary effort following the conclusion of the contest, offensive lineman Keith Van Horne said, "We were all just shaking our heads in amazement." Meanwhile, Walter Payton called McMahon's performance "unbelievable."

## Notable Achievements

- Passed for more than 2,000 yards twice.
- Completed more than 59 percent of passes four times.
- Posted touchdown-to-interception ratio of better than 2–1 once.
- Posted passer rating above 90.0 once (97.8 in 1984).
- Ran for more than 250 yards three times.
- Averaged more than 5 yards per carry four times.
- Led NFL quarterbacks with three game-winning drives in 1987.
- Ranks among Bears career leaders with 1,513 pass attempts (5th), 874 pass completions (5th), 11,203 passing yards (4th), and 67 touchdown passes (4th).
- Five-time division champion (1984, 1985, 1986, 1987, and 1988).
- 1985 NFC champion.
- Super Bowl XX champion.
- 1985 Week 1 Offensive Player of the Week.
- Member of 1982 NFL All-Rookie Team.
- 1985 Pro Bowl selection.
- 1985 Second-Team All-NFC selection.

# 50

## — GEORGE HALAS —

O ften called "the father of professional football," George Halas helped pioneer the growth and expansion of the NFL, with his many contributions to the league making him arguably the most iconic figure in the history of the game. The Bears owner for more than six decades, Halas also proved to be one of the league's most successful head coaches, spending parts of 40 seasons guiding the team to six NFL championships and an overall regular season record of 318-148-31. Yet, prior to reaching legendary status, the man who came to be known affectionately as "Papa Bear" spent his early years in the league excelling for the Bears as a two-way end, performing well enough on both sides of the ball to gain All-League recognition once and earn a spot on the NFL 1920s All-Decade Team.

Born to Czech-Bohemian immigrant parents in Chicago, Illinois, on February 2, 1895, George Stanley Halas attended local Crane High School, before enrolling at the University of Illinois, where he played baseball, basketball, and football, starring on the gridiron as a receiver on offense and an end on defense. Continuing his athletic career while serving as an ensign in the Navy during World War I, Halas played for a team at the Great Lakes Naval Training Station, earning 1919 Rose Bowl MVP honors by catching a touchdown pass and returning an interception 77 yards during a 17–0 win over the Mare Island Marines of California.

Attempting to pursue a career in baseball following his discharge from the military, Halas ended up appearing in 12 games as an outfielder with the New York Yankees in 1919, before suffering a hip injury that effectively ended his career on the diamond. Turning his attention to football, Halas subsequently spent one year playing semipro ball, before moving to Decatur, Illinois, where he took a job as a sales representative with the A. E. Staley Company, a starch manufacturer. In addition to his work in sales, Halas served as player-coach of the company-sponsored football team called the Decatur Staleys. While fulfilling that dual role in 1920, Halas represented the Staleys at a meeting held in Canton, Ohio, that resulted in the formation of the American Professional Football Association (APFA), which became the NFL two years later.

Leading the Staleys to a record of 10-1-2 in the league's inaugural season, the 6-foot, 182-pound Halas earned Second-Team All-APFA honors by doing an outstanding job at wide receiver and defensive end. Assuming full control of the team in 1921, Halas moved the Staleys to Chicago and took on teammate Dutch Sternaman as a partner. Making an impact on the field as well, Halas recorded an unofficial total of three touchdowns, with his solid play helping the Staleys compile a regular season record of 9-1-1 that earned them the league championship. After renaming his club "the Bears" the

George Halas is often called "the father of professional football." Courtesy of RMYAuctions.com

following year, Halas, who also handled ticket sales and the business of running the franchise, continued to function in the dual role of player-coach until 1929, when he chose to focus exclusively on his coaching duties. Although the NFL did not keep an official record of any statistics until after Halas retired as an active player, he has been unofficially credited with 10 career touchdowns, with six of those coming on pass receptions, two on fumble returns, one on an interception return, and one on a run.

Halas, whose earlier recruitment of college star Red Grange helped legitimize the NFL, decided to turn over head coaching duties to Lake Forest Academy's Ralph Jones prior to the start of the 1930 campaign. However, he returned to the helm in 1933 as a way of reducing costs during the Great Depression. Halas then spent the next 10 years coaching the Bears, during which time he guided them to six Western Division titles and three NFL championships. During his second tenure as head coach, Halas also combined with University of Chicago coach Clark Shaughnessy to perfect the T-formation, which created a revolutionary style of play on offense.

With the United States having entered World War II several months earlier, Halas enlisted in the Navy late in 1942. He subsequently spent the next three years supporting the welfare and recreational activities of the Seventh Fleet, serving overseas for 20 months under the command of Admiral Chester Nimitz, where he eventually rose to the rank of captain.

Returning to the Bears in 1946, Halas coached the team for another 10 years, winning his fifth league championship his first year back. Following a brief two-year hiatus, Halas began his final stint as head coach in 1958, claiming his sixth and final NFL title in 1963, before retiring for good five years later with more victories than any other head coach in league history (he has since been surpassed by Don Shula). In his 40 years at the helm, Halas endured only six losing seasons, earning in the process NFL Coach of the Year honors on two separate occasions. A pioneer both on and off the field, Halas not only mastered the T-formation, but also made the Bears the first team to hold daily practice sessions, analyze film of opponents to find weaknesses and means of attack, place assistant coaches in the press box during games, place tarp on the field, publish a club newspaper, and broadcast games by radio. Halas also played a huge role in the introduction of revenue sharing, realizing that those teams located in smaller cities did not have the ability to match the huge sums of money made by the big-market Bears.

After retiring as head coach following the conclusion of the 1967 campaign, Halas spent his remaining years in the front office, becoming the only person to be involved with the NFL throughout the first 60 years of its existence. Inducted into the Pro Football Hall of Fame as part of its inaugural class of 1963, Halas later received the additional honors of being recognized by ESPN as one of the 20th century's 10 most influential people in sports, and as one of the greatest coaches.

Halas remained the Bears' principal owner and general manager until he finally succumbed to pancreatic cancer at the age of 88, on October 31, 1983. Following his passing, former Green Bay Packers guard Jerry Kramer said of the man who coached his team's greatest rival, "George Halas was a towering figure in the NFL. Without question, Coach Lombardi had a lot of respect for Halas. More than respect, even a reverence."

Kramer then added, "We were pretty successful back then, but it was always a battle with Chicago and Papa Bear. Ugly, tough games, like 9–6. George was a rascal and could give you some lip along the sideline, usually not fit to print. . . . But they were two great coaches who had a lot of respect for each other and the Packers-Bears rivalry."

## CAREER HIGHLIGHTS

### Best Season

Making his greatest impact as a player during the early stages of his career, Halas earned Second-Team All-APFA honors in 1920, when he helped lead the Decatur Staleys to an outstanding 10-1-2 record.

### Memorable Moments/Greatest Performances

Halas made a pair of touchdown receptions during a 28–7 win over the Hammond Pros on November 21, 1920, collaborating with Jimmy Conzelman on scoring plays that covered 15 and 26 yards.

Halas gave the Staleys a 7–0 victory over the Dayton Triangles on October 23, 1921, when he scored the game's only touchdown in the fourth quarter on a 10-yard pass reception.

Halas made the most memorable play of his career during a 26–0 win over the Oorang Indians on November 4, 1923, when he stripped an aging Jim Thorpe of the football at the Chicago 2 yard line, scooped up the loose pigskin, and returned it 98 yards for a touchdown.

Halas scored twice during a 30–12 victory over the Pottsville Maroons on November 13, 1927, lighting the scoreboard for the first time when he recovered a fumble in the end zone, and scoring again on a 33-yard pass from Joey Sternaman.

Halas contributed to a 27–14 victory over the Duluth Eskimos in the 1927 regular-season finale by scoring a touchdown when he intercepted a pass in the Duluth end zone.

Halas scored the final touchdown of his career when he caught a 25-yard TD pass from Bill Senn during a 14–7 loss to the Detroit Wolverines on November 25, 1928.

### Notable Achievements

- 1921 APFA (American Professional Football Association) champion.
- 1920 Second-Team All-APFA selection.
- NFL 1920s All-Decade Team.
- #7 retired by Bears.
- Elected to Pro Football Hall of Fame in 1963.

# SUMMARY
## AND HONORABLE MENTIONS
### (THE NEXT 25)

Having identified the 50 greatest players in Chicago Bears history, the time has come to select the best of the best. Based on the rankings contained in this book, the members of the Bears' all-time offensive and defensive teams are listed below. Our squads include the top player at each position, with the offense featuring the two best wide receivers, running backs, tackles, and guards. A third-down back has been included as well. Meanwhile, the defense features two ends, two tackles, two outside linebackers, two inside linebackers, two cornerbacks, and a pair of safeties. Although Brian Urlacher spent his entire career playing on the inside, he has been inserted here as an outside backer due to my desire to include him on the team. And he most certainly had the speed, size, and range to man any of the linebacker positions. Special teams have been accounted for as well, with a placekicker, punter, kickoff returner, and punt returner also being included. The punter and placekicker were taken from the list of honorable mentions that will soon follow.

| OFFENSE | | DEFENSE | |
|---|---|---|---|
| Player | Position | Player | Position |
| Sid Luckman | QB | Richard Dent | LE |
| Walter Payton | HB | Steve McMichael | LT |
| Bronko Nagurski | FB | Dan Hampton | RT |
| Gale Sayers | 3rd-Down Back | Doug Atkins | RE |
| Mike Ditka | TE | Lance Briggs | LOLB |
| Johnny Morris | WR | Mike Singletary | LILB |
| Harlon Hill | WR | Dick Butkus | RILB |
| Joe Stydahar | LT | Brian Urlacher | ROLB |
| Dan Fortmann | LG | Charles Tillman | LCB |

| OFFENSE | | DEFENSE | |
|---|---|---|---|
| Clyde "Bulldog" Turner | C | Gary Fencik | SS |
| Stan Jones | RG | Roosevelt Taylor | FS |
| George Connor | RT | George McAfee | RCB |
| Kevin Butler | PK | Bobby Joe Green | P |
| Devin Hester | KR | Devin Hester | PR |

Although I limited my earlier rankings to the top 50 players in franchise history, many other fine players have worn a Bears uniform over the years, some of whom narrowly missed making the final cut. Following is a list of those players deserving of an honorable mention. These are the men I deemed worthy of being slotted into positions 51 to 75 in the overall rankings. Where applicable and available, the statistics they compiled during their time in Chicago are included, along with their most notable achievements while playing for the Bears.

# 51—ED HEALEY (OT, DT; 1923–1927)

Public domain, photographer unknown

## Notable Achievements

- Four-time First-Team All-Pro selection (1923, 1924, 1925, and 1926).
- NFL 1920s All-Decade Team.
- Elected to Pro Football Hall of Fame in 1964.

# 52—MARK BORTZ (G; 1983–1994)

Courtesy of George A. Kitrinos

## Notable Achievements

- Six-time division champion (1984, 1985, 1986, 1987, 1988, and 1990).
- 1985 NFC champion.
- Super Bowl XX champion.
- Two-time Pro Bowl selection (1988 and 1990).
- Two-time Second-Team All-NFC selection (1988 and 1990).

# 53—FRED WILLIAMS (DT; 1952–1963)

Courtesy of MEARSonlineauctions.com

## Bears Numbers

2 Interceptions, 65 Interception-Return Yards, 9 Fumble Recoveries.

## Notable Achievements

- Two-time division champion (1956 and 1963).
- 1963 NFL champion.
- Four-time Pro Bowl selection (1952, 1953, 1958, and 1959).
- 1958 First-Team All–Western Conference selection.

# 54—WALLY CHAMBERS (DT; 1973–1977)

Courtesy of MEARSonlineauction.com

**Notable Achievements**

- Recorded 14 sacks in 1975.
- Recorded more than 100 tackles three times.
- 1973 NFL Defensive Rookie of the Year.
- UPI 1976 NFC Defensive Player of the Year.
- *Football Digest* 1976 NFC Defensive Lineman of the Year.
- Three-time Pro Bowl selection (1973, 1975, and 1976).
- 1976 First-Team All-Pro selection.
- Two-time Second-Team All-Pro selection (1974 and 1975).
- Three-time First-Team All-NFC selection (1974, 1975, and 1976).

# 55—BILL OSMANSKI (FB; 1939–1943, 1946–1947)

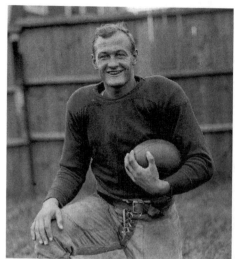

Courtesy of Boston Public Library, Leslie Jones Collection

## Career Numbers

1,753 Yards Rushing, 12 Receptions, 170 Receiving Yards, 1,923 Yards from Scrimmage, 285 Kickoff-Return Yards, 2,247 All-Purpose Yards, 20 Rushing Touchdowns, 21 Touchdowns, 4.8 Rushing Average, 4 Interceptions, 32 Interception-Return Yards.

## Notable Achievements

- Led NFL with 699 yards rushing in 1939.
- Led NFL with rushing average of 5.3 yards per carry in 1941.
- Finished second in NFL with seven rushing touchdowns and rushing average of 5.8 yards per carry in 1939.
- Finished third in NFL in rushing touchdowns once, touchdowns once, yards from scrimmage once, and all-purpose yards once.
- Five-time division champion (1940, 1941, 1942, 1943, and 1946).
- Four-time NFL champion (1940, 1941, 1943, and 1946).
- Three-time Pro Bowl selection (1939, 1940, and 1941).
- 1939 First-Team All-Pro selection.
- 1946 Second-Team All-Pro selection.
- NFL 1940s All-Decade Team.

# 56—MARK CARRIER (DB; 1990–1996)

Courtesy of SportsMemorabilia.com

## Bears Numbers

20 Interceptions, 197 Interception-Return Yards, 587 Tackles, 10 Forced Fumbles, 7 Fumble Recoveries, 1 Touchdown.

## Notable Achievements

- Recorded 122 tackles in 1990.
- Led NFL with 10 interceptions in 1990.
- Finished second in NFL with five forced fumbles in 1990.
- Led Bears in interceptions twice and tackles once.
- 1990 division champion.
- 1990 Week 9 NFC Defensive Player of the Week.
- Member of 1990 NFL All-Rookie Team.
- 1990 NFL Defensive Rookie of the Year.
- Three-time Pro Bowl selection (1990, 1991, and 1993).
- 1990 Second-Team All-Pro selection.
- 1990 First-Team All-NFC selection.
- 1994 Second-Team All-NFC selection.

# 57—JULIUS PEPPERS (DE; 2010–2013)

Courtesy of Kevin Moore

## Bears Numbers

175 Tackles, 37½ Sacks, 3 Interceptions, 15 Interception-Return Yards, 10 Forced Fumbles, 7 Fumble Recoveries, 1 Touchdown.

## Notable Achievements

- Recorded more than 10 sacks twice.
- Finished second in NFL with four fumble recoveries in 2012.
- Led Bears in sacks four times.
- 2010 division champion.
- Two-time NFC Defensive Player of the Week.
- Two-time NFC Defensive Player of the Month.
- Three-time Pro Bowl selection (2010, 2011, and 2012).
- 2010 First-Team All-Pro selection.
- 2012 Second-Team All-Pro selection.

# 58—RAY BRAY (OG, DT; 1939–1942, 1946–1951)

Courtesy of MEARSonlineauctions.com

## Notable Achievements

- Five-time division champion (1940, 1941, 1942, 1946, and 1950).
- Three-time NFL champion (1940, 1941, and 1946).
- Four-time Pro Bowl selection (1940, 1941, 1950, and 1951).
- Two-time Second-Team All-Pro selection (1949 and 1950).
- 1948 Second-Team All-NFL/AAFC selection.

# 59—KEITH VAN HORNE (OT: 1981–1993)

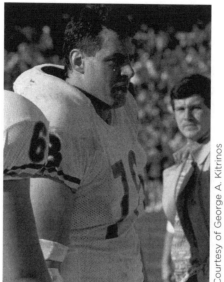

Courtesy of George A. Kitrinos

## Notable Achievements

- Ranks among Bears career leaders with 186 games played (tied-5th).
- Six-time division champion (1984, 1985, 1986, 1987, 1988, and 1990).
- 1985 NFC champion.
- Super Bowl XX champion.

## 60—KEVIN BUTLER (K; 1985–1995)

Courtesy of George A. Kitrinos

### Bears Numbers

1,116 Points Scored, 243 Field Goals Made, 332 Field Goal Attempts, 73.2 Field Goal Percentage.

### Notable Achievements

- Scored more than 100 points five times, topping 120 points twice.
- Posted field goal percentage above 80.0 once (83.8 in 1985).
- Led NFL with 144 points scored in 1985.
- Finished second in NFL in field goals twice and points scored once.
- Finished third in NFL in field goals once and points scored once.
- Holds Bears single-season record for most point scored (144 in 1985).
- Ranks second in Bears history in field goals made and points scored.
- Five-time division champion (1985, 1986, 1987, 1988, and 1990).
- 1985 NFC champion.
- Super Bowl XX champion.
- Member of 1985 NFL All-Rookie Team.
- Two-time NFC Special Teams Player of the Week.
- Two-time NFC Special Teams Player of the Month.
- Two-time Second-Team All-NFC selection (1985 and 1989).

# 61—WILLIE GAULT (WR; 1983–1987)

Courtesy of George A. Kitrinos

## Bears Numbers

184 Receptions, 3,650 Receiving Yards, 144 Yards Rushing, 885 Kickoff-Return Yards, 60 Punt-Return Yards, 4,739 All-Purpose Yards, 27 Touchdown Receptions, 28 Touchdowns.

## Notable Achievements

- Returned one kickoff for a touchdown.
- Amassed more than 1,000 all-purpose yards twice.
- Averaged more than 20 yards per reception three times.
- Finished second in NFL in average yards per reception once and kickoff-return average once.
- Led Bears in receptions once and receiving yards five times.
- Ranks among Bears career leaders in receiving yards (9th) and touchdown receptions (8th).
- Four-time division champion (1984, 1985, 1986, and 1987).
- 1985 NFC champion.
- Super Bowl XX champion.

# 62—PADDY DRISCOLL (QB, RB, K; 1926–1929)

Public domain

**Bears Numbers**

14 Touchdowns, 14 Field Goals, 32 Extra Points, 158 Points.

**Notable Achievements**

- Led NFL with 12 field goals and 86 points scored in 1926.
- Two-time First-Team All-Pro selection (1926 and 1927).
- 1928 Second-Team All-Pro selection.
- NFL 1920s All-Decade Team.

# 63—ROBBIE GOULD (K; 2005–2015)

Courtesy of John Martinez Pavliga

## Bears Numbers

1,207 Points Scored, 276 Field Goals Made, 323 Field Goal Attempts, 85.4 Field Goal Percentage.

## Notable Achievements

- Scored more than 100 points eight times, topping 120 points five times.
- Posted field goal percentage above 85.0 six times.
- Led NFL with 32 field goals in 2006.
- Finished second in NFL in field goals twice and points scored once.
- Holds Bears single-season record for most field goals (33 in 2015).
- Holds Bears career records for most field goals and points scored.
- Three-time division champion (2005, 2006, and 2010).
- 2006 NFC champion.
- Three-time NFC Special Teams Player of the Week.
- Two-time NFC Special Teams Player of the Month.
- 2006 Pro Bowl selection.
- 2006 First-Team All-Pro selection.

# 64—BENNIE MCRAE (DB; 1962–1970)

Courtesy of SportsMemorabilia.com

## Bears Numbers

27 Interceptions, 485 Interception-Return Yards, 6 Fumble Recoveries, 4 Touchdowns.

## Notable Achievements

- Recorded at least five interceptions twice.
- Amassed 116 interception-return yards in 1965.
- Led Bears in interceptions twice.
- Ranks among Bears career leaders in interceptions (5th), interception-return yards (4th), and touchdown interceptions (tied-3rd).
- 1963 division champion.
- 1963 NFL champion.
- 1965 Second-Team All-Pro selection.
- 1965 First-Team All–Western Conference selection.

# 65—DICK GORDON (WR; 1965–1971)

Public domain, photographer unknown

## Bears Numbers

238 Receptions, 3,550 Receiving Yards, 50 Yards Rushing, 1,362 Kickoff-Return Yards, 90 Punt-Return Yards, 5,054 All-Purpose Yards, 35 Touchdown Receptions.

## Notable Achievements

- Amassed more than 1,000 all-purpose yards twice.
- Averaged more than 20 yards per reception once.
- Led NFL with 71 receptions, 13 TD catches, and 13 TDs in 1970.
- Finished third in NFL with 1,026 receiving yards in 1970.
- Led Bears in receptions and receiving yards three times each.
- Holds Bears single-season record for most TD catches (13 in 1970).
- Ranks among Bears career leaders in receiving yards (11th) and touchdown receptions (3rd).
- Two-time Pro Bowl selection (1970 and 1971).
- 1970 First-Team All-Pro selection.
- 1970 First-Team All-NFC selection.
- 1971 Second-Team All-NFC selection.

# 66—DONNELL WOOLFORD (DB; 1989–1996)

Courtesy of SportsMemorabilia.com

**Bears Numbers**

32 Interceptions, 212 Interception-Return Yards, 552 Tackles, 3 Forced Fumbles, 2 Fumble Recoveries, 1 Touchdown.

**Notable Achievements**

- Recorded at least five interceptions three times.
- Recorded 101 tackles in 1993.
- Finished third in NFL with seven interceptions in 1992.
- Led Bears in interceptions four times.
- Ranks fourth in Bears history in interceptions.
- 1990 division champion.
- Member of 1989 NFL All-Rookie Team.
- 1993 Pro Bowl selection.
- 1994 Second-Team All-NFC selection.

# 67—BRANDON MARSHALL (WR: 2012–2014)

Courtesy of Chris Usalis

**Bears Numbers**

279 Receptions, 3,524 Receiving Yards, 31 Touchdown Receptions.

**Notable Achievements**

- Surpassed 100 receptions twice.
- Surpassed 1,000 receiving yards twice, topping 1,500 yards once.
- Made more than 10 touchdown receptions twice.
- Finished second in NFL with 118 receptions in 2012.
- Finished third in NFL with 1,508 receiving yards in 2012.
- Led Bears in receptions twice and receiving yards once.
- Holds Bears single-season records for most receptions (118) and most receiving yards (1,508), both in 2012.
- Ranks among Bears career leaders in receptions (9th), receiving yards (12th), and touchdown receptions (tied-5th).
- Two-time Pro Bowl selection (2012 and 2013).
- 2012 First-Team All-Pro selection.

# 68—JIM MCMILLEN (OG, DT; 1924–1928)

Courtesy of the Library of Congress

## Notable Achievements

- Two-time First-Team All-Pro selection (1925 and 1928).
- 1924 Second-Team All-Pro selection.

# 69—ED O'BRADOVICH (DE; 1962–1971)

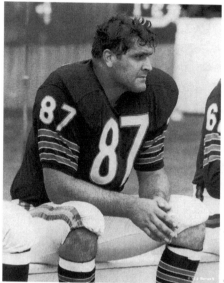

Courtesy of MEARSonlineauctions.com

## Notable Achievements

- Scored one defensive touchdown during career.
- Recorded 9½ sacks in 1970.
- Led NFL with five fumble recoveries in 1962.
- Ranks among Bears career leaders with 13 fumble recoveries (tied-9th).
- 1963 division champion.
- 1963 NFL champion.

# 70—DOUG PLANK (DB; 1975–1982)

Courtesy of SportsMemorabilia.com

## Career Numbers

15 Interceptions, 166 Interception-Return Yards, 14 Fumble Recoveries, 1 Safety.

## Notable Achievements

- Finished fourth in NFL with four fumble recoveries in 1981.
- Led Bears in tackles as a rookie in 1975.
- Ranks among Bears career leaders in fumble recoveries (tied-7th).

# 71—JAY CUTLER (QB; 2009–2016)

Courtesy of Mike Morbeck

### Bears Numbers

23,443 Yards Passing, 154 TD Passes, 109 Interceptions, 61.8 Completion Percentage, 85.2 Passer Rating, 1,227 Yards Rushing, 6 Rushing TDs.

### Notable Achievements

- Passed for more than 3,000 yards five times.
- Threw more than 20 touchdown passes four times.
- Completed more than 60 percent of passes five times, topping 65 percent once.
- Led NFL quarterbacks with four game-winning drives in 2015.
- Holds Bears career records for most pass attempts, pass completions, yards passing, and touchdown passes.
- 2010 division champion.
- Two-time NFC Offensive Player of the Week.

# 72—ALSHON JEFFERY (WR: 2012–2016)

Public domain

## Bears Numbers

304 Receptions, 4,549 Receiving Yards, 26 Touchdown Receptions.

## Notable Achievements

- Surpassed 80 receptions twice.
- Surpassed 1,000 receiving yards twice.
- Made 10 touchdown receptions in 2014.
- Led Bears in receptions once and receiving yards three times.
- Ranks among Bears career leaders in receptions (7th), receiving yards (3rd), and touchdown receptions (9th).
- 2013 Pro Bowl selection.

# 73—MIKE BROWN (DB; 2000–2008)

Courtesy of Jauerback via Wikipedia

## Bears Numbers

17 Interceptions, 275 Interception-Return Yards, 512 Tackles, 5 Sacks, 8 Forced Fumbles, 7 Fumble Recoveries, 7 Touchdowns.

## Notable Achievements

- Recorded five interceptions in 2001.
- Amassed 116 interception-return yards in 2005.
- Amassed 106 fumble-return yards in 2002.
- Led NFL in TD interceptions once and fumble-return yards twice.
- Led Bears in interceptions twice.
- Ranks among Bears career leaders with four touchdown interceptions (tied-3rd) and seven defensive touchdowns (2nd).
- Three-time division champion (2001, 2005, and 2006).
- 2006 NFC champion.
- Member of 2000 NFL All-Rookie Team.
- Two-time NFC Defensive Player of the Week.
- 2005 Pro Bowl selection.
- 2001 First-Team All-Pro selection.
- 2005 Second-Team All-Pro selection.
- 2005 First-Team All-NFC selection.

# 74—CURTIS CONWAY (WR; 1993–1999)

Courtesy of George A. Kitrinos

## Bears Numbers

329 Receptions, 4,498 Receiving Yards, 265 Yards Rushing, 678 Kickoff-Return Yards, 63 Punt-Return Yards, 5,504 All-Purpose Yards, 31 Touchdown Receptions, 31 Touchdowns.

## Notable Achievements

- Made 12 touchdown receptions in 1995.
- Made 81 receptions in 1996.
- Topped 1,000 receiving yards twice.
- Led Bears with 81 receptions and 1,049 receiving yards in 1996.
- Ranks among Bears career leaders in receptions (tied-4th), receiving yards (6th), and touchdown receptions (tied-5th).

# 75—BOBBY JOE GREEN (P; 1962–1973)

Public domain, photographer unknown

## Bears Numbers

35,057 Yards Punting, 42.1 Yards Per Punt Average, Career Long—72 Yards.

## Notable Achievements

- Averaged more than 43 yards per punt three times.
- Led NFL with 3,358 yards punting in 1966.
- Finished second in NFL in yards punting twice and average yards per punt once.
- Finished third in NFL in yards punting once and average yards per punt twice.
- Ranks second in Bears history in total punt yardage.
- 1963 division champion.
- 1963 NFL champion.
- 1970 Pro Bowl selection.

# GLOSSARY

## ABBREVIATIONS AND STATISTICAL TERMS

**C.** Center.

**COMP %.** Completion percentage. The number of successfully completed passes divided by the number of passes attempted.

**FB.** Fullback.

**FS.** Free safety.

**HB.** Halfback.

**INTS.** Interceptions. Passes thrown by the quarterback that are caught by a member of the opposing team's defense.

**KR.** Kickoff returner.

**LCB.** Left cornerback.

**LE.** Left end.

**LG.** Left guard.

**LILB.** Left-inside linebacker.

**LOLB.** Left-outside linebacker.

**LT.** Left tackle.

**MLB.** Middle linebacker.

**NT.** Nose tackle.

**P.** Punter.

**PK.** Placekicker.

**PR.** Punt returner.

**QB.** Quarterback.

**QBR.** Quarterback rating.

**RB.** Running back.

**RCB.** Right cornerback.

**RE.** Right end.

**REC.** Receptions.

**REC YD.** Receiving yards.

**RG.** Right guard.

**RILB.** Right-inside linebacker.

**ROLB.** Right-outside linebacker.

**RT.** Right tackle.

**RUSH YD.** Rushing yards.

**SS.** Strong safety.

**ST.** Special teams.

**TD PASSES.** Touchdown passes.

**TD RECS.** Touchdown receptions.

**TDS.** Touchdowns.

**TE.** Tight end.

**WR.** Wide receiver.

**YD from SCRIMMAGE.** Yards from scrimmage.

# BIBLIOGRAPHY

## BOOKS

Chicago Tribune Staff. *The Chicago Tribune Book of the Chicago Bears: A Decade-by-Decade History*. Chicago: Agate Midway Publishing, 2015.

Davis, Jeff. *Papa Bear: The Life and Legacy of George Halas*. New York: McGraw-Hill Education, 2004.

Dent, Jim, *Monster of the Midway: Bronko Nagurski, the 1943 Chicago Bears, and the Greatest Comeback Ever*. New York: Thomas Dunne Books, 2013.

Freedman, Lew. *Bears by the Numbers: A Complete Team History of the Chicago Bears by Uniform Number*. New York: Sports Publishing, 2017.

——. *Chicago Bears: The Complete Illustrated History*. Minneapolis: MVP Books, 2010.

——. *Game of My Life: Chicago Bears—Memorable Stories of Bears Football*. New York: Sports Publishing, 2006.

Gorr, Beth. *Bear Memories: The Chicago-Green Bay Rivalry*. Charleston, SC: Arcadia Publishing, 2005.

Jones, Danny. *More Distant Memories: Pro Football's Best Ever Players of the 50's, 60's, and 70's*. Bloomington, IN: AuthorHouse, 2006.

Taylor, Roy. *Chicago Bears History*. Charleston, SC: Arcadia Publishing, 2005.

Wilson, Otis, with Chet Coppock. *If These Walls Could Talk: Chicago Bears: Stories from the Chicago Bears Sideline, Locker Room, and Press Box*. Chicago: Triumph Books, 2017.

## VIDEOS

*Greatest Ever: NFL Dream Team*. Polygram Video, 1996.

*SportsCentury: Jim McMahon 1985 Chicago Bears*. ESPN, 2001.

## WEBSITES

Biographies, online at Hickoksports.com (hickoksports.com/hickoksports/biograph)

Biography from Jockbio.com
(jockbio.com)

CBSNews.com
(cbsnews.com)

ESPN.com
(sports.espn.go.com)

Hall of Famers, online at profootballhof.com
(profootballhof.com/hof/member)

Inductees from LASportsHall.com
(lasportshall.com)

LAYTimes.com
(articles.latimes.com)

Newsday.com
(newsday.com)

NYDailyNews.com
(nydailynews.com/new-york)

NYTimes.com
(nytimes.com)

Pro Football Talk from nbcsports.com
(profootballtalk.nbcsports.com)

SpTimes.com
(sptimes.com)

StarLedger.com
(starledger.com)

SunSentinel.com
(articles.sun-sentinel.com)

The Players, online at Profootballreference.com
(pro-football-reference.com/players)